Tempest in the Temple

BRANDEIS SERIES IN AMERICAN
JEWISH HISTORY, CULTURE, & LIFE

Jonathan D. Sarna, *Editor*

Sylvia Barack Fishman, *Associate Editor*

For a complete list of books that are available in the series,
visit www.upne.com

Susan G. Solomon
  Louis I. Kahn's Jewish Architecture:
    Mikveh Israel and the Midcentury American Synagogue
Amy Neustein, editor
  Tempest in the Temple: Jewish Communities and Child Sex Scandals
Jack Wertheimer, editor
  Learning and Community:
    Jewish Supplementary Schools in the Twenty-First Century
Carole S. Kessner
  Marie Syrkin: Values Beyond the Self
Leonard Saxe and Barry Chazan
  Ten Days of Birthright Israel: A Journey in Young Adult Identity
Jack Wertheimer, editor
  Imagining the American Jewish Community
Murray Zimiles
  Gilded Lions and Jeweled Horses: The Synagogue to the Carousel
Marianne R. Sanua
  Be of Good Courage: The American Jewish Committee, 1945–2006
Hollace Ava Weiner and Kenneth D. Roseman, editors
  Lone Stars of David: The Jews of Texas
Jack Wertheimer, editor
  Jewish Education in an Age of Choice
Edward S. Shapiro
  Crown Heights: Blacks, Jews, and the 1991 Brooklyn Riot
Marcie Cohen Ferris and Mark I. Greenberg, editors
  Jewish Roots in Southern Soil: A New History

Tempest in the Temple

Edited by AMY NEUSTEIN

JEWISH COMMUNITIES & CHILD SEX SCANDALS

Foreword by RABBI DR. ELLIOT DORFF
Preface by RABBI DR. JEREMY ROSEN
Epilogue by PROFESSOR DANE S. CLAUSSEN

BRANDEIS UNIVERSITY PRESS
Waltham, Massachusetts
Published by University Press of New England
Hanover and London

BRANDEIS UNIVERSITY PRESS
Published by University Press of New England
One Court Street, Lebanon, NH 03766
www.upne.com
© 2009 by Brandeis University Press
Printed in the United States of America
5 4 3 2 1

Library of Congress Cataloging-in-Publication Data
Tempest in the temple: Jewish communities & child sex scandals /
edited by Amy Neustein. — 1st ed.
    p.   cm. — (Brandeis Series in American Jewish History, Culture, and Life)
Includes bibliographical references and index.
ISBN 978-1-58465-671-5 (cloth: alk. paper)
1. Child sexual abuse by clergy — United States. 2. Rabbis — Sexual
behavior — United States. 3. Authority — Religious aspects — Judaism.
4. Abused children — United States. 5. Jewish ethics. I. Neustein, Amy.
HV6570.2.T46   2009
296.3'8 — dc22   2008054080

University Press of New England is a member of the
Green Press Initiative. The paper used in this book meets
their minimum requirement for recycled paper.

In memory of

RABBI DR. ABRAHAM NEUSTEIN,

my beloved father, mentor,

and spiritual guide

Contents

RABBI DR. ELLIOT N. DORFF

Foreword

I was as uninformed and naïve about child sexual abuse as virtually everyone else. I had had the good fortune of having terrific parents, and even though I knew as I was growing up that some of my Jewish friends had more issues with their parents than I did with mine, none of what they complained about even approached sexual abuse. It was completely off the radar screen. The same was true for all the Jewish families that I knew as my wife and I were raising our own children.

Then, in 1993, when California law changed to make teachers mandated reporters of child abuse, the University of Judaism (now the American Jewish University) and Jewish Family Service of Los Angeles (JFS) jointly published *Shalom Bayit: A Jewish Response to Child Abuse and Domestic Violence*, edited by Dr. Ian Russ, Sally Weber, and Ellen Ledley, to inform teachers in Jewish schools about the requirements of the new law, how to recognize abuse, and what to do about it when you saw evidence of it. The editors asked me to write an essay on Judaism and sexual abuse as part of that book, and the research for writing that essay was my first foray into this entire area. Yes, I knew that among its more than sixty programs, JFS, of which I was a board member at the time and later president, runs two shelters for battered women and children, but I thought that this was a project that JFS had undertaken as a service to the general community, for we were told in a report to the board several months earlier that at that time none of the residents of those facilities were Jews. This just confirmed my mistaken impression that child sexual abuse simply does not happen among Jews.

How wrong I was. In consulting with the editors, all of whom were therapists who had direct experience in counseling survivors of abuse, I found out that domestic abuse of all sorts existed in the Jewish community, including the sexual abuse of children, that it affected people affiliated with all denominations of Judaism and secular Jews as well, and that it ran across all levels of income and education. Although solid statistics about the prevalence of this phenomenon among Jews are hard to come by, there seems to be no reason to presume that Jews are any less affected by this than the general population, that as many as one in four girls and one in six boys are sexually abused before reaching the age of eighteen, most between ages seven and thirteen. Shocking and depressing, to say the least. My heart ached for these children that I had never met.

For that reason, I decided to continue the research that I had done to write the short article for the UJ/JFS project and ultimately wrote a long rabbinic ruling dealing with all aspects of family violence. Specifically, I described and defined the types of abuse and their Jewish legal, moral, and theological status; and I indicated how a Conservative approach to Jewish law has an important effect on how we can and should interpret and apply traditional Jewish law in responding to abuse. I then analyzed from a Conservative Jewish legal point of view the issues involved in spousal abuse, child abuse, and parental abuse, including sexual abuse and verbal abuse as well as nonsexual physical abuse. I dealt with the reasons victims of abuse often fail to report abuse or get help to extricate themselves from it, including their reticence to defame the perpetrator and the family, shame and misplaced feelings of guilt, and the traditional ban on informing civil authorities. I described the duties of witnesses to abuse; I discussed the obligations of the abuser to get help to stop abusing others and to make amends to the greatest extent possible; and, finally, I wrote about the degree to which the Jewish community has a duty to enable abusers to return to the good graces of the community (while still protecting everyone from possible further abuse) and the role of rabbis, educators, and lay leaders in all aspects of this issue in our community. My ruling was approved by the Conservative Movement's Committee on Jewish Law and Standards in September 1995, and then distributed in hard copy by mail to each and every Conservative rabbi. It now is available to anyone who wants to read it on both the Internet and in book form, and it has become the basis of the work done within the Conservative Jewish community to inform both rabbis and lay people of this phenomenon and to teach them how to respond to it.[1]

It is from the perspective of that experience, then, that I read the manuscript of this book. Precisely because child sexual abuse is so devastating to its survivors — in my ruling I call it "akin to murder" — this book does us all a real service in describing this particular form of abuse in its various forms, the communal structure that enables it to happen and then to be hidden from public view, and the ways in which the Jewish community can and should respond to it. Although some of the essays in this book speak to the phenomenon of the sexual abuse of children in all segments of the Jewish community, particularly remarkable is the extent to which Orthodox writers in this book have come forward to describe the problem in their community, the particular features of their community that make it even more secretive and harder to deal with than it is in the general community, and the ways in which it nevertheless must and can be addressed.

In my mind, though, the most important contribution of this book is the open and positive tone in which it is written, prompting us all to face the problem squarely and to do what we need to do to repair the damage that has already been done and to stop any future injury of this sort. Hiding our heads in the sand on this issue simply will not work to resolve it and effectively makes us all accomplices of the perpetrators. Yes, we should be ashamed of those of our community who do these things to children, and yes, acknowledging this problem and dealing with it will mean that we must look at ourselves (and others will look at us) as less than the ideal, family-oriented community that we would like to be; but both Jews and non-Jews will think much better of a Jewish community that recognizes the problem and takes concrete steps to resolve it than one that pretends it does not exist at the price of letting more and more of its children suffer terribly.

I would like to close this foreword with a declaration that comes from another area of family violence — namely, spousal abuse — but that states some important truths about child sexual abuse as well. As a result of my involvement in Jewish Family Service of Los Angeles and my rabbinic ruling on domestic violence, I was asked to participate in a project of the FaithTrust Institute, an interfaith organization whose mission is to fight dating and marital abuse. In the early 1990s, Congress created an office within the Department of Justice specifically to help police officers and judges recognize and respond to spousal abuse, and the FaithTrust Institute was awarded the government grants to run those training sessions. In the early 2000s, though, they discovered that abusers least likely to change their ways were referred to intervention programs by the courts; the next least likely to change were referred by family members; and the most likely to change were referred by clergy. So the FaithTrust Institute created a clergy task force, on which I served, to create a call for action among religious leaders to fight domestic violence. That declaration, ultimately signed by representatives of forty-two religious groups, including all four Jewish denominations, Sunni and Shiite Muslims, and evangelical as well as mainline Protestants, and still open to both clergy and lay leaders to sign, says the following:

> *National Declaration by Religious and Spiritual Leaders*
> *to Address Violence against Women (April 5, 2006)*
>
> We proclaim with one voice as national spiritual and religious leaders that violence against women exists in all communities, including our own, and is morally, spiritually, and universally intolerable.
>
> We acknowledge that our sacred texts, traditions, and values have too often been misused to perpetuate and condone abuse.
>
> We commit ourselves to working toward the day when all women will be safe and abuse will be no more.
>
> We draw upon our healing texts and practices to help make our families and societies whole.
>
> Our religious and spiritual traditions compel us to work for justice and the eradication of violence against women.
>
> We call upon people of all religious and spiritual traditions to join us.[2]

As this declaration states, we must clearly strive to eliminate violence against women in our society; we must all the more protect our children, who have even fewer means of defense and whose violation causes even more deeply rooted problems. May this book inform us about the nature and prevalence of child sexual abuse, and may it motivate us to eradicate it from within our midst so that we can truly be "a kingdom of priests and a holy nation" (Exodus 19:6).

April 2008

ELLIOT N. DORFF, Rabbi, PHD, is rector and distinguished professor of philosophy at the American Jewish University, immediate past president of Jewish Family Service of Los Angeles, and chair of the Conservative Movement's Committee on Jewish Law and Standards, for which he wrote the rabbinic ruling on sexual and other kinds of abuse, which governs the Conservative Movement's understanding of abuse and its responses to it.

NOTES

1. Elliot N. Dorff, "Family Violence," at www.rabbinicalassembly.org, under the heading "Contemporary Halakhah." Published in Elliot N. Dorff, *Love Your Neighbor*

and Yourself: A Jewish Approach to Modern Personal Ethics (Philadelphia: Jewish Publication Society, 2003), chapter 5 (pp. 155–206).

2. *Faith Trust Institute,* www.faithtrustinstitute.org, under the tab "Take Action, Sign the Declaration."

RABBI DR. JEREMY ROSEN

Preface

This important and courageous collection of essays tackles an issue that, in recent years, has been brought out of the shadows into the glare of common interest. More and more cases of sexual abuse in all its varieties, particularly of children, have come to the public's attention. These cases have spanned virtually every religion, socioeconomic class, and ethnic group. Research, as well as anecdote, has made us aware that what we have seen is just the tip of the iceberg. Yet the subject is so controversial that it generates a great deal of anger, defensiveness, and ill feeling.

Most societies, particularly the more closed ones, react badly to the idea of having their dirty laundry washed in public and try their best to avoid bad publicity. It is often easiest to blame the messenger. All means are used to obstruct, obscure, and silence both those who have suffered and, just as much, those who try to publicize the wrongs and attempt to have them rectified. Everyone's rights and feelings seem to be regarded as more important than those of the victims.

Religions all prescribe high ethical standards for their followers. So it is a disturbing thought that they almost all exhibit examples of a failure of moral leadership. Religious authorities, of whom one has every reason to expect more, and communities themselves try their best to cover up scandals, particularly in the realm of sexual abuse in all its varieties and manifestations.

The narrative of child sexual abuse described in this book is essentially a North American one. However, it is also one that has been and continues to be replicated in virtually every community I have worked in as a rabbi and teacher around the Jewish world. People entrusted with fragile and vulnerable children abuse their power to varying degrees. The victims are further victimized by being blamed. They and their families (when a family member is not the guilty party) are often hounded out of communities and isolated.

Strenuous efforts, usually involving the most senior of religious leaders, are made to prevent the matter reaching the civil courts, under the pretext that such matters are best dealt with internally. Sadly, all the evidence shows that this leads to the matter being closed unsatisfactorily.

I am not qualified to comment on the psychological aspects of this issue or on the different clinical analyses of cause and effect. Neither can I comment on the nuances between various types of sexual abuse, from pedophilia right across the spectrum, or about the likelihood of re-offending. But my experiences as a pulpit rabbi and as a school principal, over many years and in different situations, have given me enough opportunities to realize the gravity and the common nature of this issue in all its varieties. It is essential that this issue should be brought into the open community and to the attention, in particular, of pulpit rabbis and those involved in educational institutions.

In some ways, sexual abuse is not very different from other forms of abuse, in that the weak suffer at the hands of the powerful. Indeed, there is often a correlation between the use of corporal punishment in very traditional schools and sexual abuse. Male-dominated societies facilitate abuse of women in the same way that differences in power and wealth lead to the abuse of the poor and weak. We are no longer surprised to learn that in more primitive societies honor killings are frequent; women who are raped become double victims because they are usually punished more than their coercers.

There is a paradox that the very urge to protect positively, an otherwise noble aim, is sometimes the very root of the evil we are discussing. Attitudes that are praiseworthy in themselves, such as not gossiping, are taken to a reductio ad absurdum that even defies the law itself. The desire, quite understandable, to protect the children and spouses of perpetrators is used against the victims and their families. The cultural preoccupation with fitting into a protective society to reap its benefits (such as a support structure, marriage partners, the means of earning a livelihood, or being taken care of charitably) is used by its members in defense of only one side of this very disturbing situation.

However much one may be tempted to put these issues down to the limitations of undemocratic societies or sociopolitical circumstances, the fact is throughout all manner of human societies betrayal takes place at virtually every level. One can argue about whether this is because of original sin or simply the tendency of humans toward self-indulgence rather than restraint, but regardless of the society, those with power, money, and influence use whatever tools they have to gain advantage, cover up crimes, and twist the judicial system. The need for religious leaders of stature to stand up and take a firm public position is therefore all the greater.

There have been times in Jewish history when religious authorities used a range of persuasive or coercive powers to deal with men behaving contrary to Jewish law and ethics. However, particularly since medieval times (reflecting external pressures, as well as the need to preserve internal authority), the overwhelming mood has been one of quiescence, a reluctance to be proactive. This might have originated in fear of offending the non-Jewish overlords. It might have owed something to the need to buttress the authority of Jewish leadership. Either way, it has now evolved into an intentional policy.

There is a dishonorable tradition of rabbinic authorities failing to take objective, immediate, and forthright stands on sexual issues, or indeed to stand up to the wealthier and more powerful members of their communities. Major rabbinic figures who might be expected to speak out are too often protected from realities by veritable courts of intermediaries. They often get filtered information that suits political as much as halakhic ends. What is worse, more and more cases keep on coming to light of rabbis themselves taking advantage of their positions in order to abuse.

Part of the issue is the extent to which charisma has been given too free a rein. This is particularly evident in evangelical religion. In Judaism, too, the explosion in outreach movements has contributed to increasing cases where religious leaders have overstepped the traditional boundaries. When constraints are removed, all kinds of excesses are excused. The current trend in Judaism toward hagiography has made matters worse, where it is considered unconscionable to even mention a person's failings on the grounds that it is gossip and contrary to Jewish law, even if Jewish law itself requires such matters to be placed in the open to avoid repetition.

This collection of essays also performs a valuable service in documenting the absolutely unequivocal position of Jewish law against any abuse, regardless of conditions of sex, position, and degree. From time immemorial — and indeed in the Bible itself — sexual abuse of one sort or another raises its ugly head, whether it is Abraham's asking Sarah to give herself to protect him; Lot's abuse of his daughters; the stories of Er and Onan, of Yehuda and Tamar, of Dina and Chamor, or of Amnon and Tamar. Jewish tradition shaped by such biblical stories makes no attempt to hide abuse in its various forms. By the same token, the Bible makes no secret of the abhorrent nature of such abuse. Rape is even compared to murder (Deuteronomy 22:26). The repeated emphasis in the Bible on the importance of an honest judicial system that does not flinch from pursuing truth and justice underlines how important the prosecution of all crimes, including those of sexual abuse, was even thousands of years ago. These same issues are with us even in the benevolent and open United States today. Yet still, within much of Judaism, there is a culture of denial. Part of what fuels this culture of denial is that unlike in the Talmudic era, during which various interpretations of biblical narratives were given, nowadays only those who whitewash or reinterpret to imply that nothing untoward happened to victims are given authority over all others.

The more closed and defensive a society, the more protectionist it is (as can be seen in the current revelations about polygamous Mormon sects). The more a religion sees itself as being under siege, the more controlling it becomes. No better examples in the history of Catholicism, say, can be found than the Counter-Reformation or the dogma of papal infallibility, which was not promulgated until the First Vatican Council of 1870, when scientific materialism was gaining in popularity throughout the Western world.

Anyone familiar with the late Jacob Katz's *A House Divided* will also know the extent to which regressive and reactive trends, particularly in Carpathian Hasidic Jewry in the nineteenth century, create a mindset opposed to any concessions or rethinking to meet differing social needs. The great revival of Orthodoxy since World War II owes more in character and makeup to these forces than to any other in Judaism and continues to exert a growing influence against anything that hints at revisionism.

Given the extremely strict views (externally, for certain) of some sectors of Judaism on matters sexual, the way sexual predators are protected is even more difficult to understand. The usual excuses have been heard: there is a long tradition of non-Jewish or nonreligious legal systems being anti-Semitic and repressive; non-Jewish agencies are animated by liberal and essentially antireligious values, so that bringing them in may result in losing the victims to the community altogether. Closed communities believe they can only survive by functioning autonomously and dealing internally with sensitive issues. There is also a significant post-Holocaust reaction against secular, non-Jewish systems in Europe and beyond, which are perceived as having stood idly by while Jews were massacred. Therefore, it is sometimes argued, one cannot be expected to trust in such systems or their values. One often hears it said that liberal values and feminists have led to the collapse of family values and to lifestyles that are seen as totally antithetic to traditional ones.

Any attitudes or pressure coming from such value systems is regarded as suspect. The fragmentation of society into conflicting interest groups and ideologies further exacerbates a state of cultural conflict in which each side protects itself from scrutiny, either though secrecy or by assaulting competing values. The result is too often that a culture of obstruction rather than cooperation prevails, where anyone from within either camp who speaks out is accused of being a traitor and an enemy. Even if some of this might be understandable, it certainly is no excuse. Many of these attitudes are dated. Besides, they represent an unconscionable challenge to open, caring, and fair societies where a just and effective legal system is the rule rather than the exception.

Of course, the issue cannot only be laid at the door of closed societies. In open, multicultural societies individuals are encouraged to make their own choices and the creation of closed religious societies within the wider free community is also facilitated. Yet this often leads to two sets of standards, because both the judiciary and law enforcement personnel are reluctant to intervene until forced to, either by dictate or by public pressure. In Europe, more so than in the United States, the judiciary is often reluctant to enforce state laws that might offend the sensibilities of more fundamentalist religious groups of citizens. Sadly, domestic abuse and even honor killings in Western societies are too often ignored as "internal affairs."

If one had the confidence that these issues were indeed being dealt with internally, I doubt the need for this publication would have been so pressing; it is precisely because this is not the case that it is. Admittedly, in recent years matters have begun to improve. Thank goodness, there are now agencies in Judaism taking these issues very seriously and professionally. But it is in the most seemingly Orthodox reaches that still at this moment the blinds are drawn and those who should be punished are protected.

I recall a conversation some years ago with Stuart Eizenstadt, then the U.S. ambassador to the European Union, later involved in helping reclaim Jewish property in Eastern Europe. He told me that he had come across properties in Poland that were originally established by Hasidic groups as refuges for battered wives in the nineteenth century. Clearly, there was a degree of openness then among some religious leaders that was very different from the mood prevailing today. But at the same time, Bertha Pappenheim attested to the blind eyes many other religious leaders turned to the sexual trafficking of children, otherwise known as the "white slave" trade, that so affected the poorer Jewish families of Poland at that time.

Doubtless, the priests and kings of ancient Judea all argued against the prophets and accused them of undermining society. They were, indeed, accused of fomenting trouble, attacking authority, showing disrespect to religious leadership. The prophets believed their task as spiritual leaders was to tell the truth as they saw it. Authority, even if it pays lip service to truth, usually has another agenda: the preservation of the status quo and the limitation of nonconformity. In truth, one needs structure, but at the same time one needs a counterbalance. Where there is injustice, it must be uncovered.

This work must not be seen as an assault on the Orthodox religious position. We who are passionately committed to Torah have a sacred obligation to ensure that it is seen in a positive light. Sometimes that means facing unpleasant realities. Current cases before the courts in the United States and Israel only go to show the matter is pressing and ongoing. The aim of this publication is not to attack Torah or its communities of followers, but to enhance them by clarifying what true Torah values really are. "Truth must sprout from the ground." Where there is light there can be growth.

May 2008

JEREMY ROSEN, Rabbi, PHD, is professor and chairman at the Faculty of Comparative Religion, Faculteit Voor Vergelijkende Godsdienstwetenschappen (FVG), Wilrijk/Antwerp, Belgium, and former director of Yakar Educational Foundation, London. He is an Orthodox rabbi, ordained at Mir Yeshiva in Jerusalem, and a graduate of Cambridge University. He has held positions as a pulpit rabbi, school principal, and academic. He now divides his time between Europe and the United States.

Acknowledgments

Compiling a list of those who encouraged and nurtured this book is almost more daunting to me than the production of the work itself. To begin with, each contributor has his or her own sources of inspiration, and how can I name those? Probably the safest course for me here is to narrate the steps that led me to the task of editing *Tempest in the Temple*, touching, as I go, on the people who were most instrumental in shaping the journey.

In the fall of 2006, I received an unexpected e-mail from Dr. Phyllis Deutsch, editor in chief of the University Press of New England. Phyllis had superbly supervised my previous book, *From Madness to Mutiny*, and wanted to know if I had the subject matter to undertake another book. At the time, *Madness* had been out less than a year and a half; the thought of starting all over again felt like getting pregnant too soon after giving birth. I e-mailed Phyllis to say that I would be appearing later that same evening on ABC's *Nightline* to discuss, with host Cynthia McFadden, child sex scandals in the Jewish community. Considering the controversy surrounding that topic, I thought my response would ensure that I would never hear from Phyllis, or from UPNE, again.

I was wrong. Phyllis let me know soon afterward that she had spoken to her colleague Jonathan D. Sarna. Dr. Sarna, besides being the Joseph H. and Belle R. Braun Professor of American Jewish History at Brandeis University, is also the editor of Brandeis's Series in American Jewish History, Culture, and Life. It turned out that Dr. Sarna and Phyllis both wanted a new book for the series — on precisely the delicate subject of rabbis, the Jewish community, and child sexual abuse.

We all knew that this was no small commitment: a book on the Jewish community's handling of child sex scandals in the prestigious Series in American Jewish History, Culture, and Life would introduce pedophilia and child sex abuse into the company of subjects that describe American Jewish reality. I knew that editing such a book would be a challenge.

I also knew it was one I could not refuse.

Since 1986, when I founded the Help Us Regain The Children legal research center, I have become privy to literally thousands of cases of suspected child sex abuse, many of them arising from within my own religious community. A shocking theme in many of these cases has been how the alleged victim was punished for speaking out, while the facts of the abuse allegations were all too often suppressed. After I organized several hearings by committees of New York's state legislature that confirmed the appalling proportions of the problem, an outraged state senator described one such case (in a letter to federal authorities) as, "an intensely ferocious effort made by judges, social service, and law guardian agencies, rabbis and elected officials to protect the alleged abuser from an investigation" and warned that "a heinous crime has been committed and is being covered up." I knew then that I could not allow those words to be the last on the subject.

My father, Rabbi Dr. Abraham Neustein, and my mother, Shirley Neustein (both now, sadly, deceased), stood by me as I fought to expose the unwelcome truth about child sex abuse — which I knew existed in Jewish communities as well as elsewhere. My father, from time to time, for dramatic emphasis, would pull down from a shelf a huge, unabridged dictionary volume and remind me: "Justice isn't just in here, Amy: it's more than a word in the dictionary!" In a very real sense, my parents provided the original inspiration for this book.

Other inspirations were those in government and the media who listened to me, trusted me, and took action in whatever capacity they could. I will name here the most important: New York governor (and former state senator) David Paterson; Jeremiah B. McKenna, former chief counsel to the New York State Senate Committee on Crime; Alan M. Vinegrad, former assistant U.S. attorney for the Eastern District of New York; Marcia A. Pappas, president of NOW New York State; Mo Therese Hannah, professor of psychology at Siena College in Albany, New York, and chair of the annual Battered Mothers Custody Conference; Judge Samuel Coleman (also a former New York State legislator) of Rockland County, New York; New Jersey congressman Donald Payne; New York congressman Jerrold Nadler; retired Brooklyn congressman Major Owens; retired USA Today columnist and editorial page editor Barbara Reynolds; New York Times metro reporter, and former Washington Post New York bureau chief, Michael Powell; New York Post political columnist Ray

Kerrison; award-winning actress and documentary producer Lee Grant; and producer Roxanna Sherwood of ABC's *Nightline* and *PrimeTime Live*.

Other inspirations have been less public figures, but of no less importance to me: Rabbi Israel Kravitz, my late father's oldest and dearest friend, who shared with him a life devoted to the rabbinate and the Jewish people; Susie Rosenbluth, who repeatedly profiled me and my work in her monthly magazine reaching Orthodox Jewish enclaves in New York and New Jersey; Naomi Maurer, a longtime friend of my family's, whose outrage over what was done to far too many Jewish children lifted me from occasional despair; Evelyn Haies, a loyal and steadfast friend who gave much-needed love in dark times; Sam Friedlander, a confidant and trusted ally; Mark Young, my dear cousin who has repeatedly shown sterling character; Eileen Stenzler, my truest friend and adopted "sister"; and Lino Virdo, a dear elderly friend who can make me laugh uproariously. To all these, and to many more, I offer my sincere thanks.

Every writer/editor needs an editor, and although I have already mentioned the role of UPNE's Phyllis Deutsch and Brandeis University's Jonathan Sarna in the genesis of this book, I want to stress here that my gratitude to both of them for the opportunity of giving life to *Tempest in the Temple* — a project they have shepherded from start to finish — is greater than I can say.

A.N.

Tempest in the Temple

AMY NEUSTEIN

Introduction

In 2002, the Catholic Church priest abuse scandal, after simmering for years, broke in the press, shocking the United States and the world. Lawsuits filed by adult males who had been abused as children prompted the resignation of Cardinal Bernard Law of the Boston Archdiocese and set off a convulsion in the Catholic Church from which it will require years to recover.

With so much attention focused on the sexual abuse of young and adolescent children by Catholic priests, the national media did not at first recognize a parallel scandal taking shape within the Jewish clergy. True, the press had reported cases of individual rabbis who had sexually victimized children. One can hardly forget the case of Baruch Lanner, the rabbinic youth leader of the National Conference of Synagogue Youth (an affiliate of the highly influential Orthodox Union), convicted in 2002 of abusing teens; or that of cantor Howard Nevison of New York's Temple Emanu-El, who pleaded guilty to the abuse of his nephew; or Richard Marcovitz, the Conservative rabbi from Oklahoma convicted of indecent and lewd acts and sexual battery of a child. Still, it was not widely recognized that clergy abuse among Jews might reach the level of scandal, as it had in the Catholic Church.

That changed dramatically several years later. First, in 2006, *New York* magazine featured a report ("On the Rabbi's Knee: Do the Orthodox Jews Have a Catholic-Priest Problem?") on an unprecedented federal lawsuit filed by several Jewish men against a former teacher and the Brooklyn yeshiva that continued to employ him decades after they say they reported being sexually abused by the teacher. Then, ABC's *Nightline*, after a three-month investigation into cover-ups of sex abuse within the Jewish clergy, reported the story of a self-styled Brooklyn "rabbi" and "counselor" charged with first-degree sodomy and child abuse who had taken refuge in Israel to escape prosecution. The following year, the *New York Jewish Week*, a mainstream Jewish weekly with over a hundred thousand readers, reported the results of a study of Orthodox Jewish women and sexual abuse whose findings had just been published in the *American Journal of Psychiatry*.[1] Debra Nussbaum Cohen, writing in the *Jewish Week* ("No Religious Haven from Abuse"), stressed the study's major findings that "sexual abuse was reported by 26% of the respondents surveyed, with 16% reporting abuse occurring by the age of 13."[2]

Child sex scandals had now finally made their way out of the Jewish closet — in stark contrast to 2002, when Jewish media were still largely silent on sexual abuse scandals among Jews (notwithstanding the front-page headlines devoted to pederasty and other abuse scandals that were permeating the Catholic Church). Back then, the editor of this book, together with Michael Lesher, one of this book's contributors, wrote a chapter in *Sex, Religion, Media* (edited by Dane S. Claussen) aptly titled "The Silence of the Jewish Media on Sexual Abuse in the Orthodox Jewish Community."[3] The chapter chronicled case after case of suppression of child sex scandals in the Jewish media, showing how an apparently deliberate attempt was made at the editorial and news levels to keep such stories out of the sight of readers.

Now that the door to the Jewish closet has been pried open, stories that have been in mothballs for years have come to the fore. Consider the landmark case of Avrohom Mondrowitz. The charismatic Brooklyn rabbi and speciously credentialed psychologist fled to Israel in 1984 to escape prosecution for thirteen counts of sodomy and sexual abuse of boys aged nine to fifteen.[4] At the time, and for years afterward, the case received little attention in the U.S. press; it was completely ignored by Jewish media. In November 2007, Mondrowitz was arrested in Jerusalem and now faces extradition to the United States, and the revival of his case has been widely reported in both mainstream and Jewish media; even the Orthodox community's foremost paper, the *Jewish Press*, editorialized that Mondrowitz's long-delayed arrest proved the need for a "more honest approach to the very real problem of pedophilia and abuse in the Orthodox community."[5]

Still, it sometimes seems that a day doesn't go by without an attempt on the part of some powerful Jewish community leaders to lock the barn door after the horses have escaped.

For example, the *New York Jewish Week*'s reportage of the *American Journal of Psychiatry*'s study of sexual abuse among Orthodox Jewish women (whose findings more or less mirror the figures for the non-Jewish population) caused such an uproar in the Jewish community that within two months of Nussbaum

Cohen's article, Rabbi Dr. Marvin Schick reserved a full-page advertisement in the same newspaper for the sole purpose of attacking the article and the study it reported. Rabbi Schick, a nationally known educator and leading spokesperson for Orthodox communities in the United States and Israel, in a full-page advertisement, slammed the study as "scholarly abuse" and up-braided its authors for what he called "reckless scholarship and statistics . . . which constitute a form of group libel and severe cruelty toward observant Jews."[6] Schick's attack prompted Long Island, New York, psychologist, author, and child abuse activist Dr. Michael Salamon to post a rejoinder to a Listserv operated by Nefesh (an international network of Orthodox Jewish mental health professionals in the United States and Canada), writing, "I am amazed at how many of us are more interested in 'shooting the messengers' than in at-tempting to use this information to help us serve our communities better."[7]

Salamon's view is reason itself, yet many in the Jewish community sympa-thize with Schick and would much prefer to keep child sex scandals locked away in a closet. While certainly not denying the existence of child sexual abuse, they argue, oddly, the merits of suppressing the issue: they question whether protecting the 25 percent of the Jewish population that may have been abused is fair to the remaining 75 percent that has not been abused and that stands to suffer, if not the trauma of sexual victimization, then at least from public shame when it becomes known that there are sexual predators within the Jewish community. For these critics, the issue is closely linked to the fear that revelations about Jewish offenders will promote anti-Semitism. This "dilemma" — whether to protect the sex abuse victim at the expense of the community — is not something new. It was recognized, and rejected, in 1990 by Irving ("Yitz") Greenberg, a New York Orthodox rabbi, in an edito-rial appearing in *Moment*. Rabbi Greenberg admonished rabbis, media, and the Jewish community facing cases of child sexual abuse:

> Spiritual leaders who ignore or even cover up the presence of sexual abuse, Jewish media that continue the conspiracy of silence by acting as if this does not happen in the Jewish community, *those who cut off or isolate victims who dare speak out*, bring upon themselves the judgment that the Torah places on the accessory and bystander: "Do not stand idly by the blood of your neighbor" (Leviticus 19:16). (April 15, 1990, p. 49) [emphasis added]

Since many Jews, even in today's North America, live in tightly knit communities, we cannot ignore or minimize the legitimate needs of Jewish communities, even when opposed to those of a child who is sexually abused by a rabbi, a teacher, a camp counselor, a parent, or anyone in a position of authority. No sensible person could argue that Jews have no right to be concerned about their public image; history has proven that Jews, like any other minority, are judged more harshly than others for such social problems as alcoholism, substance abuse, domestic violence, mental illness, or juvenile delinquency. A century ago, immigrant Jews were so ashamed to admit to poverty that many rejected government benefits to which they were rightfully entitled.

However, much of the community's sensitivity to public scandal derives less from fear of anti-Semitism than from the general fear of shame (in Yiddish, *shonda*), a blight that can easily ruin a family's name, its status in the community, and the marriages of its children for generations. *Shonda*, which has traditionally served as a useful mechanism for social enforcement of community values, norms, ethics, and propriety, has a disadvantage: fear of public shame can loom so large in the eyes of the Jewish community that many of its leaders and lay members will deny the existence of a scandalous secret like sexual abuse. Worse, they will vilify the victim who speaks out as a traitor to the community.

More than American Catholics — members of another religious minority, but one that tends to define itself as "American" before "Catholic" — Jews still identify strongly with other Jews. This means that when dealing with Jewish child-sex scandals, we cannot ignore the psychosocial dynamics of the Jewish community as an integral part of the problem, as well as a necessary part of the solution. It is precisely this ingrained ethos of Jewish communities, regulated and controlled by the fear of *shonda*, which the contributors to *Tempest in the Temple* seek to analyze, dissect, and explore with a frankness never before devoted to the issue of child sex abuse within the Jewish clergy.

To accomplish this task, the essayists are at pains to strip away the façade that has too long protected Jewish communities from incisive critique. Such candor by no means implies that these essayists have embarked on an attack against Jews. On the contrary, the contributors to this book demonstrate a well-informed, professional, sensitive, and respectful posture in examining Jewish institutional values, the norms that have helped to shape Jewish cultural life since the Middle Ages. These are not writers who are looking for a flashy headline or for a chance at "Jew bashing." Nor do they automatically accept as true every abuse accusation; they carefully examine the facts of each case, well knowing the irreparable damage that can be done to a clergyman who is falsely accused. The contributors, drawn from the three branches of Judaism (Orthodox, Conservative, and Reform), are experienced professionals who have earned good reputations in their respective fields.

Joining the discussion is Barbara Blaine, an attorney and social worker, who, as a survivor of abuse by a priest, founded SNAP (Survivor Network of those Abused by Priests), the world's leading activist group on this issue, which broke the wall of silence about sexual abuse in the Catholic Church. Her work has been instrumental in raising public consciousness about the pervasiveness of child sexual abuse committed by priests — and has also paved the way for Jews to confront pedophiles and child sex abusers within their own communities. In this connection, I would like to mention that Blaine's contribution to a collection of essays focusing on Jewish clergy abuse was specifically praised by Rabbi Dr. Saul J. Berman, an eminent Modern Orthodox rabbi and director of Continuing Rabbinic Education at Yeshivat Chovevei Torah (YCT) Rabbinical School in New York, when he reviewed the manuscript at the publisher's request. Rabbi Berman observed:

> The article by Barbara Blaine, entitled, "My Cross to Bear," [which serves] as a fascinating tale of generating some responsiveness and accountability on issues of abuse within the Catholic Church . . . was [of] definite value in preserving the account of what had happened in another religious community as a model for what needed to, and could, happen in the Jewish grass roots response to this matter.

Given the caliber of the contributors and their approach to this delicate subject, *Tempest in the Temple* naturally offers an open discussion of some of the deep-rooted fears in the Jewish community, fears that at times have been the reason for serious misapplications of biblical precepts and Talmudic law. These principles were never intended to protect the guilty and convict the innocent; most certainly, they were not meant to shield pedophiles within the Jewish clergy while sacrificing their victims on the altar of community shame. Anything less than a candid analysis would be a grave disservice to victims of abuse, to Jewish communities (which must take a proactive role in helping to heal the victims), and to the sexual offenders in our communities whose criminal behavior must be stopped.

This book will not be pleasant reading; at times, it will stir readers to want to rationalize or even deny the accounts of the cruel mistreatment of abuse victims by those who, all too often, defend and support abusive rabbis. The contributors have made a deliberate decision not to hold back what they know firsthand about clergy abuse and its poisonous effects on its victims, while at the same time realizing how difficult it may be for readers to digest this material.

The contributors are practicing rabbis, educators, pastoral counselors, sociologists, mental health professionals, and legal advocates for abuse victims; they rank among the most eminent professionals who work on the front lines of sexual abuse committed by rabbis and others in positions of religious leadership. The editor undertook to gather as diverse a group of voices as possible for this work, so as not to skew the book in any one direction by favoring one branch of Judaism over another. There is no question that pedophilia and sexual abuse exist across *all* branches of Judaism. It happens that some of the most heartrending accounts of sexual victimization (and of powerful institutionalized denial) come from within the Orthodox sector of Judaism, even though Orthodox Jews make up only 20 percent of U.S. Jewry. In addition, the editor found within Orthodox communities some of the most passionate voices urging that the problem of child sexual abuse be faced head-on. Similar voices from within non-Orthodox communities — some of whom are represented in this book — will doubtless emerge in larger numbers. It is the editor's prayerful hope that *Tempest* will prove only the beginning of the written discussion of this topic, a discussion that is bound to include a larger proportion of Conservative and Reform Jews than is found in this volume.

The makeup of this book was arguably shaped by the zeitgeist. A succession of high-profile clergy abuse cases, principally within the Orthodox community, have recently attracted headlines: Lanner, Kolko, Mondrowitz. Professionals closely connected with these cases participated in this project, providing reflections and proposing reforms to prevent future victims.

That these cases arose in Orthodox communities is perhaps not very surprising. Orthodox children spend many hours each weekday in religious schools (yeshivas); many also have an additional half day of school on Sunday. This gives a potentially abusive teacher or counselor much more exposure to children than in other Jewish communities. Besides this, Orthodox youth often participate in such extracurricular activities as basketball and other sports, exclusively organized and run by members of the religious community. It follows naturally that parents in Orthodox communities have expressed particular interest in exposing and stopping the abusive rabbis (many of whom are teachers) among them.

Such people also express anger at the special Jewish institutions to which many Orthodox Jews turn before going to any secular authority, in cases of alleged child sexual abuse as in other cases. Author and lecturer Rabbi Dr. Bernhard Rosenberg, who is Orthodox by training, ordination, and religious practice — though now the rabbi of a Conservative New Jersey congregation — is a case in point. Rabbi Rosenberg wrote a scathing letter to the *Jewish Press* in July 2000 about the case of Rabbi Baruch Lanner. Rabbi Rosenberg wrote: "My anger is not only with him [Rabbi Lanner], but with the rabbis, head advisors . . . who supposedly had knowledge of his actions and protected him by their silence. . . . Why did [child agencies] not act? Was it because they received testimony from rabbis who covered up for him?"[8]

Rosenberg articulated what many others have suspected: well-organized rabbis can affect the performance of secular law enforcement officials. Traditional Jewish communities exhibit bloc voting patterns: followers often take directions from their leaders in choosing candidates for office. This gives Orthodox rabbis in many large communities unusual political power and thus possible influence even over secular law enforcement. And it is clear that many of the communities they lead and represent are vehemently opposed to charges of child sex abuse leaving the four corners of the community. In a large religious enclave outside of London, an eighteen-year-old rabbinic student named Eli Cohen was convicted of indecently assaulting a young girl. The day after his sentencing, "between 100–200 people threw missiles at the home of the family of the victim . . . shouting 'informers'"![9] Chapter 8 of this book deals with a case in which rabbinic influence affected a district attorney's decision to drop serious charges against a rabbi in a child sex abuse case.

This book of eleven contributors is divided into three sections. The first section, titled "Breaking Vows," addresses Jewish clergy who break their "vows" (sacred obligations)[10] through active pedophilia, including serious acts of child sexual abuse. The section begins with the story of how a Conservative Massachusetts synagogue survived a sex abuse scandal (the cantor was convicted of abusing a mentally retarded girl), an ensuing prosecution by state authorities, and a protracted civil lawsuit brought against the synagogue and its officers by the abused congregant's family. This chapter is followed by discussions of the psychodynamics of sexual abuse by clergy, offered by mental health professionals and educators who elucidate why leaders fall prey to sexual transgressions, what makes them commit acts of sexual abuse, and what pastoral counselors, therapists, and rabbinic educators can do to thwart or prevent such behavior. The contributors to this section examine sexual boundary violations from both a psychological and a Jewish standpoint. The second section, titled "Sacrificing Victims," enucleates the community dynamics surrounding abuse: how a community unwittingly encourages co-enablers who allow abusers to continue to abuse; how victims of abuse are all too often ignored or cast off by their religious communities (suffering serious psychological injury as a result); and how powerful religious institutions protect their own, even when the rabbis they protect are child molesters. In this section we are joined by Barbara Blaine, founder of SNAP, for a moving personal account of how the Catholic Church, as a religious institution, protects its own at the expense of its victims. The third section, titled "Let Me Know the Way," addresses in detail how as a community we can overcome ignorance, bias, corruption, and prejudice associated with clergy sexual abuse. Solutions — those that have already succeeded, as well as new solutions that have not yet been tried — are explored here.

While this book is the first to hold a magnifying glass to child sex scandals in temples and synagogues, its purpose is not to blame or shame Jews as such. Rather, its purpose is to examine this horrific problem with as much clarity and precision as possible so that the best remedies can be offered to the community as a whole. No Jew among us can afford to step aside and let the next person carry this burden. We must all contribute to stopping child sexual abuse in temples, religious schools, and synagogues, camps, youth groups, or wherever there are children and adolescents, because wherever there is power, seduction, and access to vulnerable children, we can be sure that sexual predators will seek their prey. For this reason, *Tempest in the Temple* is likely to be as timely in the future as it is now, since as long as sexual pathologies exist society will have to deal with sexual predators in search of their next victims. And why should we ever have thought our clergy was immune?

NOTES

1. R. Yehuda, M. Friedman, T. Y. Rosenbaum, E. Labinsky, and J. Schmeidler, "History of Past Sexual Abuse in Married Observant Jewish Women," *American Journal of Psychiatry* 164 (2007): pp. 1700–1706.

2. October 26, 2007, p. 10

3. See Dane S. Claussen, ed., *Sex, Religion, Media* (Lanham, Md.: Rowman and Littlefield, 2002), pp. 79–87.

4. While Mondrowitz's "diploma" in psychology from Columbia University proved to be false, it is not clear whether he similarly faked his rabbinic credentials. He has never produced a certificate of rabbinic ordination from any qualified institution, but that does not rule out his having been ordained privately. In any case, he was known in Brooklyn as "rabbi," and his right to the title was never questioned until after the news spread about the charges against him. See Tina Kelley, "22 Years Later, a Child Abuse Suspect's Extradition is Sought," *New York Times*, November 16, 2007, p. B4.

5. "Justice Delayed — and Possibly Denied," *Jewish Press*, November 22, 2007, p. 78.

6. *New York Jewish Week*, December 21, 2007.

7. Posted to Nefesh Listserv December 30, 2007, and later obtained from Dr. Salamon.

8. Rabbi Dr. Bernhard H. Rosenberg, "The NCSY Incident," letter to the *Jewish Press*, July 14, 2000, p. 79.

9. *Guardian*, August 2, 1991, p. 2.

10. In Judaism, clergy do not take *formal* vows as in some other religious traditions.

Breaking Vows

LOEL M. WEISS & MARK ITZKOWITZ

Unholy Waters

How a Massachusetts Synagogue Found Its Way to
Shore after a Sex Abuse Scandal, a Prosecution, and a
Lawsuit — As Narrated by the Synagogue's Rabbi
and Its Legal Counsel

BEGINNINGS

The Rabbi

The journey started on February 6, 2003, and ended May
28, 2006. It was a journey of sadness, frustration, and hope. It was a journey
that allowed us to meet and interact with some wonderful people but also to
see behaviors that left us saddened and angry.

February 6 was a Thursday and I was at home. My father had just had major
heart surgery and I was dealing with my fear and my mother's fear and concern.
Dad spent most of the next sixteen weeks in the intensive care unit before
dying. Either situation, the story that was about to unfold at Temple Beth Am
or my father's illness, would have been more than enough. Together, I can't
imagine how I got through that winter and spring. It was only through the tremendous support of family and friends, as well as the temple president, Scott
Belgard, and the temple's attorney, Mark Itzkowitz, that I was able to "walk
through the valley of the shadow of death," and emerge on the other side.

Our synagogue, Temple Beth Am, is located in Randolph, Massachusetts,
an inner suburb of Boston. At the time this story begins, we had been reading
daily newspaper reports of accusations of sexual abuse allegedly committed
by Catholic clergy and documented instances in which the Catholic hierarchy,
including Cardinal Bernard Law, had allegedly known about many of these

incidents, had chosen to hide them from the public, and had allegedly moved the perpetrators to different parishes to escape responsibility for their actions. When I think back on what happened at Temple Beth Am, I reflect on those scandalous stories emerging from the Catholic Church and ask myself how they affected me. I believe they made a difference. I cannot be certain how we would have reacted to our own situation had it not been for these sordid revelations; but I suspect that if I hadn't been jolted by what Cardinal Law had apparently done, I too would have tried to handle the sex abuse accusation privately. I would have tried to convince the accuser and her family that this was a *shonda* (an embarrassment). It wouldn't have been hard: in fact, when the victim's family first made me aware of the accusation, they themselves expressed concern about the image of the temple and the Jewish community. It was I who encouraged them to call the police and to move forward. I was not going to repeat the errors of the Boston Archdiocese.

That fateful first call came on a Thursday. It was from a couple I knew well, both of them congregants. They said that there was something very important that they needed to discuss with me — could I come right over to their house? I had a previous engagement and suggested that we meet on Friday morning in my office. They agreed to a Friday morning meeting but insisted that it had to be in their home. This was an unusual request and during the evening I tried to guess what issue might cause them to need to see me immediately and in their house. I couldn't have imagined.

I drove to the house on Friday morning after minyan and was ushered into the living room. Already gathered were my congregants, two young women who were reintroduced to me as two of their daughters, and a friend of the family who I subsequently learned worked for an attorney but was not an attorney. Their third and youngest daughter, who regularly attended Shabbat services with her mother, was not present.

I sat down. After some preliminaries, they said their youngest daughter had reported being raped by our *hazzan* (cantor).

I was stunned.

At that time, the hazzan had worked for Temple Beth Am for twenty years, two years longer than I. He was almost seventy years old and was beloved by the congregation. In fact, a meeting of the Board of Directors scheduled for that coming Sunday was expected to recommend that the congregation ap-prove an extension of his contract. In addition, the hazzan and his wife were personal friends of the family who had just accused him of sexual abuse.

I hardly remember the next few minutes. The other daughters were very angry. While both parents were concerned about their youngest daughter, the father was also was concerned about the effect this charge would have on the community as a whole.

I asked who else had been told and was informed that the daughter's psychologist had been told earlier in the week. The daughter was in her thirties at the time; she was mentally retarded and functioned at a minimal level. She was living at home and had a job at a local nursing home. I remember being surprised that the psychologist had not informed the authorities, for he was a "mandated reporter" under Massachusetts law (though I, as a clergyman, was not). When I inquired on that point, the family said that they had told the psychologist that they needed time to tell me and to decide what else to do. They said their psychologist had given them a week before he would act.

I told them that if they believed their daughter's allegation, they should call the police. Knowing that this woman was mentally retarded, I admit to having had some doubts about her reliability. Nevertheless, especially in light of the scandal in the Catholic Church, I felt that I could not simply ignore the charges. As Mark Itzkowitz, the temple's attorney, said later, the temple does not have the personnel or the expertise to investigate the charges; that is up to the authorities.

Although it was the family's responsibility to call the police, it was my responsibility to inform the president of the shul. I excused myself, went into a different room, and used my cell phone to inform Scott Belgard what I had just been told. We agreed that we needed to separate the hazzan from the community until the situation was resolved. Scott said that he would contact Mark Itzkowitz. While I was not involved in that discussion, I found out later that Mark had concurred in our decision.

Immediately afterward, remembering that it was Friday morning, we informed the shul's ritual chairperson, Judith Freedman Caplan, that the hazzan would not be able to perform his duties that Shabbat and that she would need to get lay people to lead services.

I also believed it was important to keep the name of the alleged victim confidential, and, from that time until the present, I have never revealed it. However, her name was in the court documents that her attorney ultimately filed; moreover, because a description of her as a woman in her thirties who was mentally retarded was printed in the newspapers after the charges were made, everyone in the community soon knew who she was. It was not in our power to prevent this.

I remained as the police arrived and began their investigation. They were told that some of the alleged incidents took place in the temple, some in the hazzan's car, and some at the nursing home where the victim worked. The officer explained what would happen next: there would be an investigation of the allegations not only by the local police but also, because the woman was mentally retarded and her parents were her legal guardians, by the county district attorney, who would handle the investigation through a special unit that dealt with sexual assault cases. Based on their findings, the district attorney would decide whether charges would be filed. The police officer also told me that the temple would be kept informed as the investigation proceeded.

I had arrived at the house at around 8:00 A.M. and left a little after 11:00 A.M. I was shaken, upset, and unsure, but so far felt that we had handled things as well as we could.

I spoke to Scott Belgard later in the day. By then he had spoken to the hazzan, had informed him of the charges, and had told him that he was being suspended from his duties as hazzan, with pay, until the investigation was completed. At that time there would be a further evaluation of the situation.

I remember feeling incredibly fortunate that the president of the temple was willing to deal with this very hard situation directly. I couldn't imagine having to tell my colleague that he was being accused of rape. I still couldn't believe that it had happened.

The Lawyer

In my legal practice, I have concentrated on representing victims of violent crime in civil cases in which they have sought financial compensation from various sources in an attempt to repair their shattered lives and persona. By way of example, I have represented many victims of incest and rape; victims whose personalities inevitably had been altered for the worse, including more than a dozen victims of both sexes and many ages who had been raped by clergy of various denominations. I even have represented Jewish clergy who have been physically and emotionally abused by spouses or "significant others." Although I had known the hazzan for more than fifteen years, had respected, liked, and trusted him, I did not doubt that he was capable of the charges alleged. Everyone is capable of them.

Nor did I doubt the honesty of the victim or her family. Although the information I had received from President Scott Belgard did not enable either of us to determine who the victim was (Rabbi Weiss had not told us her name, age, or mental disabilities), my twenty years of experience representing rape victims has confirmed the scientific and anecdotal evidence consistently reported by police, social service, and victim rights organizations. This evidence shows that reports of sexual abuse and rape are overwhelmingly accurate and not contrived; that details of rape incidents often emerge slowly and incompletely over time as the victim increasingly regains a sense of personal safety and is able to confront and disclose — to persons that she comes to trust — the specifics of the trauma(s); that the damage caused by rape is far greater than commonly understood, not only to the victim but to those closest to the victim and, indeed, to the community as a whole; that no individual is incapable of victimizing and no individual is incapable of being victimized; and that incidents of rape are grossly underreported, not exaggerated.

Scott Belgard was not able to reach me until midmorning Friday to advise me of the allegations against the hazzan and of the fact that the police had been involved at Rabbi Weiss's suggestion. By then, Scott had already spoken with the hazzan, a man he and his family had grown to know, respect, and love over more than twenty years. Scott advised me that he and the rabbi had determined that the hazzan had to be separated from the congregation, at least for the time being, in order to protect the congregation from any potential danger, and that he had informed the hazzan that he was suspended from the performance of his duties and was not to enter the temple until further notice. In hindsight I am deeply impressed by the remarkable judgment, sensitivity, and courage these two men (rabbi and president) showed in taking such steps, given the long-term relationship between the hazzan and the congregation — especially since at the time neither Scott nor Rabbi Weiss could bring himself to believe the allegations against the hazzan.

That, however, was just the start. Immediate steps were required to ensure the protection of the community from myriad dangers from a variety of sources. This required both identifying "the community" at risk and identifying the risks. Most immediate was the risk of additional physical/sexual harm to the primary victim from the accused. The rabbi already had addressed that issue by convincing the family to contact the police, which had the effect of separating the hazzan and the victim. We would find out later that the victim's parents, against the advice of their other children, had waited two days before contacting the victim's long-term psychotherapist; against the advice of their other children and the victim's therapist, had waited four days before contacting the rabbi, and then only at the insistence of the psychotherapist; and had waited five days before contacting the police, and then only at the urging of the rabbi. Due to her mental disabilities, the victim had earlier been assigned a state agency caseworker who had as her function the protection of mentally disabled persons; the family did not contact that agency or caseworker.

The victim and her family required immediate assistance to help them deal with the effects of the trauma. To their credit, the family had rallied to the defense of their daughter and sister, not questioning her allegations due to the manner in which the victim had reported them. This, one would expect, at least saved the victim the additional trauma suffered by so many rape victims of being disbelieved by those to whom they turn for protection and support. The family as a whole had been victimized, not only by the vicarious harm which they were suffering as the result of the victim's trauma, but by the betrayal of the friendship and trust that they had placed in the hazzan, both as leader of the temple community and as close personal friend for many years. The rabbi was able to report that the family already had sought the assistance of the victim's psychotherapist to help the family address their shared trauma. In addition, they also had sought legal assistance from a friend who was a paralegal and from that friend's employer. The rabbi would remain in close contact with the family and with the victim herself in an attempt to provide religious counseling and support for as long as the legal posture of the case permitted.

The hazzan and his family also would require assistance. Not only had the hazzan and his wife been active in the community, they had raised their children and grandchildren within the community of Temple Beth Am. Whether there was any truth to the allegations against the hazzan, there were no allegations against his family. Most assuredly, they would be traumatized by the allegations and their aftermath and would require community support.

Then there was the rabbi himself. The scope of the rabbi's duties needed to be investigated. The rabbi, in consultation with his colleagues, was in the best position to determine the requirements of halacha (Jewish law), and he did so. Legal counsel was required to research quickly the requirements of civil law. Statutes and regulations had to be investigated rapidly as there is a legal duty to report "immediate[ly]" allegations of sexual abuse disclosed to persons identified as "mandated reporters" by Massachusetts law. Indeed, one of my clergy abuse cases involved allegations that mandated reporters had failed in their reporting duties for a period of approximately thirty-six hours, during which the perpetrator sexually assaulted a second victim, my client. At the time of the allegations against the hazzan, clergy were not deemed "mandated reporters." (That was changed by an amendment to the law before the case concluded, as a result of the disclosures of widespread sexual abuse within the Boston Archdiocese, abetted by the repeated failures of Catholic leadership to report and/or to prevent the abuse.)

The community at risk included, of course, the congregation of Temple Beth Am, where the hazzan had officiated for two decades. Scott Belgard's immediate decision to suspend the hazzan minimized any possibility of future abuse, at least until additional information could be obtained and further action taken. However, the community included not only those who could be at risk of molestation in the future but those who might have been abused in the past. Such people needed to be identified, protected, and assisted, as did their families and close contacts. Moreover, the risk of harm to the community was not only sexual, physical, and emotional; it included the harm that was sure to follow from the disruption of the normal religious functioning of the temple. It included the harm that would come from a rapid flow of rumors, innuendo, misinformation, and misconceptions. The risk of factionalism and disintegration of the community could not be underestimated. It would be an injustice to the sexual abuse victim to call the larger temple community "victims," but there could be no question that all would be affected by the allegations and by everything that would follow from them.

Finally, the community at risk included the Jewish community of Greater Boston, the Jewish community of Massachusetts, the Jewish community of the United States — indeed, in some sense, Jews everywhere. By February 2003, when the allegations against the hazzan were reported, more than 550 victims of clergy sexual abuse within the Boston Archdiocese had asserted civil claims against the leadership of the Catholic Church. The Massachusetts attorney general was preparing a report that would be released within the following six months, documenting over 1,000 such victims within that archdiocese between 1940 and 2000. We all knew that allegations of sexual abuse by a single Jewish clergyman might lead to many more such accusations and, no matter what the facts were, could encourage anti-Semitic calumnies.

To address these concerns, we made fruitless efforts to obtain guidance from the United Synagogue of Conservative Judaism (USCJ), the umbrella organization of Conservative Judaism. (Ultimately, we learned that USCJ did not have any written policies to address the situation.) I already knew from my own cases dealing with clergy abuse that the Catholic Church's response had generally depended on its ability to hide information from the public. When information could be hidden, the Church did not hesitate to make false promises to victims to remove abusive priests from ministry in exchange for promises of silence by the victims and their families. After the scope of the abuse no longer could be hidden, the Church did not hesitate to issue public press releases referencing vague general accusations of misconduct by unnamed victims against specifically identified priests. I did not want that way to be our way.

To help protect the community from disruption, the decision was made to funnel all inquiries to the rabbi, Scott, or me, and to have only one of the three of us respond. The Ritual Committee chairperson, Judith Freedman Caplan, was told promptly that the hazzan would be unable to perform his duties for the indefinite future and that arrangements would have to be made among lay people to cover his responsibilities. She became the unsung fourth member of the congregation to assume an inordinate amount of responsibility over the next several years to ensure that the congregation continued to function in as normal a fashion as possible.

I was also concerned about disruption of the congregation as a result of the criminal investigation. Congregants could be subjected to police interrogation, records could be subpoenaed, and the synagogue's computer system could be seized pursuant to search warrant. The loss of the computers and their records could paralyze the operation of the temple office. But at the same time, I wanted to perform our own investigation of the scope of the hazzan's criminal sexual misconduct, if any. I knew we would never be in a position to determine definitively whether any criminal misconduct had occurred. The investigation would focus on whether there had been prior allegations of sexual misconduct or other nonsexual misconduct, prior conduct that could have given rise to such allegations, and the temple's response to such allegations and conduct, if any. This seemed to me the best way to do the right thing on behalf of all of us.

FIRST STEPS

The Rabbi
On Shabbat, we told people that the hazzan was not able to be in shul. Remarkably, no one questioned us further.

On Sunday morning, the president, Scott Belgard, asked the members of his Executive Committee to come into my office fifteen minutes before the scheduled start of the Board of Directors meeting. Mark Itzkowitz was there as well.

Members of the board were told as much as we knew and that the hazzan's contract extension would be removed from the table. We asked them to be very discreet because the lives and reputations of many people hung in the balance. In executive session, a formal motion was made to reconsider whether to renew the hazzan's contract. The motion to reconsider renewal of the contract was passed unanimously.

The next week was filled with meetings. (In between them, I visited my father in the hospital in Boston almost every day.) I confess that at the time I wanted to stonewall, to circle the wagons and share as little as possible. Mark, however, insisted that we do just the opposite: that at every possible moment, by phone, e-mail, and regular mail, we keep everyone informed as to what was happening. As it turned out, Mark was 100 percent correct. That we chose to follow this advice was probably the single most important decision we made.

Over the next two weeks, the police investigated the allegations, including interviewing me and performing various DNA tests in parts of our temple building. This was quite upsetting, thinking that evidence of rape would be found in our chapel!

On Friday, February 21, 2003, exactly two weeks since I had first spoken with the victim's family, the police called to inform me that the hazzan was being arrested that day.

A news story appeared in the *(Quincy, Mass.) Patriot Ledger* on Shabbat, the next day, informing everyone as follows:

Robert Shapiro, the hazzan or cantor at Temple Beth-Am, pleaded innocent Friday to three counts of rape and four counts of indecent assault and battery on a mentally retarded woman.

The incidents allegedly took place over the past year, some of them at a Canton nursing home.

Shapiro, 69, was released on personal recognizance after his arraignment in Quincy District Court. Assistant District Attorney Lisa Beatty's request for $2,500 cash bail was denied, according to David Traub, spokesman for Norfolk County District Attorney William Keating.

Shapiro was ordered to stay away from the Meadowbrook Skilled Nursing and Rehabilitation Center in Canton and to have no contact with the alleged victim and her family. He was also ordered to report every two weeks to the court probation department, according to Traub.

The incidents allegedly took place over the past year at both the nursing home and the temple, according to attorney Bruce Namenson of Quincy, who represents the alleged victim.

After Shabbat services on Saturday morning, Scott, Mark, and I stayed to provide everyone the opportunity to express their feelings and ask questions. The next day, Sunday, we had a congregational meeting. The sanctuary was packed. Again, questions were asked, comments made. The attitude was subdued but with an air of unfocused anger. Mark quietly and gently answered every question and tried to help people understand what he knew and that this was going to be a very long and arduous process. I remember thinking of something I'd heard quoted from Supreme Court Justice Potter Stewart, that the last thing he wished for even his worst enemy was to be a party in a lawsuit in the American judicial system. I think he was right.

The Lawyer

Soon after the article in the *Patriot Ledger*, I read a statement to a meeting of the congregation in which I explained that Hazzan Shapiro had been arrested and charged with three counts of rape and four counts of indecent assault and battery on a mentally retarded woman. I gave the facts as simply and directly as I could, and then added that, as I saw it, we all had a moral obligation to try to protect the safety and reputations of everyone in our temple "family." Therefore, I suggested that anyone approached by reporters should "exercise the utmost circumspection," bearing in mind the teaching of Rabbi Elazar ben Shamua in *Pirkei Avot*: "Let the honor of your student be as dear to you as your own; the honor of your friend as cherished as your respect for your teacher; and your respect for your teacher as great as your awe of heaven." I hoped that would do for the moment.

THE STRAIN

The Rabbi

The next few weeks were again filled with meetings. This time, however, they were not practical but emotional. I spent a large part of my day listening to congregants. Most could not believe the charges. A few claimed to have had suspicions. Most, like mourners sitting shiva, just had the need to retell the story.

From that first Friday when I was made aware of the allegations, I had made the decision to be in contact with both the hazzan and the victim and her family. Each week, I would call and visit. Even after his arrest, I continued to support the hazzan; partly because I believed in his innocence, partly because he was a friend, and partly because everyone deserves support, even wrongdoers.

As I listened to congregants and spent time with the hazzan, I began to realize that he and the victim were by no means the only ones affected. In fact, the entire community became victims, including the hazzan's wife and family. Unfortunately, I was never able to speak to his family without him present.

The victim and her family were in need of much support. In truth, many congregants tried to give it to them. Others felt as though the situation was the family's fault. How could they do this to our beloved hazzan? As I have mentioned, the victim, her family, and the hazzan's family had been very close for a very long time. They had spent a lot of time together at both families' houses; therefore, it never excited much attention that the hazzan would drive the alleged victim to synagogue for Friday evening services or take her for ice cream or seek her out when he visited patients at the nursing home.

Many congregants noted that during the kiddush following Shabbat morning services less than a week before making her allegations public, the alleged victim had behaved with the hazzan in a way that had seemed very flirtatious, holding onto his shoulder or holding his hand. No one had given this much thought, because at all times the alleged victim's mother was present and because, again, people knew that the families were very close. Now everything was changed.

There were other people to deal with outside the congregation. We were especially concerned about our students, both those still living in the community and those away at college. No matter how much we understood that the alleged victim was an adult and not a child, because she was mentally retarded and functioned at a very minimal level and because of the situation with the Catholic Church, I couldn't help but be concerned about our students. I sent a letter to all of our college students, noting that this was a very difficult time for Temple Beth Am, and adding this:

Judaism teaches us many things: not to gossip, to respect the legal process which means that people are innocent until proven guilty and not to bear false witness. More than ever, this is a time for our community to come together to support each other, Hazzan Shapiro and the alleged victim. If you would like, feel free to contact the Hazzan, he needs our support. Because of the confidentiality of the situation, it is impossible to contact the victim, but rest assured she is being cared for as well.

I concluded the letter by asking anyone with questions to feel free to contact me. Of course I knew that there would be questions. I didn't yet know how many there would be.

The Lawyer

Sometimes, the hardest thing to do is that which you know must be done. We wanted, first and foremost, to provide honest information. But that is a difficult thing to do when one does not have the full story, and when both too much disclosure and too little disclosure can be harmful. It is especially difficult when people want to know "the truth" and the truth is hidden. It is even more difficult when information must be shared in stages, with ever-increasing numbers of people receiving each disclosure, not all of whom share similar goals or sensitivities. It is agonizingly difficult when one realizes that, at each stage, the people receiving the information can misuse it.

Ritual can be an ally in such a situation. Symbols and procedures that stress the unusual importance of a situation convey that significance to the listener. For that reason, when we delivered information, we chose to use procedures that we had seldom, if ever, used before, to inform our listeners that we were using them and why we were using them, and to obtain their assent and their cooperation in their use.

Our system for sharing information about the sex abuse allegation was detailed and unusual. First, we shared information with each other. Next, we informed the six members of the Executive Committee, the officers of the temple who executed decisions of the Board of Directors. Next, we informed the twenty-four-member board, the decision-making body of the congregation. Next, we informed the congregation as a whole. Then, we confirmed the substance of the disclosures in written statements shared with the members of the congregation who had not been able to attend the meetings. At each stage, we impressed upon our listeners the dangers of further disclosure: inadvertent and/or deliberate *lashon hara* (gossip); the potential to ruin the reputations of everyone involved; the spread of gossip and incorrect/false information; the danger of worsening the emotional harm that had occurred and that would continue to occur; the danger of dividing the congregation; the danger of interfering with legally required investigations, which themselves were required to occur in accordance with legal procedures; the danger of damaging the standing of the temple in the town of Randolph and in the Greater Boston Jewish community; and the danger of harming the standing of the Greater Boston Jewish community and inadvertently encouraging anti-Semitism. We used these informational sessions not only to provide information but to educate in Jewish values. The rabbi began sermonizing about *lashon hara* and its dangers. We used examples and lessons from Jewish philosophy and history to illustrate points.

We addressed the Board of Directors in executive session. This meant that nonmembers were excluded, doors were closed, and minutes of meetings only noted the convening of executive session. In the eight years I had served on the temple's Board of Directors, this was the first time we had made use of such a procedure.

After we made statements to the congregation — often reading from prepared texts to ensure that we said exactly what we meant to say — we took questions until the listeners had run out of questions. The most painful question asked of us at the first congregational meeting, both for its accusatory tone and for its false premise, was "Why were you covering it up?" By the end of the meeting, I believe we had dispelled that erroneous assumption. Not only did people appear satisfied that we really were trying to do the right thing, but they offered to help us by heeding our warnings and by providing us with information and with leads to more information.

At the suggestion of a psychologist member of the congregation, the rabbi invited several psychotherapists and mental health counselors to make themselves available to the congregation for counseling, and indeed they conducted a counseling session for the congregation as a whole. The rabbi advised congregants to remain in individual contact with the affected parties. Since we had not disclosed the victim's identity, the rabbi suggested that people send cards and letters to the rabbi directly, which he then would bring to the victim and her family.

We tried to be particularly solicitous of the needs of teens, children, and their parents. Although the hazzan was not accused of pedophilia, and at no time did we receive information alleging such behavior, younger community members likely would see themselves as having been at greatest risk of abuse by the hazzan and easily could misconstrue the hazzan's past involvement with them. Older congregants did not understand how children and their families could have felt at risk since the allegations involved an adult. However, in the climate of the Catholic Church scandal, which overwhelmingly involved child and teen victims, it hardly could be otherwise. The other question that I clearly remember from the congregational meeting was from a parent: "How do we tell our children?" Our answers were less than satisfactory, I am afraid, but the genuineness of our concern helped avoid divisions between older and younger congregants.

Our full cooperation with law enforcement led to some of my most painful experiences: sitting silently and in deep humiliation with detectives on the staircase outside the darkened chapel while state crime scene investigators conducted tests for semen in the pews and on the *bimah* (pulpit); escorting detectives through the empty synagogue, at times when the sanctity of the building would not be disturbed, to ensure them of our cooperation and to discourage them from investigating at times that would be embarrassing to the congregation. I also interviewed potential witnesses about any knowledge of possibly wrongful conduct by the hazzan at any time in the preceding two decades. I maintained contact with the district attorney's office and with local police detectives in the hope of avoiding further surprises and being able to anticipate telephone calls from the press.

At every stage of these processes, it was necessary to continue to educate people about the dangers of spreading rumors and false information. Most people understood readily, but some required great investments of time, effort, and patience. At different stages of the long process, the rumor mill would grind, but, on the whole, the congregation understood the need for discretion and self-censorship and maintained an impressive degree of both. As compensation for the congregation's restraint, the rabbi, Scott, and I made ourselves more available perhaps than ever before, so that congregants would always be able to find us to ask for updated information, to question, to vent, and to provide us with leads and information.

For similar reasons, we coordinated our responses to press inquiries but made a point of responding to the press when queried. Fortunately, the local press obtained the story before the Boston press did. As a consequence, the Boston media paid less attention to the developing story than it otherwise would have. The *Boston Globe*, for example, has a policy of giving short shrift to local stories the *Globe* itself does not break. Since the two main Boston papers were busy covering the Catholic Church scandal and since neither had reported the hazzan's arrest before the *Patriot Ledger* had, the two Boston papers only reported our scandal occasionally and in passing. Only once did *Boston Herald* reporters appear in our parking lot; congregants uniformly and without being requested told the reporters that it would be inappropriate to discuss such matters on Shabbat. No congregant was quoted or cited in the story.

We did not have such success with other media outlets. The local Jewish press was hungry for the story, apparently seeing it as a means of becoming part of the press coverage of the Boston clergy abuse scandal. We had to conduct long off-the-record discussions with some reporters to impress upon them the damage that they could cause to the entire Jewish community by excessive or inaccurate reporting. The local press similarly was invested in the story, albeit to a lesser extent. It was necessary to provide reporters with limited information, carefully worded, so that they would have something to report and so that they would not consider themselves stonewalled in their journalistic investigations and thereby search harder and more recklessly for stories. President Belgard wisely saw this as a good opportunity to invite reporters to temple cultural, social, and religious activities so that they could see the congregation functioning normally. Nevertheless, we received hostile press coverage mainly in Ku Klux Klan, Nazi, and Islamic publications (*Jews for Allah*), taking advantage of the scandal to assure their readers that Jews inherently are evil and sexually debased.

THE FALSE CALM

The Rabbi

Things began to settle down. We continued to meet with congregants. But since nothing new was happening, the newspapers lost interest.

The one fear we all had was that now that the allegations had become public, there might be others who would come forward to assert similar charges. There had never before been any suggestion of inappropriate behavior on the part of the hazzan, but you never know what can be lurking in the shadows. In addition, when the hazzan was hired in 1982, background-check standards were very different. Issues of sexual improprieties were not on the radar screen. Thankfully, no further allegations were ever made.

We also continued to cover all of the hazzan's duties. Lay people came forward to lead our services and I took over bar and bat mitzvah training. The entire congregation pulled together to help.

We had little idea of what was in store for us.

The Lawyer

One of the issues raised at the congregational meeting had been whether and how long the hazzan should be compensated when he was unable to perform his functions. Fortunately, the hazzan was sensitive to this issue himself. Among the sadder responsibilities the president and I performed was to meet with the hazzan in his home study to inform him that he would not be able to return to the temple to perform his duties. Our efforts to be gentle and his incredulity meant that, in the end, it was his wife who finally explained it in a manner he was able to comprehend. As we parted in sad silence, Scott said that that had been one of the hardest things he ever had been called upon to do. Sensitive to the situation, the hazzan's attorney suggested an acceptable arrangement that enabled the contract to end amicably and the hazzan to retire with dignity to focus his efforts on his defense. The congregation was able to hire a new cantor shortly afterward.

Then everything changed.

THE LAWSUIT

The Rabbi

Right before Passover, Mark called to inform me that he had been served with notice of an impending suit by the alleged victim against the temple, Scott Belgard, and me. He said that the plaintiff (the alleged victim) could choose to sue the entire Board of Directors and all previous presidents, but this was not yet in the offing (and, indeed, never did occur).

The threat of a lawsuit is frightening. I checked my personal insurance coverage and, since the suit arose out of my professional duties, my insurer would not defend me. The Rabbinical Assembly, my professional organization, had consistently told us not to carry malpractice insurance because it would encourage lawsuits, so I did not have any. The president and I felt very vulnerable.

Mark said that he would receive all legal documents so we wouldn't have to worry that a sheriff would knock on our doors. Also, he and the other lay leaders began to research the temple's insurance to ascertain what it would and would not cover.

Massachusetts law limited the liability of not-for-profit organizations like Temple Beth Am to a maximum judgment of $20,000, so it made sense for the alleged victim and her family to sue individuals. What Scott and I feared, though, was that while the temple might have coverage, we would not. Luckily, the insurance carrier agreed to cover all parties to the suit, and they provided an attorney. Mark continued to represent the temple without compensation; I can only imagine how many nonbillable hours he put into this job. From the beginning, I felt that he and the insurance company's attorney, Peter Kober, believed that we were not responsible and worked "above and beyond" not simply because it was their job but because they believed we were right. It was a great source of comfort to both Scott and me.

As Passover of 2003 came and went, we began actively looking at our documents and interviewing congregants who were responsible for hiring the hazzan in 1982. We also heard from congregants who felt that the hazzan might have interacted with them or their children in an uncomfortable way.

Interestingly, Scott, Mark, and I all had children (four boys, two girls), five of whom had studied with the hazzan as they became bar and bat mitzvah. None of us felt that anything had been improper. In fact, we all felt he had been very warm and supportive. So did a large majority of our congregants.

On the other hand, perception can sometimes be more important than fact. What I mean is that certain behaviors that were appropriate and acceptable in the past are no longer seen as such. The hazzan, being an older man, grew up in an age where hugging children and adults was considered appropriate — not to do so would have been viewed as cold and uncaring. We now live in a time when you cannot touch a child on the shoulder as a sign of support. Still, everyone we spoke to felt very comfortable with the hazzan. All of them believed that the hazzan had never done anything improper with their children, and in interviewing the children, we got the same result.

Though I felt we were handling this matter the best way we could, there were many times over the three and a half years of the process that I felt angry. I was angry at the hazzan for his actions. While I didn't believe he had raped the woman, he had acted in a way that had given the appearance of impropriety (*marit ayin*). I was angry at the family of the victim for suing the temple, Scott, and me. They were active members of the community. They came to Shabbat services. They saw my look of shock when they first told me about the allegations. How could they believe that any of us had known about the hazzan's alleged behaviors and had done nothing to stop them? And I was very angry at the plaintiff's attorneys. Having interviewed the family, they had to have known that the case was weak or nonexistent. Nevertheless, in the hope of making money, they put me through hell. I wasted hundreds of hours of time preparing for and defending myself. And they put my family in financial jeopardy.

Yet all of that paled next to one of the saddest consequences of the lawsuit; because I was being sued, I was instructed by counsel not to have any dealings with the family or the alleged victim. No more phone calls. No more visits. Even if I met them in the supermarket or on the street, I was to be cordial but cool. This was very hard for me and, as I found out later, only intensified the family's anger against me and the temple. From friends of theirs, I have heard that, until this day, they have not been able to understand the connection between their lawsuit against me and my pulling back from contact.

In addition, when word of the lawsuit against the temple became public, a number of congregants also expressed anger against the family and severed contact. I understand why the family sued; but I regret the unintended consequences for them and for us.

The Lawyer

One of the very few benefits to synagogue counsel being personally involved as a synagogue member is that involvement conveys a knowledge of the parties and of the underlying situation that would not be available to uninvolved counsel.

Once the temple was sued, I, as temple counsel, could assist the attorneys appointed by the temple's insurance company in preparing a defense. As a consequence, I was able to help prepare overall defense strategy and questions to the plaintiffs that would expose the weakness of their position to their own counsel and force the plaintiffs to confront the implications of the litigation they were pursuing.

For example, proving that the temple knew or should have known of the hazzan's proclivities to abuse the victim was one of the elements the plaintiffs were required to prove to succeed in their negligence claims against the temple, the rabbi, and Scott Belgard. Hazzan Shapiro had a reputation of being a "touchy-feely" person, one who often hugged congregants and their children, rubbed their backs and arms, and generally made himself at home in what now is known as that person's "personal space." Plaintiffs' counsel easily could have interpreted such information as identifying potential misconduct by the hazzan (undue familiarity or worse), which obviously would have been known to temple members, clergy, and officers. However, the plaintiffs were as familiar with such conduct as everyone else in the temple and never thought that there was anything improper about it. To defuse any potential use of this information by plaintiffs' counsel — such as, as the basis for deposing large numbers of congregants in the hope of finding those that objected to the behavior — I, as temple counsel, helped formulate requests for admissions (approximately 250), a litigation device that forced the plaintiffs to admit that they knew of such behavior by the hazzan, did not consider it offensive or harmful, and did not consider it a basis for keeping their daughter, the victim, away from the hazzan. As a consequence, plaintiffs' counsel was denied the opportunity to try to make more of the behavior than the plaintiffs ever had, was unable to use it to investigate further, and was forced to confront the fact that the temple did not have greater knowledge of the hazzan's behavior than did the plaintiffs themselves. Similarly, some of the requests for admission forced the plaintiffs to confront the fact that their suit was directed at the personal assets of the rabbi and President Belgard, rather than at the temple's insurance coverage. Unfortunately, those requests did not have the desired effect of making the plaintiffs abandon the claims against the rabbi and Scott Belgard.

Involvement in the process also enabled me, as temple counsel, with the court's permission, to address issues that insurance counsel were barred from addressing due to legal conflicts of interest. For example, insurance counsel could not address issues of insurance coverage. Only I could inform the court of the potential effect of the criminal case upon the temple's insurance coverage, which would be to strip the temple of any defense, notwithstanding the facts at issue in the suit. Due to an insurance policy exclusion, coverage would not be available if it was proven that any abuse of the victim began before a certain date. The victim could not supply dates because of her mental deficiencies. Evidence in the criminal case likely would supply the dates in a way that would decide the insurance issue. If the criminal case concluded before the parties had a chance to investigate the civil case, the insurer likely would have refused to defend the temple, the rabbi, and President Belgard, regardless of their liability, making the costs of defense prohibitive. I was able to explain this to the court and thereby to prevent the plaintiffs from obtaining a complete stay of the civil proceedings until the criminal case concluded, which is customary in cases of this type. As a result, by the time of the hazzan's guilty plea in the criminal case, the parties had been able to conclude all of the discovery in the civil case except for the deposition of the hazzan himself, and insurance counsel, with input from me as temple counsel, had prepared a motion for summary judgment that was designed to resolve the claims against the temple, the rabbi, and President Belgard without trial. Although the motion was denied in order to enable the plaintiffs to depose the hazzan, by that point so much work had been done by insurance counsel that the insurance company decided not to abandon the defense, but to continue it through trial.

Of course, such involvement by temple counsel came at a price. I was obliged to attend all court hearings, depositions (nine witnesses, twelve days in our case), and deposition preparation sessions, or to obtain coverage from other attorneys who were members of the synagogue. Complicating the expenditure of time was the fact that only insurance counsel "officially" represented the temple in the litigation. Schedules were coordinated between the court and counsel of record for the plaintiffs, the hazzan, and the temple; notice to me as temple counsel was provided only as a courtesy by insurance counsel, not as a requirement of the litigation. Accordingly, it often was necessary for me to reschedule matters previously scheduled in my other cases to accommodate the schedules of the court and the parties in this case.

THE LONG LEGAL PROCESS — AND A GUILTY PLEA

The Rabbi

It was fully fifteen months after the beginning of the civil suit before Scott and I actually gave deposition testimony.

Scott and I had no idea what was involved in a deposition. Our attorneys, Mark for the temple and Peter Kober for the insurance company, spent hours teaching us what to say and how to say it, all the while "telling the whole truth and nothing but the truth."

Being deposed is quite an ordeal. You answer questions simply but truthfully. For example, if the question is, "Do you have the time?" The answer is, "Yes." It's up to the attorney to ask the next question, "What time is it?" Only then do you give the time. This is very stressful until you get used to it and, even then, there were times that I volunteered too much information. Mark took great satisfaction from a comment the questioning attorney made to Scott: "Help me out here. I can see that you've been well prepped." The one thing that made it easier for Scott and me was that the truth was on our side. We had no need to try to evade the truth because we had done nothing wrong.

I must say that my one strong impression of the deposition was that there were four attorneys present. I kept on thinking of the amount of "billable hours" in the room and how sad it was for everyone concerned. After the fact, the other major thing I remember is that the last question I was asked was if I believed that the hazzan was guilty. I answered, "No."

Scott's deposition lasted one day, mine was held over two days. In addition, a parent and two bar mitzvah students who had expressed concern about the hazzan's physical contact with them were deposed. They, too, had to be prepared by Mark and Peter Kober to be ready for the deposition. They, too, shared nothing that indicated that we should have known about the situation beforehand.

The hazzan was involved in both a civil suit and a criminal trial. The criminal trial comes first, since a person cannot be forced to testify and thus possibly incriminate himself. The hazzan's deposition had to wait until after the criminal proceedings were over.

By the spring of 2005, all of the depositions had been taken except the hazzan's, which still was waiting for the criminal case to end. Our attorneys decided that there was no evidence that could reasonably point to our responsibility, so they filed a motion for summary judgment. Simply put, that motion asks the judge to rule that the plaintiff's case is so weak that it's a waste of the jury's time to go to trial. Scott and I were cautioned not to expect a positive result. We were assigned a trial date for September 2006, the week before Rosh Hashanah; three and one-half years after I was first made aware of the allegations.

The judge rejected our arguments, but he did so because the hazzan's deposition had not been completed. He told us we could refile the motion for summary judgment later.

In the fall of 2005, I happened to meet a court officer who was working in the court that was hearing the criminal case. He told me that there was a deal in the works. I immediately called Mark; he checked on it and confirmed that this was true.

A few days later, I was in for the shock of my life. The hazzan had agreed to a plea bargain that included admitting to charges of being sexually involved with a mentally retarded woman. In return, the rape charges were dropped and he was sentenced to one year of house arrest and ten years probation, and he had to register as a sex offender.

I was devastated. He had admitted his guilt. Some congregants rationalized the guilty plea by saying that he really didn't do it but he had to take the plea lest he be found guilty at trial and sentenced to real jail time.

For me, the guilty plea meant just what it said. I had been wrong when I had said that I did not think he was guilty. And I began to replay everything over in my mind. Could I have known? Should I have known? What could I have done differently? Now we had a real victim and I could not help her because I was still being sued. Now I was angry and sad: angry at the hazzan, angry at the situation, and sad for the victim, the congregation, and the hazzan's wife and family.

Up until that moment, I had really believed that he was innocent. That he would be proven innocent and therefore our civil case would simply go away. Now, that was not going to happen.

The Lawyer

Since we were not parties to the criminal proceedings, we had no right to formal notice of upcoming events and often received information from friendly sources either immediately before an event occurred or contemporaneously with it. To preempt press coverage and to prevent unpleasant surprises to our congregants, several times we were compelled to drop whatever we were doing and collaborate on e-mails, which we circulated to the congregation as soon as we completed them. By this time, Scott Belgard's term of office had expired. The new president, Nathalie Weinberg, continued to work closely with the three of us to continue in the same vein the work that we had been doing for over two years.

The first such occasion occurred just before Rosh Hashana, when we learned that the hazzan was pleading guilty to the criminal charges.

We immediately drafted an e-mail that notified the congregants of what had happened: Hazzan Robert Shapiro had pleaded guilty to fourteen counts of indecent assault and battery upon a mentally retarded person; the seven rape counts charged against him had been dismissed; he was being sentenced to ten years' probation, the first year of which would be served under house arrest. There would be no prison time, but he would have to register as a sex offender and receive sex offender counseling. He was also prohibited from having contact with mentally retarded persons. The e-mail went on to describe some other troubling things that had emerged from the litigation:

> The victim's parents also alleged that they had been ousted from the Temple and shunned by our members after they came forward with their allegations.
>
> . . . Although we ended our formal relationship with Hazzan Shapiro, we did not end our relationship with the victim's family. To the contrary, the victim's family chose to end their relationship with the Temple; a fact which we first learned when we received the plaintiffs' discovery responses in the civil lawsuit which they commenced against the Temple, Rabbi Weiss, and Scott Belgard, as well as against Hazzan Shapiro.

Finally, the e-mail informed everyone that a congregational meeting would be held after Yom Kippur to discuss the situation, and warned the congregants of the likelihood of more press interest.

As it turned out, fewer people attended this meeting than the first one. We interpreted this as a sign that the congregation was satisfied that we had been keeping them informed, and that life was returning to normal for the vast majority.

Shocking though the hazzan's guilty plea was, it made perfect sense for reasons that had nothing to do with the accuracy of the charges against him. Not long before, Father John Geoghan, one of the most notorious of the abusive Catholic priests and one of the few prosecuted in Massachusetts for his crimes, had been beaten and suffocated to death in prison by an incarcerated murderer, who claimed to be avenging the priest abuse victims. The murder was not lost upon the hazzan's criminal defense counsel, who were among the most respected and sought-after in Massachusetts. Arguably, their client's life could have been jeopardized had he been sent to prison.

Besides, although the hazzan was required by the criminal law to admit his guilt as part of the procedure, his admission was to a carefully scripted text prepared jointly by his criminal and civil attorneys and the district attorney. It said a great deal formally but provided little additional information. Technically, his guilty plea meant that the prosecution had borne its burden of proof; not necessarily that the defendant was "guilty."

For our purposes, though, the hazzan's deposition testimony after his conviction was more to the point. With the criminal process at an end, the plaintiffs deposed the hazzan, now under house arrest, at his home. His wife remained in their bedroom so as not to be exposed to the disturbing testimony. Listening to it and analyzing it in the context of the case against the temple was one of the hardest things that I ever have had to do in my professional practice.

The hazzan admitted his sexual abuse of the mentally handicapped plaintiff, even as he disputed aspects of his plea testimony. Despite the lack of physical evidence, which had been a great relief to the three of us who had been aware of the extent of the CSI investigation, the hazzan admitted to a few instances of sexual misconduct with the victim in the chapel after Friday evening services. He admitted his sole responsibility and specifically absolved the victim of responsibility:

Q: Are you suggesting that it's [the victim's] fault that this happened?
A: No. No.
Q: Surely you don't hold her responsible for what happened, do you?
A: No. I was responsible.
\
Q: Did [the victim], at some point, begin to react to your touching?
A: Never.
Q: Never?
A: Never.
Q: Not positively, not negatively? Nothing? No reaction at all?
A: Just clinging.
Q: Do you think she knew what was going on?
A: I thought so.
\
Q: Did she ever, ever ask you to touch her sexually?
A: No.

At its most disturbing, the hazzan's testimony illustrated how easily someone considered a pillar of communal responsibility and looked to as a moral example could gradually surrender his moral and intellectual reasoning to baser instincts. The hazzan testified that for several months he was "aware of feeling some sort of sexual feeling about [the victim]" before he acted upon those feelings. Nevertheless, he did not "even think about getting help" for himself, although he admitted to waking up in the middle of the night and thinking "this is a mentally challenged young girl, and I'm having these feelings about her, and that's not a good thing." Despite engaging in sexual misconduct for "at least two years," he never advised the victim's parents not to continue bringing her to his house. Nor did he discuss his behavior with anyone at the synagogue or with a professional counselor. He revealed the process of his thoughts about the continuing abuse in this remarkable passage:

Q: Did you at any point in time appreciate the risks to which you exposed the Temple should you be caught?

A: No.

\

Q: What were you thinking?

A: I can't, other than what I've said to you. I mean, except that I knew within my heart and soul that I was doing wrong.

Q: Were you concerned about the consequences?

A: I never thought that what I was doing was hurting [the victim] or thought it [*sic*] my mind that it was assault. It didn't — that didn't occur to me.

Q: Do you still think that?

A: No.

Q: Do you know now that it was an assault?

A: It was a crime.

\

Q: Did it occur to you that what you were doing was immoral?

A: Yes.

\

Q: [H]ow did you feel hearing Rabbi Weiss say he didn't believe the allegations?

A: I didn't feel good about it.

Q: I think Mr. Belgard said the same thing. Do you remember that? He also didn't believe it. How did you feel hearing him say it?

A: I didn't feel good about it.

In due course, a civil jury would find the hazzan liable for sexually abusing the victim and would award over five million dollars as compensatory damages to her and to her family. Again, we would drop everything upon learning of the verdict and prepare an e-mail to the entire congregation so that they would receive the information from us, before it might be reported on the evening news. The size of the award, if ever collected, would expose not only the hazzan but his family to financial ruin. Those consequences do not, of course, make the award less than meritorious given the harm inflicted upon the victim.

The Rabbi

Finally, all of the depositions had been completed. No new facts had come to light concerning the temple's role. We refiled our motion for summary judgment, asking the judge to dismiss the case against the temple and against us as individuals. I attended the court hearing on this motion. Even I could see that the arguments of the plaintiffs' lawyers were pretty weak. Our lawyers felt we had a good chance of succeeding, especially concerning the claims against Scott, who by virtue of being a volunteer leader of a not-for-profit corporation, was protected by a much higher standard of proof.

About a month later, I got a call from Mark. The judge had issued his ruling. He had granted summary judgment for Scott, for the temple, and for me. His ruling said that, based on the facts, no reasonable person could have known what was happening between the hazzan and the victim.

The plaintiffs had thirty days to appeal. We were told that they had no plans to do so. But we waited. Thirty days later, we celebrated. The ordeal was over.

But it really wasn't. As Mark has consistently said, as long as the victim and her family feel estranged from the temple, the case is not over.

Still, we celebrated, because the truth did prevail. But we knew that the victim, the hazzan, his family, and the entire temple would not be the same. Everything we did from now on would be held up to scrutiny because of this case. Even today, six years later, the emotions of those years keep flooding back to me.

The Lawyer

Massachusetts state court judges rotate between courthouses periodically. The judge who had issued the decision enabling discovery to proceed concerning the claims against the temple, Rabbi Weiss, and President Belgard was the same judge who decided the summary judgment motion. The same factors that had impressed him initially, and in large measure had convinced him to permit discovery to proceed, now led him to grant summary judgment to "the Temple defendants," as we were called. He noted in particular our immediate decisions to encourage the family to notify the police and to separate the hazzan from the temple. Justice Charles Hely, explaining his decision to dismiss the case against us, summarized the significant facts in the second paragraph of his decision:

Robert Shapiro was employed by the Temple as a hazzan for about twenty years. The Temple defendants first learned of [the victim]'s report of sexual abuse by Mr. Shapiro on February 7, 2003. The Temple defendants suspended Mr. Shapiro the same day. His contract was not renewed. He was never again employed by the Temple.

The judge concluded:

Considering all the summary judgment evidence presented in this case, there is no basis from which a fair-minded jury could find that there was negligence by the Temple defendants and that such negligence was a cause of the plaintiffs' injuries.

He dismissed the plaintiffs' claims that the temple defendants had acted "maliciously or wilfully" as "frivolous" and their claims of "gross negligence and wanton or reckless conduct" as baseless.

The district attorney had reached the same conclusion during the investigation of the criminal charges against the hazzan. No charges ever were brought against the temple, Rabbi Weiss, President Belgard, or any temple officer, director, or employee other than the hazzan himself.

Commenting to the press after the verdict against the hazzan, plaintiffs' counsel, Adam Satin, stated: "It became clear as the case was pending that [Shapiro] had concealed his acts from the [T]emple."

I believe this result owed much to the wisdom, resolution, and courage of Rabbi Weiss and Scott Belgard.

Nevertheless, as I reported to the Board of Directors at the conclusion of the litigation, the temple truly cannot be said to have "won" until the victim and her family and the family of Hazzan Shapiro feel comfortable enough to return to the congregation.

LESSONS LEARNED

The Rabbi

A few weeks after the other "Temple defendants" and I were dismissed from the lawsuit, I summoned the courage to call the family of the victim. Now that I was no longer being sued, Mark said it was okay to do this. I wasn't quite sure what I expected, but I felt I had to reach out. I think I deliberately chose a time when I assumed they wouldn't be home. I guess I thought that if this was going to work, it wasn't fair to them to have me call unannounced. So I left a voice mail for them.

They never returned the call.

Months later, I found out that they did receive my message, but they felt that if I couldn't be with them throughout the process, I really wasn't there for them any longer. How sad.

So now we look back. What did we learn? Here is what I would say:

Take things seriously. Do not dismiss allegations, no matter how hard they are to believe.

Do the right thing, no matter how painful.

Be deliberate, but act resolutely after deliberating.

Always protect the greatest possible number of potential victims, recognizing that allegations of this type victimize everyone and not just the persons most immediately involved.

Action cannot claim the luxury of waiting for judicial determinations of guilt or innocence. The duty to act arises from the allegations, if not from prior suspicions.

Know your place and carry out your responsibilities, not those of others. Police, attorneys, judges, juries, and psychotherapists all will play a role. Do not try to preempt them by trying to perform their investigations or to make their decisions about evidence, guilt, and innocence. That is not your role. Your role is to protect the congregation and the community. Protect it — understanding at all times that it is comprised of many people of widely differing interests and beliefs, and that all must be protected to the greatest extent possible.

Be respectful of all persons at all times. Ensure that the congregation behaves the same. Discourage gossip, rumors, and speculation.

Instill trust by your behavior, especially by your seriousness, openness, honesty, and fairness to all.

Don't try to hide or stonewall.

Be truthful.

Be careful.

Be honest.

Be patient.

Be forthcoming.

Have someone whom you can trust and with whom you can share your feelings. Keep the community informed. Let them have a chance to express their feelings and to vent. Throughout this experience, except for the victim and her family, the congregation lost no members. In addition, members volunteered to help out and support the organization. During the last two years, Scott was no longer president. The new president informed us that the temple would stick by us and support us, emotionally and financially. That was a wonderful tribute to Scott's leadership and the sense that what we did was done for the good of everyone.

Get the congregation's help in restoring normalcy. One person cannot do everything. The more members of the congregation who are involved in teaching, leading services, helping with bar/bat mitzvah training, the more they feel positively invested in the community and in the situation. However, the congregation has designated certain people (the president, the rabbi, the attorney) to make decisions. It is very important to keep the congregation completely informed; they should never feel they are being stonewalled. But at the same time, the congregation needs to know that the leadership is responsible for all decision making. Keeping the congregation informed does not require repeating remarks that often are hurtful, by design or by accident. The leadership can convey the substance of information without repeating details that can exacerbate harm. Likewise, we can respond to members' questions and even solicit advice when appropriate (e.g., from other attorneys or psychologists), but we take responsibility for the outcome. This approach allows the entire community to feel involved, yet spares them the burden of making (or of taking responsibility for) difficult decisions that may be distasteful to them personally. For example, the decision to separate the hazzan from the congregation undoubtedly was distasteful to many who had come to love him over the years. Since the leadership made that decision, those members of the congregation who would have found it difficult to reach the same conclusion were spared responsibility for that decision.

Understand the risk of the congregation factionalizing over their belief/disbelief of the allegations. Do your utmost to include and unify the congregation in all matters, to maintain normal activities, and to avoid friction between congregants. Ensure that the congregation knows the risks of disunity and acts for the benefit of the whole community.

Teach. All of life is a learning experience, especially when the lessons are

important and unpleasant. Do not forego the opportunity to learn and
to teach.

Bring honor to the Jewish people when it is accused of dishonorable
behavior. Honest, resolute action to protect the community demonstrates
kiddush ha-Shem (sanctification of God's name). Covering up criminal
behavior so as not to "shame" the community, when doing so guarantees
further emotional and possible physical injury to the alleged victim and
risks increasing the number of victims, demonstrates the opposite, *hillul
ha-Shem* (a desecration of the name of God).

Be realistic. The charges will not go away because you ignore them.
Investigators and reporters will not give up the search for truth because
you do not cooperate. Cooperate willingly and humbly when doing so
will help the community.

There is no "cookie cutter" way to handle something like this. Each situation
is different and requires a different strategy. But I think the above principles
are universally applicable. Judaism has been teaching moral and courageous
behavior in difficult circumstances for four thousand years. Apply what you
have learned. Jewish teaching does not apply only during services.

And so it ends. But not really.

Scott, Mark, and I will always carry this with us. The members of the
congregation will always remember that a beloved hazzan betrayed them and
their trust. A wonderful woman lost her relationship to a congregation that
had provided her with caring and support. There are so many victims. But in
the end, I feel proud that we acted properly; that a community came together
to help itself and to support its members; that we came away from this terrible experience with a sense that even when bad things happen, the human
spirit can survive, and with God's help we can "walk through the valley of the
shadow of death" and come out, bruised but whole.[1]

NOTES

1. More recently the hazzan asked me if he (and his family) could return to the
temple. I thought for a while but sadly had to decline. Though I believe in *tshuvah*
(penitence), the wounds his return would reopen for the congregation would far
outweigh his *tshuvah*.

MICHELLE FRIEDMAN

Crossing the Line

What Makes a Rabbi Violate Sexual Boundaries —
And What Can Be Done about It?

INTRODUCTION

Sexual misconduct by rabbis violates an interconnected series of secular and sacred boundaries. Offending rabbis, who may also be charismatic leaders and gifted teachers, breach core Jewish values. In addition, they betray communal trust, abuse the privilege of authority, and profoundly damage their victims.

This essay explores the power and perils of rabbinic charisma from an educational perspective. For rabbis to be successful, they need to maintain their own spiritual energy and to mobilize commitment and religious activism in community members. Regardless of the rabbi's intent, powerful emotions often lead to unpredictable impulses and behaviors. I suggest that the question to pose in the future ought not to be what to do *if* charged, unexpected, and/or erotic feelings develop between rabbi and congregant, but what to do *when* such feelings occur. Rabbis deserve formal training as to how to anticipate and respond to boundary challenges. Such training, while undoubtedly important for all clergymen, is equally crucial for anyone who will be in contact with children and who may experience sexual feelings in that connection, so as to allow problems to be detected as early as possible and appropriate steps to be taken. At the same time, rabbis deserve encouragement and support in order to explore their own personalities as fully as possible. I will present an overview of basic psychodynamic aspects of the rabbinate and describe New York–based Yeshivat Chovevia Torah (YCT) Rabbinical

School, a Modern Orthodox academy, as one model of education in rabbinic boundary sensitivities.

A discussion of professional boundaries begins with examining the multiple roles of a rabbi. These include teacher, lifelong student, religious exemplar, ritual director, wise advisor, community organizer, counselor, source of spiritual inspiration — the list goes on and on. Each role demands and deserves energy and dedication. Whatever their individual personalities and talents, effective rabbis must get psychologically and spiritually close to the people with whom they hope to connect. At the same time, it is wise to be wary of rabbinic charisma and of the emotional power invested in rabbis. Clergy, like all of us, feel the very human emotions of need, disappointment, and loneliness.

The unique position of the rabbi renders him privy to congregants' secrets and deepest feelings.[1] The powerful mix of congregants' trust coupled with the rabbi's personal vulnerability can be volatile and unpredictable. The rabbi must be vigilant in assessing his own state of mind in order to regulate the distance from listening sympathetically to crossing the line into inappropriate intimate behavior.

Mental health professionals, who presumably receive formal training in boundary awareness, struggle with managing the powerful erotic tensions that regularly arise in their work. A psychologist, however, generally has an office and designated office hours, and does not regularly socialize with his patients. The rabbi's work offers far fewer formal demarcations between personal and professional life. He may pray next to a congregant in the morning and counsel that same person about devastating illness or marital strife just moments after the completion of services. The rabbi may need to interact with a high school sophomore who studied with him for her bat mitzvah and is a star youth group leader who appears to be struggling with an eating disorder. At a crowded kiddush, a congregant divulges impending financial catastrophe. On the rabbi's side, he or members of his family may be going through academic or personal troubles visible to the local community. In short, the complex nature of the rabbi's profession exposes him to constant emotional demands while affording him little distance or privacy from the very people who generate these feelings. In order to meet the challenge, rabbis and those who care about their education and welfare need grounding in basic psychological principles of power, charisma, and abuse.

Charisma, whether quiet and unassuming or dazzling, even flamboyant, implies the capacity to inspire enthusiasm, devotion, and purposeful action. No matter whether a rabbi is naturally endowed with charismatic gifts or needs to work at interpersonal skills, he must always respect the profound power differential inherent in the rabbinic position. Rabbi and congregant are never two individuals on an equal footing. No matter how similar or dissimilar they are in terms of age, background, temperament, and goals, the unique role of the rabbi sets him apart from congregants in fundamental ways.

Key to this appreciation is an understanding of the concepts of *transference* and *countertransference*. These terms, coined by modern psychoanalysis, identify paradigms of human interaction operative from time immemorial. "Transference" refers to the largely unconscious compendium of feelings, memories, and associations elicited in a person by relationship with another individual. It is important to underscore that this dynamic is constantly operative and underscores all human interaction, normal as well as pathological. To illustrate in a rabbinic context: A middle-aged, happily married adult congregant, Ms. A, may experience her forty-five-year-old rabbi as vaguely reminding her of an autocratic grandfather, a kindly Hebrew school principal, a dashing celebrity, or a work authority. She may feel shades of wishing to please, flatter, flirt with, and rebel against — all with the very same rabbi. A seventeen-year-old girl, Ms. B, may see her twenty-nine-year-old rabbi as a perfect husband and father, in contrast to her own cold and unavailable parent. In addition, his smile reminds her of a character in a popular TV series who dates a younger girlfriend.

"Countertransference," in turn, refers to that similar set of psychological phenomena evoked in the rabbi. At different times, Ms. A may touch off pleasant notes of her rabbi's sister or evoke the critical personality of his third-grade teacher. Ms. B's rabbi, whose marriage is strained with a new baby that has serious medical complications, finds himself looking forward a great deal to chats with Ms. B. He feels younger, freer, and more attractive when she is around.

Despite these intimations of boundary troubles, the above examples describe normal responses. Psychodynamic theory posits that transference and countertransference are always operative — that first impressions and subsequent feelings we all experience are rooted in the emotional bedrock of our earlier selves. Our rabbis must remember that their female congregants are responding to a whole host of associations projected onto them, onto what they represent for each congregant, and are not responding exclusively to the rabbis as individuals in the present moment. Equally important, a rabbi needs to pay attention to the private sources of his own powerful reactions so that he can discriminate the emotional residue of past impressions from feelings generated in present-day encounters. Recognizing strong feelings that depart from the rabbi's baseline constitutes the rabbi's critical first step to understanding his own psychology and making choices about his subsequent behavior. Whether anticipation of a congregant's visits generates pleasurable excitement or antipathy, the rabbi needs to take stock honestly of what he feels. With this starting point, he can establish personal standards that meet conventional expectations for his role as rabbi and to get help when he feels he is in distress.

A rabbinic appreciation of transference/countertransference maintains respect for the tendency of people to admire and sometimes idealize persons of authority. At the opposite pole, a rabbi may experience congregants' anger, disappointment, or cynicism. The astute rabbi realizes that he is the recipient of all sorts of projections that have little to do with his actual physical being, personality, or knowledge. Congregants of both sexes may seek to be close to the rabbi for reasons unrelated to their conscious goals of religious study, counseling, or synagogue involvement. A grieving widow may find the rabbi to be the most consoling person in her sorrowful world, an unpopular adolescent may experience the rabbi as uniquely appreciating her intellectual creativity, a man emotionally estranged from his spouse may try to enlist the rabbi as his advocate in a bitter domestic saga. What does the rabbi do if the widow reaches for a hug and the hug turns into an embrace? What if the teenage girl asks to meet the rabbi at an unusually late hour or if the distraught husband suggests that a large donation will be forthcoming if the rabbi is successful in brokering a domestic resolution that favors the husband's point of view? Rabbis are bombarded by all sorts of contradictory expectations — to comfort and to rebuke, to engage and to distance, to praise and to reproach, and so on. In order to maintain psychological and spiritual balance, the rabbi must be aware of multiple psychological forces operating at any given time. Most of all, the rabbi needs to be in tune with his own emotional life.

While a rabbi optimally uses his own reactions as a barometer of feelings, he must be careful to monitor his assessments of situations and his choices of interventions. Is the advice the rabbi offers intended to guide an individual seeker toward deeper understanding and responsible, independent choice? Does the rabbi feel he needs to actively persuade a congregant to make a specific choice or follow one direction? Life circumstances offer the rabbi infinite opportunities to enter congregants' lives at emotionally charged and highly vulnerable moments. At the same time, the rabbi is subject to peaks and valleys in his own personal life. His marriage may be disintegrating, his health compromised, his dreams of success withering. Whatever the state of his emotional, sexual, financial, and family circumstances, the rabbi should never exploit congregants to satisfy his own personal needs. No matter how compliant or even enticing a congregant may appear, the rabbi must stay mindful of the sacred privilege of his rabbinate.

In order to establish boundaries between guidance, manipulation, and exploitation, the rabbi needs to consider and define the scope of his role with a set of basic parameters. Here I borrow from the mental health literature in referring to a series of guidelines.[2] These parameters establish an atmosphere of safety and predictability in which the rabbi/congregant can flourish. While the rabbi is always responsible for boundary maintenance, these guidelines are meant to protect both rabbi and congregant from violations that might arise from sexual feelings. I will address the categories of *role, time, place, cloth-ing, name, language, gifts, self-disclosure,* and *physical contact.*

A core concept in understanding professional boundaries is the notion of "role." This refers to the rabbi's conception of himself vis-à-vis congregants. No matter what the denomination, the rabbi/congregant relationship is hierarchical. While the best rabbis cultivate personal humility, students and congregants look to them for inspiration and leadership. Communities' wishes oscillate between the rabbi as charismatic leader who opens the door of Jewish experience and that of the clergyman who is more a facilitator, a teacher and consultant who empowers congregants to assume more active Jewish lives.[3] Attention to defining his role will establish the basic rules and framework for the rabbi's relationships with congregants. The rabbi's notion of his role surely will evolve and change over time, but he should always have the general question "Is this what a rabbi does?" in mind. This query is not meant to inhibit impulses of genuine interest or specific concern, but rather to shape appropriate rabbinic responses. For example, some rabbis engage in extensive counseling with congregants, while others prefer to refer them to professionals. Some rabbis are comfortable playing sports, going out socially, or traveling with congregants, while others are not.

"Time" refers to the actual hours when the rabbi is available and to the length of contact, whether these involve counseling sessions, home/hospital visits, or phone calls. Many rabbis feel that they are expected to be available at all hours. Another commonly held belief is that if a rabbi spends enough time and energy in a prolonged session, thorny issues can be resolved. Such attitudes are fraught with pitfalls. While cases of true emergency demand rabbinic availability in the middle of the night, such situations are rare. In fact, what is much more likely to result from meetings at unusual times of day or overly lengthy sessions is chaos in the rabbi's schedule and resentment growing in his family for the intrusions into private time. Another serious concern of time mismanagement is that exceptional treatment of certain congregants might be interpreted as, or lead to, inappropriate intimacy between them and the rabbi. Extensive late-night conversations, for example, whether in person or on the phone or Internet, are not standard professional practice and thus violate the "this is what is a rabbi's role" precept.

Attention must be paid to physical locations of rabbi/congregant encounters. While meetings with congregants need to be conducted in a private fashion, interviews should be held in an office or other public room (study, *beit midrash*, classroom). The rabbi's office should have a window to the outside or to a reception area. Office décor might include a small table positioned between armchairs. These details convey respect and safety that facilitate divulgence of serious matters as well as indicating boundaries. The presence of other staff people in proximity to the rabbi's private office also sets a tone of professionalism. When the rabbi needs to make a home visit, he should try to meet with congregants in more public rooms, such as kitchens or living rooms. If the congregant is bedridden, the rabbi should leave the bedroom door open and sit on a chair at a respectful distance from the bed. If a rabbi is driving with congregants, he should be mindful of the cozy feeling often generated on car rides. Some trips with congregants might be better made with additional passengers and advance planning as to the seating arrangements. If a rabbi decides to participate in recreational activity with congregants, he needs to consider the situation carefully from different perspectives. For example, Ms. W invites the rabbi to accompany her to a chamber music concert that her date/husband/friend can't attend. Even if his relationship with Ms. W has been completely correct, Rabbi X would do better to decline the offer politely. If she were to offer him both tickets, he might accept them, offering to pay their cost. If a group of teens invite their favorite Judaic studies teacher — who happens to be single — to a concert/movie or other nonacademic entertainment, he would do well to consider the event's content and venue before accepting. This rabbi might run the matter by a colleague or his principal to get another point of view. If the rabbi decides that he wants to go with the group, he might bring a companion. These measures help maintain rabbinic boundaries for rabbi and congregants as well as protecting against the appearance of impropriety to casual observers.

The category of "clothing" includes the rabbi's appearance as well as the expectations he sets for congregants' apparel when participating in small meetings or synagogue activities. In deciding what to wear, a rabbi should remember the adage "they see you before they hear you." People want to feel that their rabbi, like their doctor, is conscientious, thoughtful, and stable. Once again, role sets the tone. Neither cutting-edge fashion nor ultracasual clothing fits the public rabbinic role. In addition, while rabbis should certainly enjoy individual taste choices, their own grooming and clothing need to be in keeping with standards of modesty held by the community. Just as with any of the other social boundary regulators under discussion, when a rabbi notices that his grooming behavior, such as dressing up or applying cologne to meet with certain female congregants, departs from his baseline, he needs to pay attention. On the other hand, congregants' choices of attire may also express mixed messages. If a woman wears a sexy outfit to meet with the rabbi, is her goal to be fashionable or seductive? Is it appropriate for the rabbi to suggest different attire or will such a comment be interpreted as insulting or suggestive? While there are no simple answers, rabbis must pay attention to their own appearance as well as to their responses to that of congregants.

By what name should a rabbi be called? Does Rabbi Joe Stein prefer to be called Rabbi Stein, Rabbi Joe, or just plain Joe? Many rabbis, especially in school or Hillel settings, feel that first-name usage imparts warmth and availability. First names evoke easy familiarity and erase the sense of rabbinic "otherness." At the same time, the level social playing field suggested by first-name usage might also invite expression of flirtatious/seductive feelings generated in the power differential of rabbi/congregant counseling. Rabbis may feel that calling adult congregants by their first names while expecting to be called "Rabbi" is undemocratic or even disrespectful. While discussion of names is always in order, the rabbi needs to consider the psychology underlying the uneven gradient between clergy and congregant. A slight sense of formality enables many people to feel that they are respecting their faith. That tinge of outsiderness, while potentially a bit lonely at times for the rabbi and his family, helps many people feel that their rabbi represents a profound Jewish tradition that is responsive to their deepest needs.

Choice of language works in tandem with name choice. Rabbis need to be thoughtful regarding the use of slang and commonly used vulgarities. Such language implies casual, even uncensored, behavior and might be interpreted as inviting other breaches of conventional boundaries.

Money, services, and gifts occupy an area that, like the others, requires common sense and tact. Payment for such rabbinic functions as performing weddings or special lessons may be completely appropriate. Congregants may suggest a kind of barter system: an accountant offers to help the rabbi with tax preparation in exchange for study time, a personnel trainer suggests some time in the gym or a massage in exchange for helping a bar/bat mitzvah child prepare their Torah portion. Gifts in recognition of special service, gratitude, achievement, etc., can also be deeply meaningful to congregant and rabbi. The rabbi needs to pay attention to whether a service or gift is inappropriately personal or expensive. If the accountant is a woman who suggests a visit in the late evening when she knows the rabbi will be alone, the rabbi would do well to turn down her request graciously. Regardless of whether the trainer is male or female, gay or straight, the rabbi needs to consider whether physical contact, however professionalized, is appropriate with a congregant.

Self-disclosure is perhaps one of the most sensitive areas of rabbinic boundary crossings. Rabbis, unlike mental health professionals, live their lives in the fishbowl of their communities. A certain portion of their lives is bound to be public information. Congregants often know a great deal about the rabbi's past, his marriage, and his children. They may know that he is hoping to publish a novel or going through a divorce, or that his child is struggling with learning difficulties. No matter how much information leaks out in the course of community life, the rabbi and his family have a right to privacy. In addition, curious though people may be about his personal life, specific knowledge of a rabbi's private struggles rarely benefits congregants. Unless the rabbi has chosen to make such issues known in his public role, counseling sessions are neither the time nor the place to divulge his struggle with alcoholism or his brother's bout with prostate cancer. Persons in counseling are much better helped by attentive, compassionate listening to their own situations. General wisdom about what has been helpful to others may be useful, even if the chief "other" is the rabbi himself. Discussion of the rabbi's own problems are often experienced as intrusive or selfish ("I can't believe it, I went to the rabbi to talk about my mother's dementia and he went on and on about his messed up relationship with his parents!"). Material about the rabbi's past that is not known to the congregation is best kept private. High school students have little to gain finding out whether their rabbi smoked pot or was sexually active when he was a teen. Far better use of discussion time would be exploring what either answer would mean to the students in the here and now.

The topic of physical contact — the Rubicon of boundary violations — deserves extensive attention. For starters, the definition of acceptable social touching between the sexes, whether it be a handshake, a hug, or a peck on the cheek, is not consistent among rabbis. To some degree, touching will be determined by denominational affiliation. In general, Orthodox rabbis will not engage in physical contact with women other than, at most, a handshake. Male rabbis from all denominations express warmth and comfort to men congregants in a wide variety of ways. Whatever their style, rabbis need to examine carefully their custom of social physical contact. They need to consider what any bodily gesture might mean to either male or female congregants. Some congregants might even be offended by differential treatment of the sexes — meaning that they prefer that their rabbi be an equal-opportunity hugger or cheek kisser or not touch anybody at all. Of course, there are times of great emotion, when a congregant is so distraught or overwhelmed that he or she spontaneously hugs or grabs the rabbi. Tact and compassion should guide the rabbi. Suppose, for example, as a recent widow weeps, she impulsively jumps out of her chair and throws her arms around a divorced rabbi's neck. The rabbi has always found this woman charming and attractive. While he may be startled and not able immediately to pry her away, he must not respond with an embrace. Rather, he should gently move toward physical disengagement and reestablish conversation. Doing so will help protect the vulnerable woman's dignity. It will also protect the rabbi from acting on tender, even romantic, feelings that he may not have been consciously aware of until that moment.

Physical contact that slides into sexual misconduct does not happen in a vacuum. At this point, a look at the distinction between boundary crossing and boundary violation is useful. "Boundary crossing" refers to a bending of conventional protocol, a discrete piece of behavior that may be unusual but is essentially benign and may even be helpful. A Hillel Foundation rabbi accompanies a distraught college student to an emergency room at midnight; a synagogue rabbi takes an isolated widower to buy new clothes; a chaplain persuades the estranged relative of a nursing home resident to come in for a visit. While none of these activities may be typical, the rabbi would readily discuss why and how they came to be.

"Boundary violations," on the other hand, refers to harmful, exploitative, repetitive behavior that a rabbi would be reluctant to discuss. The slippery slope of sexual misconduct usually begins with relatively minor boundary violations.[4] In other words, frank sexual activity takes place in a scene prepared by earlier breaches of protocol. A female congregant asks for counseling early in the morning when no other staff is present. She and the rabbi converse several times a week by phone or e-mail. They begin to call each other by pet names or endearments. The rabbi starts talking about his own marital woes. A fond gesture becomes a caress and escalates into planning a weekend in Las Vegas. Another scenario: A sixteen-year-old boy confides his homosexual longings to a youth group rabbi privately struggling with his own homoerotic attractions. They exchange reading material and start meeting outside of group programs. During a religious youth retreat, they take a walk in the woods and in that secluded setting engage in sexual activity.

From the outset, this chapter has focused on the individual rabbi's obligation to stay mindful of and chaperone proper boundary management. While the responsibility for maintaining professional standards always rests on the rabbi, we need to consider what sorts of character types are most susceptible to committing sexual misconduct.[5] Here, the correlation between narcissism and charisma is worth noting. Healthy narcissism, a necessary trait in all character formation, allows us to value our own needs and achievements. A solid core of narcissism is found in successful leaders who use their charismatic gifts to take on difficult tasks and inspire others to do the same. Narcissism slides into pathology when the need for personal fulfillment and self-aggrandizement blocks out restraint, judgment, and empathy. Unhealthy narcissists lack remorse and blame others or outside situations for their own inappropriate behaviors.[6]

Patterns of behavior over time indicate character structure and pathology. Reverend Dr. Marie Fortune, a significant writer in the area of clergy abuse and founder of the FaithTrust Institute, suggests a continuum of clerical sexual abusers: At one end is "the wanderer," who lacks self-control and, in certain opportune moments, wanders across boundaries. At the other extreme is "the predator," the serial offender and sociopath who purposefully seeks out victims and feels little shame or guilt.[7] While sexual boundary violations committed by those all along the spectrum may at first glance appear similar, frequency and patterns of abuse imply different recovery possibilities for rabbis who commit such offenses.

This essay is not focused on the investigation of abuse accusations. Suffice it to say that if an accusation is made, appropriate measures must be taken to protect the privacy and reputations of the alleged victim and the accused rabbi. During an investigation, the rabbi's behavior must conform to safety precautions determined by the community and governing agencies, such as the rabbinic association to which the rabbi belongs. These might include chaperoning the rabbi during meetings, arranging for certain activities to be conducted by the associate rabbi at the synagogue or temple, or even temporarily suspending the rabbi from all of his duties. Any rabbi found guilty of sexual abuse cannot remain in his former professional position. The damage to each individual victim, her family, and the community as a whole will take a long time to heal.

Rehabilitation of the rabbi who has committed a sexual violation is a complex topic. The capacity for an abuser to truly do *teshuvah* — i.e., to acknowledge his wrongdoing, feel remorse, apologize, and make amends — probably correlates to some degree with future behavior. Most likely, rabbis who feel shame and contrition about the abuse will fall into the "wanderer" category. Rabbis who have committed multiple boundary violations and/or have abused children — that is, "predators" — have a very poor prognosis for insight or rehabilitation.

Other factors, such as sexual addiction (including perversions such as pedophilia), alcohol and/or drug abuse, and specific psychiatric illnesses (most notably the manic phase of a manic-depressive disorder), may contribute to disinhibition and impulsivity. The presence of any of these conditions can seriously impair judgment and lead to sexual boundary violations. As mentioned earlier, an otherwise stable and ethical rabbi who is going through personal distress can slip into inappropriate intimacy with a congregant. It must be repeated that psychological impairment, loneliness, or even naïveté are never excuses for rabbinic abuse. Hopefully, awareness of such situations can help rabbis in distress seek appropriate treatment and prevent the tragedy of sexual boundary violations.

YCT (Yeshivat Chovevei Torah) Rabbinical School, an Orthodox Jewish seminary in New York City, offers one plausible model — among other models used at rabbinic institutions in the three major branches of Judaism — of rabbinic preparation that integrates pastoral counseling education into *all four years* of the training program. This commitment of time and resources rests on the knowledge of the importance of psychological self-awareness for rabbis at all levels. Students and faculty regularly discuss topics having to do with the classical text tradition as well as modern scholarship and psychology. Faculty and administration understand that all rabbinic practice, including boundary regulation, is founded on the individual rabbi's spiritual and emotional health.

In this regard, a seminary's admissions procedure is the critical first step toward cultivating rabbinic boundary awareness. While no screening tools guarantee detection of sociopathy, malignant narcissism, or sexual addiction, careful and methodical protocols can weed out potentially troubled candidates. It is far more difficult to eject a student once he is enrolled in the program than to reject an applicant during the admissions process. In any case, of course, the challenge of out-counseling or expelling unsuitable students pales in comparison to containing the pain and destruction wrought by rabbis who commit boundary violations in a community.

The YCT Admissions Committee solicits and reviews transcripts, letters of recommendation and other relevant materials. "Red flags" such as incomplete academic work and undocumented gaps in time require solid explanations. All candidates are interviewed by several male and female faculty and staff members. Besides exploring the nature of the applicant's call to the rabbinate and his skill level with religious texts, interviewers ask about formative religious experiences, influential relationships with rabbis or religious teachers, and the nature of the applicant's struggles with religious life. Admissions personnel are as interested in the applicant's comfort level in responding to these questions as in the specific content of his answer.

Once admitted, students at YCT Rabbinical School experience three components of the pastoral counseling program throughout the entire four years of training: the didactic curriculum, pastoral fieldwork, and structured personal and group exploration. The formal curriculum of the first year focuses on the nature of the helping interview and specifically on the role of the rabbi.

We discuss the fears and fantasies that people bring, often without conscious awareness, to rabbis. Through role play we explore how congregants project a multiplicity of expectations on their rabbi — as wise authority, critical parent, representative of God, absolver of sin, free therapist, friend, to name but a few. We emphasize that while these projections may have little or nothing to do with the rabbi's actual age, looks, or personality, he needs to be mindful of their potential influence in the rabbinic encounter. As students explore the interaction of personal style and rabbinic role, significant class time is devoted to the specifics of rabbinic boundaries discussed in the earlier section of this chapter. In addition, we discuss the limits of pastoral counseling, when to refer, and the parameters of rabbinic confidentiality.

Throughout the curriculum, we emphasize that in any situation the rabbi needs to stay in touch with his own emotional pulse. Does a particular situation generate feelings of empathy or disgust? Does he find a congregant particularly alluring or off-putting?

Does the rabbi feel anxious or inadequate in the face of a situation, pressed to come up with some kind of immediate and wise response? We impress on the students the need to assess urgency and the imperative of not jumping to premature intervention. Beginning rabbis underestimate the enormous healing benefit they have to offer through active, compassionate listening. The first year continues with sessions on major areas of psychological distress that rabbis are likely to encounter. These include psychotic states, depression, anxiety, obsessive-compulsive disorder, and trauma.

The second-year didactic curriculum concentrates on hospital chaplaincy as well as marital and family counseling, the areas of most common rabbinic pastoral involvement. Third- and fourth-year classroom time is devoted to a life-cycle curriculum starting with the spiritual life of young children and moving all the way through end-of-life issues. All along we include the theme of awareness of rabbinic boundary titration. How should a rabbi handle the issue of teens' sexual exploration? What kinds of transferences arise with college students, young adults, and mature persons reckoning with illness, mortality, and loss? Sexual boundary issues are explicitly discussed by Rabbbi Mark Dratch and his faculty from J safe.

Master classes offer senior students the opportunity to present challenging clinical situations to guest experts. Countertransference issues and boundary questions underscore many of the fourth-year students' concerns. One student described a situation in which he was a bus counselor for a religious summer program. Walking to the back of the bus on a routine check, he spotted an ultrareligious adolescent girl openly masturbating in her seat. Needless to say, the student was taken aback and had no idea to what to do. Certain that she had seen him observing her activity, he went to the front of the bus, waited a few minutes, and returned to the rear of the bus for a second look. Once again, her skirt was raised and her masturbatory activity clearly visible. Class discussion, facilitated by a child psychologist, explored the high level of anxiety generated by this vignette. Examination of motivation, age-appropriate and age-inappropriate sexual self-stimulation, and possible interventions followed acknowledgment of the delicacy of the situation.

The pastoral fieldwork component aims to translate classroom discussion and role play into actual rabbinic settings. Starting in the second year, students at YCT spend significant time in a variety of placements. In the chaplaincy rotation, all students shadow experienced hospital chaplains and then make independent visits on acute-care units. Rabbinic students and their mentors process the complex feelings that arise in medical environments. Patients' talk of anger, hopelessness, and lost faith often challenges young rabbis' sense of competence. Rabbis might try to assuage spiritual pain with words or gestures that cross conventional professional boundaries. Again, not every boundary crossing leads to transgression. The more open our students become with doubt and crisis, the more they can reach for meaningful responses that respect patients' autonomy. Other fieldwork opportunities include rabbinic internships in communities, university Hillels, and schools, and rotations through such social service agencies as Alcoholics Anonymous and bereavement groups. During class reviews, students are expected to discuss boundary challenges in their fieldwork situation along with other aspects of the experience.

In addition to the didactic and fieldwork components already described, YCT includes a process group, a unique experience that is the heart of the pastoral counseling program. Each class of students is assigned a psychologist/psychiatrist who meets with that group weekly all four years of yeshiva. That mental health professional has no other academic contact with the students and keeps the substance of the meetings confidential. During their tenure in yeshiva, students confront religious and political differences, institutional struggles, personal travails and triumphs, and whatever else they choose to explore. Present goals include providing a moderated forum for open discussion and helping students to better understand the group process.

As participants and observers in the process group, our future rabbis can put into practice the theories that they learn in the classroom. For example, in facing conflict with peers, most people choose either to avoid the disputed topic or to head into direct confrontation. Both tactics generally have unhappy outcomes. Process group teaches students that expressing difficult feelings in responsible, first-person language can be constructive and lead to some degree of compromise or resolution. Taking a longer view, we hope that group trust develops that will survive the yeshiva years. We hope that our students will call on each other for support in situations of all sorts, including troubled private times and boundary slips or crossings, or violations.

Recognizing that the support and happiness of our students' spouses are keys to YCT rabbis' success, we have a wives' support group that meets monthly. The women represent a range of ages, professions, and attitudes toward their role as *rebbetzins*. Some have children, others do not. These differences pale next to the shared experience of being the wives of future rabbis. Their support group offers an opportunity to consider current and future issues unique to rabbinic couples.

While pastoral counseling classes house most of the specific boundary awareness curriculum, the support and participation of YCT's entire faculty and administration are crucial for educational impact. Psychological sensitivity needs to be cultivated in all yeshivas and seminaries for students and teachers to feel safe enough to explore their vulnerabilities and flaws. The overall institution needs to reflect regularly on its process as a collective as well. YCT uses several modalities to assess its organizational health and responsiveness. Regular student reviews of their teachers and instructors identify faculty members' individual strengths and weaknesses that can be addressed in more specific ways. Rabbinical training institutions must work at creating an environment of trust and respect, modeling for the students the idea that no problem is too shameful to be discussed. At YCT, personal psychotherapy is encouraged and referrals are regularly made for individual, premarital and marital therapy. Again, we hope that long after they have received *s'micha* (rabbinic ordination) our students will turn to the faculty and to each other for support and guidance.

While our goal is that the relationship-oriented focus and intensive curriculum at YCT Rabbinical School will prepare our students for the challenges of their vocation, we know that some *musmachim* (ordained rabbinic graduates) will commit boundary violations. *When* — not *if* — this happens, our hope is that an offender will not retreat into isolation and further offense. Rather, we hope that he will somehow let a colleague know that he is in trouble. That rabbi, probably a YCT graduate, will offer support and at the same time counsel his friend toward immediate interventions. These would include stopping the inappropriate behavior and getting professional help. Yeshiva faculty and other agencies might become involved. We hope that throughout what is certain to be a long and difficult process, respect for the privacy of the victim(s), the rabbi's family, and, to the extent possible, the rabbi can be maintained.

CONCLUSION

Caring, inspired commitment poses constant challenges to rabbis of all temperaments and character types. Whether achieved through psychotherapy or other modalities of self-exploration, awareness of his personal character is critical to a rabbi's judgment and stability.

Rabbinic sexual boundary violations thrive on secrecy. Some are committed by individuals with severe psychological impairment who intentionally and repeatedly seek out vulnerable subjects. Other rabbis slide down less obvious slippery slopes into sexual impropriety. Times of personal darkness render a rabbi vulnerable to impulsive, potentially destructive activity.

Rabbinic education and post-*s'micha* programming must explicitly deal with the power and perils of rabbinic authority and charisma. Whether clergy work aims toward comforting the afflicted or afflicting the comforted, transference and countertransference issues are ineluctable companions of rabbinic involvement. Rabbis must anticipate the ubiquity of transference projections and learn how to recognize boundary crossings and violations. When they find themselves in danger of transgression, rabbis need to know how to correct the situation, make amends, and get longer-term help. All yeshivas and seminaries must institute mandatory courses in boundary sensitivity for rabbis-in-training. Once in the field, graduate rabbis need support and ongoing supervision. Establishing confidential lines of communication and responsibility should provide forums for discussing and addressing inevitable boundary crossings and violations. Such a foundation will support thorough investigative procedures when accusations of sexual abuse arise.

Current sex abuse scandals in the rabbinate across the denominations regularly find their way into the media and raise public protest. Community reactions range from blanket denial and vilification of accusers to protests of journalistic anti-Semitism and the undermining of trust of rabbis in general. My hope is that bringing these devastating human situations to light ushers in a new era of openness and honesty about rabbinic power and its perils.

NOTES

1. As most instances of rabbinic boundary violation are perpetrated by male clergy, I will use male pronouns when referring to rabbis. Certainly, an exploration of the boundary issues of women rabbis would be meaningful, but it is outside the scope of this essay.

2. Thomas G. Gutheil and Glen O. Gabbard, "The Concept of Boundaries in Clinical Practice: Theoretical and Risk-Management Dimensions," *American Journal of Psychiatry* 150.2 (February 1993): pp. 188–96.

3. Tzvi Blanchard, "In Defense of Magic Dust," *Sh'ma* 37/636 (December 2006/ Tevet 5767), p. 12.

4. Gutheil and Gabbard, "The Concept of Boundaries in Clinical Practice."

5. Charlotte Schwab, *Sex, Lies and Rabbis: Breaking a Sacred Trust* (Bloomington, Ind.: First Books Library, 2002): pp. 214–22.

6. Naomi Mark, "Charisma and Narcissism in the Jewish Community," *Sh'ma* 37/636 (December 2006/Tevet 5767), pp. 3–4.

7. Marie Fortune, *Is Nothing Sacred?* (New York: Harper Collins, 1992) and Fortune, *Clergy Misconduct: Sexual Abuse in the Ministerial Relationship*, reprinted in Elizabeth Schüssler Fiorenza and M. Shawn Copeland, eds., *Violence Against Women* (Maryknoll, N.Y.: Orbis, 1994): pp. 109–18.

ERICA BROWN

Straying the Course

Can Jewish and Secular Leadership Archetypes
Rein in Religious Leaders?

Clergy abuse hurts in many ways. It not only hurts its direct victims, it also tarnishes — often irrevocably — the influence of religious leadership generally and can diminish the power of faith. I will never forget a picture that appeared in a weekly news magazine after the Reverend Jim Bakker's infidelities were made public. It was a black-and-white photo of a female congregant who had collapsed on the stairs of the church. In looking at this emotional shell of a once–diehard defender of the faith, I saw, in miniature, the collapse of religion, too, entrusted as it was to a charismatic man who manipulated devotion.

Abuse by clergymen of their congregants is one of the thorniest leadership issues we face today. We tend to view this problem through the lenses of religion, law, and psychology: What happened to the victim? What happens to faith after abuse? Can justice be achieved? Will the scars ever heal? Has the religious institution to which the clergyperson belonged accepted accountability, where appropriate? And yet, in connection with this sensitive issue, we rarely ask *leadership* questions of the clergy involved, or of the leaders, lay and professional, who ignore their own intuitive suspicions or the painful confessions of the victims and their families.

Some of the leadership questions that are central to clergy abuse include:

\ Do the clergy in question fully understand the extent of the *authority* and *trust* they hold, especially given the high moral esteem with which they are regarded by their constituents and society in general?

- \ Can clergy separate personal temptation from their public leadership responsibilities?
- \ Do faith leaders mask clergy abuse with silence or needless defenses in order to protect the dignity of the position generally or to protect the particular offender in question?
- \ Do we as congregants hold religious leaders accountable and have strict ethical governance structures in place?
- \ Do we as congregants evaluate and monitor the performance of clergy generally and regularly, or do we allow mistakes to fester under an imagined notion of clerical infallibility?

We need to pose these difficult questions in connection with all parties involved in cases of abuse by clergy. No one within a congregation, youth group, or school where there is suspicion of abuse is free to walk away from responsibility. Not our leaders. Not ourselves.

Within the Jewish community, clergy abuse is rarely heard about or discussed, even though there have been highly visible cases that have brought shame upon us. I believe that these have been, so far, isolated instances — and I would not want to see the natural reaction to such cases evolve into a general distrust of all religious institutions and their leadership. Still, we cannot say that child sex abuse by rabbis does not happen or that, if and when it does, the Jewish community always responds appropriately. Denial, wavering, intentional neglect of wrongdoing, and the penalization of the victim or his or her supporters are often found in Jewish abuse cases. Sexual harassment and abuse by Jewish leaders may be very unusual, but the lack of responsiveness, too often seen, and the need for greater accountability still require enhanced vigilance.

Three related issues are at the core of any discussion of Jewish leadership and clergy abuse: the problem of charisma in religious leaders, the difference between public and private morality and its relationship to the clergy, and the importance of creating Jewish institutional environments that deal comfortably with error. In the ideal world, community members and lay leaders need not try to protect the reputation and honor of religious offenders who function in environments where the admission of wrongdoing is safe, acceptable, and a sign that one lives by the principles of atonement and forgiveness that are tenets of one's faith. On the other hand, contrition may not be enough: you foster hypocrisy as a leader when what you say and the way you live occupy two separate moral universes.

One of the persistent defenses of clergy who abuse is a new form of the old theory that the ends justify the means. Charismatic priests and rabbis bring their flocks to higher levels of devotion and observance. Even if the price is high — so high that it may include abuse — the overall achievement for religion is greater, or so some people reckon. From an empirical standpoint, having been closely involved with such a case for years, I can now say openly, "You are wrong. The ends never justify the means." People have trouble separating charisma from content, package from substance, and means from ends. But these *must* be analyzed for what they are. The fact that a rabbi who abuses congregants or students in a youth group, synagogue, or school setting may *also* be an acclaimed teacher or mesmerizing lecturer is not beside the point. It *is* the point. The charisma such leaders exude may be the very reason they are able to abuse others and get away with it. We allow charismatic religious leaders to flourish and grow unchallenged, sometimes to a dangerous extent, when we do not question them or put reins on their influence. We cannot ignore or reward charisma that leads to repugnant behavior. We, as a society, have to teach ourselves to place less emphasis on personal magnetism and more on personal authenticity and ethics.

The impact of charisma on leadership has received interesting treatment in one of the most influential books on business leadership today: Jim Collins's *Good to Great*.[1] Collins and his team sought to isolate characteristics of great companies over a span of fifteen years, with the goal of minimizing the role of leaders in this study of greatness. (Over a time span of fifteen years, it can be assumed that companies may enjoy the leadership of several CEOs.) What Collins and the others found was the impossibility of separating corporate greatness from great leadership, and they identified two qualities that they deemed essential to what they called "level-5 leaders": tremendous will combined with profound humility. This combination assured that the leader had the drive to succeed but that the success was for the company, rather than for the leader. Level-5 leaders are not self-promotional; they want the mission of their company to shine, while they generally avoid the spotlight.

Companies often hunt celebrity CEOs to bring market attention to their products or services. Collins sees this as an error of judgment. Such CEOs can amass power for themselves and often care more about their personal success than about the success of the company.

Collins does not believe that charisma helps leaders. In fact, he calls it a liability. Why? Charisma, that rare personal quality attributed to leaders who arouse fervent popular devotion and enthusiasm, would seem to be a natural and desired leadership quality. Personal magnetism or charm helps leaders better communicate their message. In the world of priests, rabbis, and imams, we find many sincere and devoted religious leaders who lack fire and passion and, consequently, have trouble communicating their message, recruiting those on the margins, or sustaining membership. The power of their message is limited by poor delivery.

But for Collins, charisma is still a liability, because leaders too often use personal charisma — in place of personal sincerity — as a magnet for attention and influence. In abuse cases, this "magnet liability" of charisma is often the operating principle that allows these individuals to expand their sphere of influence and enjoy undeserved protection.

Charisma on the side of the abuser often promotes silence on the part of the victim. Silence is the great emotion-numbing mechanism that allows abuse to grow like a cancer.

True, when accusing a religious leader of abuse we have to ensure scrupulously that there is sufficient evidence to come forward and that we approach religious institutions and their leaders with respect. However, there is an obligation in the Torah to expose any leaders who abuse their power. Maimonides, the great medieval Jewish thinker and physician (1135–1204), wrote extensively on Jewish leadership, weaving together demands from the Bible and Talmud into statements about the responsibility of such leaders as kings, priests, and judges, as well as the responsibility of the nation when those leaders are not people of the utmost integrity. According to Maimonides, every effort should be made to ensure that all members of the Sanhedrin (the Jewish high court) be of mature age, imposing stature, and good appearance, and be able to express themselves clearly and with well-chosen words.[2] Maimonides also believed that leaders must disdain money, must fear God, be humble, love people, love truth, and worry about maintaining a reputation for scrupulousness.[3] Those who take bribes, who judge with an agenda, who make errors of judgment with serious repercussions, or who ignore their communal responsibilities are not only to be chastised but to be singled out publicly. In such cases, the public must be aware that an individual once held up for admiration is now condemned for improper behavior. We do no one a service by protecting such an individual. In fact, we do ourselves a disservice by becoming less caring individuals who cannot hear the plight of others and end up tarnishing our own reputations in the process. According to one popular leadership guide,

> Calloused fingertips lose their sensitivity. Your listening becomes less and less acute, until you fail to hear the real messages from people around you, and cannot identify the songs beneath their words. You listen to them only strategically, as resources or obstacles in the pursuit of your objectives. In the effort to protect yourself, you risk numbing yourself to the world in which you are embedded.[4]

When leaders protect other leaders, they also sustain an environment that, over time, promotes more malfeasance by not identifying and stopping immoral behavior. The danger is even greater in connection with the sacred spaces of churches and synagogues. On the one hand, they are places whose inhabitants strive to lead better moral lives. On the other hand, they are also places of forgiveness that promote outreach and acceptance. A central principle in Jim Brown's *The Imperfect Board Member* is that it is easier for a leader to ask for forgiveness after the fact than facetiously to ask for permission to engage in immoral behavior.[5] Simply stated, leaders may believe that the bad acts they do can be facilely wiped away with apologies afterward, well knowing that they would never have been able to get away with such bad behavior had they asked permission first. We find this kind of after-the-fact remorse most common among politicians who publicly decry their mistakes, pretending to act contritely to all those whom they may have hurt, knowing all along that a good apology does wonders with the public.

In a way, we have encouraged this duplicity: we like to see our leaders in this humble posture of forgiveness. In a sense, it is cathartic, as such acts of public contrition offer us a modicum of much-needed ethical correction. But what if we knew ahead of time that public apologies were all premeditated acts, or even a ruse employed by leaders who well understood that they could easily get away with deplorable behavior as long as a soulful apology accompanied such behavior afterward? But, is this not what our biblical prophets harangued the public about in their remonstrations, by chastising those who repeatedly brought sacrifices to compensate for bad behavior instead of staying on the straight and narrow in the first place? One well knows that if any one of these leaders had had to ask permission before engaging in immoral behavior, such license would never have been given to them in the first place.

So why then do we accept "forgiveness" from our leaders after the fact, especially when it comes to matters as serious as clergy sexual abuse?

In relation to clergy abuse, we find that asking forgiveness from victims or congregations without accepting punishment or offering recompense offers the patina of redemption for many abusers and can even seem humanizing in a sanctuary or cathedral setting. Yet this kind of response to abuse simply feeds into the melodrama often deliberately created by charismatic leaders: they present themselves as their own biggest outreach project. Congregants must be wary of individuals who use their own sins as a platform for a theater of redemption. Leaders who sin are not the same as congregants who do so. They must be held to a higher standard because they have placed themselves on a public, moral pedestal. Again, we turn to Maimonides for guidance:

> There are behaviors in the category of profaning God's name that are specifically problematic when done by a person learned in Torah and known for piety. . . . [E]ven though these acts are not sins, they are still a profanation of God's name.[6]

Maimonides lists relatively minor offenses here, including being in the wrong company, not greeting someone with the appropriate politeness, or behaving irascibly. He advises everyone in the religious public eye to go out of his way to be a model of truth and piety. If this is true for minor offenses, how much more so must public religious figures worry about the effect on their reputations of major biblical transgressions.

Maimonides based his words on a famous passage in the Talmud that highlights the consequences of clergy abuse:

> If someone studies Scripture and Mishnah [Jewish oral law supplementing the written laws in the Hebrew Scriptures] and serves the disciples of the wise but is dishonest in business and discourteous in his relations with people, what do people say about him? "Woe unto him who studies Torah — woe unto his teacher who taught him Torah!" This man studied the Torah but look how corrupt his deeds are, how ugly his ways. . . .[7]

The operative word in this passage is "ugly." The beauty of all that is holy is made ugly by a person who uses his or her faith to exploit the vulnerable. Not only does such a person bruise others emotionally, he also can also bring about the collapse of decency and the shattering of faith for coreligionists.

The liability of charisma raises another leadership issue. If leaders have to live constantly under a microscope, will good leaders come forward to lead at all? Asked differently: what happens when standards are so high for a leader's behavior that they discourage people from assuming positions of religious communal responsibility?

One of the most fascinating questions about leadership generally — and leadership within a faith or religious community, in particular — is the role of public versus private morality and its contribution to the authentic self of leadership. Today, under intense media scrutiny, we are seeing an almost complete blurring of the two. Moral blemishes in private are flashed on screens worldwide, as if to say, "Can you trust this person if he or she does X?" It is a fair question on one level and a loaded question on another. We naturally assume that private sin easily translates into public betrayal; spousal infidelity or neglectful parenting means that the unfaithful or neglectful person will one day betray a religious organization as well. In other words, any indiscretion establishes a pattern of behavior that may apply to many other leadership situations.

It is not surprising, then, to learn that two leadership experts, Jim Kouzes and Barry Posner, found that of the four characteristics most admired in leaders — honesty and integrity, a sense of the visionary, the ability to inspire, and competence — honesty and integrity were rated the highest.[8] Such qualities are associated with someone who has high personal moral expectations; as a leader, he or she will turn those expectations into a modus operandi for an institution.

> Character generates moral authority, a powerful form of influence within an organization. As with shared vision and values, these leaders are principle-centered, believing in and demonstrating loving-kindness, dignity and respect for everyone, honesty and integrity, fairness and forgiveness, service about self, excellence and humility. They are particularly noted as being ethical, perhaps even "noble." Character enables the authentic leader to engage moral authority to elevate and pull followers toward the shared vision. Authentic leaders also live a congruent life of spiritual synchronicity that enhances their influence even further.[9]

Unquestionably, in an age of cynicism about leadership, stressing "character" as a necessary and sufficient aspect of leadership seems natural. James

O'Toole, in his important book *Leading Change: Overcoming the Ideology of Comfort and the Tyranny of Custom*, discusses the importance of leaders having respect for followers. In his words, effective leaders "always keep faith with their people: they must never lie to their followers nor break the laws they are charged with upholding."[10] Having said this, O'Toole questions the current wisdom of the adage "private behavior predicts public behavior" as a disqualifier for leadership positions:

> A review of any list of great leaders will reveal that almost all were flawed human beings with notable private failings. . . . If we insist on perfection of character, we are unlikely to find many exemplary leaders, and our analysis will end in despair.[11]

How much can we separate private and public failings when it comes to clergy? The Hebrew Bible suggests that flawed individuals can make great religious leaders. Story after biblical story presents us with characters who are jealous, angry, self-absorbed, or who make decisions by fiat; these qualities may actually help them navigate political challenges. While rabbinic tradition contains admonitions aplenty to avoid politics for a life of silence, scholarship, and near-saintliness, the Bible is filled with stories of leaders who engaged in little of this self-imposed isolation. One of the enduring appeals of biblical texts is their portrayal of the rawness of the human condition; we are almost forced to see our ancient leaders as flawed, even tragic, possessed of both a frail and a noble humanity. As a result, we are able to relate to these figures and see in their religious growth a window to our own. The subtle message is unavoidable; the outcomes are more complex than we want to believe.

The distinction between private and public morality is displayed memorably in the early chapters of Genesis, after the flood waters of Noah's Ark recede. Noah plants a vineyard, grows grapes, and produces wine. "And he drank of the wine and was drunken, and he uncovered himself *in the interior of his tent*."[12] The pressures on this man were, no doubt, very great. Charged with the building of an ark, the saving of his family and of representatives of the animal kingdom, and then burdened with the task of constructing a new world — one that would not suffer the fate of the last — Noah faced a daunting challenge that would lead anyone to drink.

While criticized in rabbinic commentaries, Noah's indiscretion is not treated harshly in the biblical text. It is arguable that this failing did not deserve public reproach because it occurred "in the interior of his tent." Only Noah's son Ham changes the nature of this private act: "And Ham, the father of Canaan, saw the nakedness of his father — and related it to his two brothers *outside*."[13] Nachmanides, an early-thirteenth-century Spanish commentator, suggests an important distinction between the inside of Noah's tent — the sphere of private behavior — and the "outside," where indiscretions become public. In this narrative, it is Ham — the one who makes Noah's private affair public — who is criticized, both by his father upon waking and by the biblical text itself.[14]

No one is suggesting that private immorality should be ignored. The Hebrew Bible is imparting a more nuanced message: when we move unfairly from a leader's public service to his inner life, we are no longer capable judges of behavior. In the public domain, a leader must exemplify the highest moral standards and be always mindful of his public responsibilities to those he serves. Franklin Roosevelt, in one of his famous fireside chats as president, said, "I never forget that I live in a house owned by all the American people, and that I have been given their trust."[15] Along these lines, O'Toole argues that "the gauge of the greatness of leaders is their public record measured over their entire lifetimes."[16] In other words, value-based leadership is not of the moment; it is a condition of great leadership measured across a lifetime.

However, it is also our responsibility to leave a leader's private life private. No doubt there will be many who disagree with me and think that anything a leader does, public or private, deserves to be in the public eye. But I believe that in our tabloid-driven culture we do not learn the personal moral failings of leaders out of a desire to create a better organization or country; we learn about them so that we can bring our leaders down several notches, gloat over failings, and sustain a gossip industry. This only makes leaders difficult to find. As O'Toole says, "If we insist on perfection of character, we are unlikely to find many exemplary leaders, and our analysis will end in despair."[17]

Compare O'Toole's words with those of the nineteenth-century German neo-Orthodox commentator, Rabbi Samson Raphael Hirsch. On the passage in Genesis in which Abraham calls his wife his "sister," Rabbi Hirsch comments that we should not be shocked by the Bible's open admission of the flaws of our leaders. It is there for a didactic purpose:

> The Torah never hides from us the faults, errors and weaknesses of our great men. Just by that it gives the stamp of veracity to what it relates. But

in truth, by the knowledge which is given us of their faults and weaknesses, our great men are in no wise made lesser but actually greater and more instructive. If they stood before us as the purest models of perfection we should attribute them as having a different nature, which has been denied us. Were they without passion, without internal struggles, their virtues would seem to us the outcome of some higher nature, hardly a merit and certainly no model that we could hope to emulate.[18]

Rabbi Hirsch adds that the sterling qualities of our biblical heroes and heroines would be lessened were we not shown examples of behavior that appear to belie them. As an example, he cites the Torah's declaration of Moses' humility in the twelfth chapter of Numbers, which is all the more significant because in the same chapter we see Moses "fly into a passion." By displaying heroes with human complexities, the Torah shows us "the result of a great work of self-control and self-ennoblement which we should all copy because we all could copy."[19] Rabbi Hirsch says of our patriarchs and matriarchs, "They do not require our apologies, nor do such attempts become them. Truth is the seal of our Torah, and truthfulness is the principle of all its true and great commentators and teachers."[20] Thus, the Hebrew Bible repeatedly illustrates that great leaders need not be perfect. True, Rabbi Hirsch also stresses that leaders will pay for private indiscretions with private suffering: "The Torah also shows us no faults without at the same time letting us see the greater or lesser evil consequences."[21] But that is ultimately a leader's own problem.

On the other hand, leaders who make facile distinctions between private and public morality are walking a tightrope and may fall disastrously. This is particularly true of religious leaders, who occupy — by choice — the domain of the sacred and holy. They may have taken vows. They may be ordained. They may wear distinctive clothes and present themselves as adhering to higher spiritual standards than those that are expected of others in areas of behavior and propriety. Individuals who make such choices cannot easily distinguish between public and private morality because they have chosen to make their private moral conduct the basis for their professional existence. When Noah got drunk inside his tent, he hurt no one except himself. He put himself in a private place where his behavior was visible to no one and affected no one. But abuse by a clergyman exploits the sacred trust placed in a confidant, guide, and advisor and affects not only the body but also the soul of the victim. It is the worst kind of abuse precisely because the public and private persona of the clergyperson cannot be easily separated. Priests, rabbis, and imams cannot put themselves in the public eye as moral exemplars and then scoff at a public who holds them accountable for just that reason.

A CULTURE OF ERROR

There are some important preventive measures that can reduce to abuse by clergy; one such measure is feedback. Annual performance reviews that are tied to salary increases and contract renewal give a synagogue board a measure of control over a rabbi or senior leader's behavior; they also serve notice to the leader that he or she must answer to the congregation.

While this may seem obvious, I cannot emphasize enough that this is *not* standard practice in congregations across all denominations. In one of the leadership classes that I conduct for board members of Jewish institutions, a woman once raised her hand and asked how her rabbi — who was no longer effective as a leader — could be reached through feedback. I asked her when his contract would be up for renewal, and she answered, "Oh, he's got a life contract." In many congregations, the annual performance review, if conducted at all, is a perfunctory activity. In one instance, an older gentleman told me that his rabbi would not be able to handle criticism. Is this an acceptable excuse for someone principally responsible for the spiritual and often emotional lives of hundreds of people? We have yet to create a culture where the performance of senior religious leaders is regularly assessed and where mechanisms for comprehensive and honest feedback are offered.

Such evaluations may help stop clergy abuse before it starts. One of the common arguments made against voicing sex abuse accusations is that the accused rabbi has been in his or her position for such a long time that seniority and tenure will weigh against any complaint. Instead of the leader's behavior being called into question, the credibility of the victim is minimized. Without regular, honest, and comprehensive evaluation of leaders, small problems turn into larger and often irreversible problems with hard-to-handle consequences. When a clergy problem can no longer be ignored, you hear those in positions of power say, "We let it go on too long."

It is also important to include every part of the congregation or community in the evaluative process. Clergymen treat different people differently. A common complaint of abuse victims is that the offender did not show his or her "true" colors to everyone, so that people in positions to affect change did not find the abuse claims credible, given their own relationship to the accused person. In a recent leadership text, we find the same point:

> In a very real sense, you are a different person with different kinds of people and in different settings. . . . Indeed, the research on different sources of feedback confirms what seems common sense — bosses, subordinates, and peers see different aspects of a person's behavioral repertoire. That's why the same leader can look so different when evaluated from each of these perspectives.[22]

Even though Judaism does not claim infallibility for its clergy, Jewish communities are often silent about their rabbis out of respect for the rabbinic position and its authority. Communities assume a relationship of trust with their rabbis that can make evaluations feel uncomfortable. But clergy abuse smashes the fragile relationship of trust, and it can only be countered with a rigorous system that allows for preventive transparency. We all have to understand that a rabbi's role is very unusual. In the words of a Jewish thinker, "One day the rabbi is relating to a board member, and the next day he or she is burying the person's dead mother."[23] If rabbis were not different from other people, they would not be trusted as faith leaders.

We must also understand that religious and professional cultures that continually mask error are a safe harbor for clergy abuse. We have already learned this lesson in another context: that of the regulation of charitable Jewish institutions. As one influential Jewish philanthropist has written:

> If success in the Jewish community were measured by the accolades of our staffs and directors, we could claim victory in the struggle for renaissance. . . . If I ask whether the accolades are backed by outside evaluation, I am usually met with blank stares. Unfortunately, too many executive directors and staffs fail to understand the need for objective evaluation at all stages of a project's trajectory.[24]

Creating a culture where mistakes are acknowledged and progress is monitored opens doors to risky conversations, healthy debate, and institutional growth. Most importantly, open institutional cultures limit the festering, halting, and hesitating approach many individuals have to questioning authority. Without the perceived freedom to question authority, abuse victims will not articulate their concerns and may even become numb to their own pain. Another theme heard repeatedly in abuse cases is "What is the point of telling anyone? No one is listening." Creating responsive religious environments with open channels of communication can change that tune.

CONCLUSION

That there are people who abuse authority for personal, immoral gain should not come as a shock. That some of these individuals have embraced a life of sacred service is extremely upsetting, but, sadly, still not a surprise. We all know leaders who lack self-awareness and self-control. We see these deficiencies in ourselves and therefore can see them in others. We recognize the power of addictions, and how even people of otherwise high moral character can stumble and falter.

What we cannot excuse are those who stand on the outside and permit abuse to continue by not stopping it, and those who even encourage abuse because they do not call it by name. The Book of Proverbs tells us, "One who hides hatred uses lying lips."[25] One who hides detestable behavior is lying to himself and to others, and ultimately corroding the beauty of all that is sacred and lofty in this world. Holiness and morality have a porcelainlike fragility; it is the task of congregational leaders to protect what is fragile.

Emily Dickinson, in one of her poems, describes the disastrous collapse of a cherished ideal:

It dropped so low in my regard,
I heard it hit the ground
And go to pieces on the stones
At bottom of my mind.[26]

The poem could well describe the moral collapse that occurs when unworthy people hold places of moral elevation. The cry of clergy abuse victims is shattering. It breaks our hearts, and it can break our faith. Religion drops low in our regard. The poet blames herself for the mistake of placing a fragile ideal in a precarious place. We must blame ourselves when we allow a religious leader to remain in place who has the power to break hearts and shatter souls.

NOTES

1. Jim Collins, *Good to Great* (New York: HarperBusiness, 2001).

2. Moses Maimonides, *Mishneh Torah*, The Book of Judges 2:6 (author's translation).

3. Ibid., 2:7.

4. Ronald Heifetz and Marty Linsky, *Leadership on the Line* (Boston: Harvard Business School Press, 2002): 225–26.

5. Jim Brown, *The Imperfect Board Member* (San Francisco: Jossey-Bass, 2006): 45.

6. Maimonides, *Mishneh Torah*, Laws of Foundations of the Torah 5:11.

7. BT *Yoma* 80a.

8. In Dean Pielstick, "A Model of the Process of Authentic Leading," *Executive Search Consultants for the Nonprofit Sector* (October 2006): 2.

9. Ibid., 7.

10. James O'Toole, *Leading Change* (San Francisco: Jossey-Bass Publishers, 1995), 35.

11. Ibid.

12. Genesis 9:21 [emphasis added].

13. Genesis 9:22. Nachmanides on Genesis 9:22 (author's translation) [emphasis added].

14. Ibid.

15. F. Roosevelt, fireside chat on economic conditions, April 14, 1938.

16. O'Toole, *Leading Change*, 35.

17. Ibid.

18. Samson Raphael Hirsch, *The Pentateuch: Translation and Commentary*, trans. Isaac Levy (Gateshead, England: Judaic Press, 1976), 236.

19. Ibid.

20. Ibid., 237.

21. Ibid.

22. Daniel Goleman, Richard Boyatzis, and Annie McKee, *Primal Leadership* (Boston: Harvard Business School Press, 2002), 135.

23. Excerpt from a conversation guided by Carl Sheingold, "Whither the Professional and Lay Leadership?" *Sh'ma* 9 (April 2004): 47–54.

24. Michael H. Steinhardt, "Accountability," *Contact* (Summer 2004): 3.

25. Proverbs 10:18.

26. Emily Dickinson, "It Dropped So Low in My Regard," *The Collected Poems of Emily Dickinson* (New York: Barnes and Noble, 1993), 63.

Sacrificing Victims

JOYANNA SILBERG & STEPHANIE DALLAM

Out of the Jewish Closet

Facing the Hidden Secrets of Child Sex Abuse —
And the Damage Done to Victims

We are at a historic moment, when there is emerging awareness of a problem that has been shrouded in layers of denial and disbelief — sexual abuse in the Jewish community. As we write these words, the first study to document prevalence of sexual abuse in a Jewish population appeared in the November 2007 issue of the *American Journal of Psychiatry* (Yehuda, Friedman, Rosenbaum, Labinky, & Schmeidler, 2007). These preliminary data in a sample in the Orthodox community suggest that prevalence rates of sexual abuse in that community parallel the rates of abuse in the larger society: approximately one-fourth of the women surveyed reported having experienced sexual abuse as child. This staggering statistic indicates that sexual abuse experiences among women are more common than obesity (20 percent of the population) and are equal to a woman's lifetime risk of breast cancer. Yet, unlike these public health problems, sexual abuse has too often been treated as a topic unfit for public discussion and largely irrelevant to the concerns of the Jewish community. This is changing.

In 2007, a series of groundbreaking articles in the *Baltimore Jewish Times* by Phil Jacobs identified multiple victim reports of sexual abuse at the hands of respected rabbis and teachers in Baltimore yeshivas, or schools of Jewish learning (see Jacobs, in references). A coalition of mental health professionals, advocates, writers, educators, and victims in Baltimore, under the auspices of the Shofar Coaliton, now energized by the newest revelations in the Baltimore community, have begun to provide direct support to Jewish victims of sexual abuse, education to the community, and research on the prevalence of this problem in the Jewish community of Baltimore. Other Jewish communities have similarly begun to open the door for a frank examination of sexual abuse in their respective communities. Among those leading this effort are Ariela Goldstein, LMSW, Dallas Jewish Family Services and Debbie Fox, LCSW, Jewish Family Service of Los Angeles. *Narrow Bridge: A Film about Sexual Abuse*, a recently released film by Israel Moskovits, portrays a fictional account of sexual abuse in the Orthodox community, and several documentaries on the topic are currently being developed.

The Rabbinical Council of Greater Baltimore summarized this new awareness in a public letter to the community on April 11, 2007: "We must acknowledge that this horrible form of abuse exists — and has existed for generations — in our community as well. This issue must be confronted directly and we believe that this discussion can be a first step towards the necessary and achievable goal of ridding our community of this scourge" (in Jacobs, May 21, 2007). The Baltimore Board of Rabbis, which includes rabbis from across the ideological spectrum, added its own voice in urging the Jewish community to accept its obligation to confront these issues.

This new awareness is motivated by the desire to help the children and adult survivors of abuse whose devastating stories have begun to surface in the community. Whether the perpetrator is a rabbi, religious teacher, camp counselor, parent, or trusted family friend, an imbalance of power exploits the vulnerable child and makes any sexual approach to the child an assault with devastating psychological consequences.

THE PSYCHOLOGICAL EFFECTS OF CHILD SEXUAL ABUSE

Being sexually abused by my father, whom I loved and on
whom I depended, exploded my world and sense of safety
into a million pieces. Nothing was ever the same.
— Jewish survivor Rachel Lev (Lev, p. 6)

The evocative term that may best capture the profound demoralization and internal devastation suffered by victims of child sexual abuse is the term "soul murder." Leonard Shengold (1999) used this term to describe the effects he found in his patients who had been victimized as children. This soul murder is characterized by a variety of psychological sequelae that have been documented in an increasingly robust literature that has found that child sexual abuse is a risk factor for a large array of mental health, behavioral, and social problems that can occur regardless of socioeconomic level. In children, these problems include sleep difficulties, nightmares, night terrors, depression, poor school performance, wetting and bowl accidents, sexualized behaviors, suicidal ideation and self-harm, dissociation, conflicting attachment to the abuser, and feelings of self-blame (Putnam, 2003; Silberg, 1998; Briere, 1998; Faller, 2003). Newer research suggests that sexual abuse may be associated as well with enduring changes to children's developing brains (Teicher, 2002).

The Case of Adina

One way to illustrate vividly the effects of sexual abuse perpetrated on a child is to tell the story of Adina, an eight-year-old girl who came to the first author's office for therapy.[1] Adina had been abused by her father, an assistant cantor in their local synagogue. Adina's case evocatively illustrates the symptoms displayed by abused children, societal forces that impede disclosure, and the potential for successful healing.

A bright and verbal child, Adina had been describing acts of sexual abuse since the age of two. While Adina's behavior had led her mother to believe that something terrible was happening to her, Adina's language was not sufficiently clear to convince the local social service agency that she was being abused. As a result, the family court ordered her to have weekends with her father after the parents separated.

At the time she came to see the first author, Adina had been forced to visit her father on weekends for six years. During these years, many people suspected that something dreadful was happening to Adina. Reports were phoned in to the social service department by teachers, nurses, and therapists. However, social services failed to substantiate any of these reports, and thus Adina was not protected. Adina's mother reported that over the years Adina became more and more troubled. Her symptoms read like a textbook on the ill effects of abuse on children. Adina had nightmares and sleep problems that resulted in her waking up in the night, screaming, "No, no, don't!" Her mother noted that she would often sleep sitting up, as Adina stated that her nightmares became worse when she lay in her bed. Adina also wet her bed at night, a symptom that persisted long after she was successfully toilet trained.

During the day, Adina's behavior was highly variable. Sometimes, she seemed sweet, cooperative, and playful. At other times, she appeared angry, oppositional, and defiant. She would sometimes go into temper tantrums that would last for hours, during which she could not be consoled. Her behavior often changed right before visits with her father; Adina's mannerisms and behavior became angrier. Sometimes right before leaving the house for the visit, Adina would go into a deep sleep, requiring her mother to carry her to the car. This variable behavior and escape from stress through sleep are symptoms often associated with dissociation, a frequent sequela of abuse among children and adult survivors (Silberg, 1998). As a further dissociative indicator, Adina reported to the first author that she felt like her mind was made of "two people," that one of them liked her daddy and one liked her mommy. Adina often had difficulty remembering what happened at the visits with her father after she got home.

Adina also displayed sexualized behavior. Adina's mother noted that she would catch Adina rubbing her genitals on furniture in the house after entering a trancelike state in which she seemed oblivious to her surroundings. Her mother reported that she would gently redirect Adina at these times.

Adina would also enter moods of deep depression, surprising for a child of her age. She talked about suicide and had many moral and philosophical questions about why the world was created and whether God was really good. Sometimes when she was in one of these moods, she would cry, withdraw to her room, and refuse to go to her weekly swimming activity — something she usually enjoyed. Adina's mother noted her daughter would repeatedly pick at sores on her skin, sometimes to the point of bleeding, and seemed to have no feeling of pain. Some days Adina would stare at her schoolwork, unable to concentrate or complete tasks she normally completed without difficulty.

In therapy, Adina quickly warmed up to seeing the first author and was able to do elaborate drawings about the internal world in her mind and the two people, "Moshe" and "Sarah," who she said lived in her imagination. Six months into treatment, while the first author explored with Adina the feelings associated with these two internal identities, Adina revealed that Moshe had a secret. In painstaking and elaborate detail, Adina described repeated sexual assaults by her father, including vaginal penetration. This time, due to the first author's careful documentation, Adina's superior language skills, and a responsive social service department in a new state, Adina was finally believed. All visits stopped, and prosecution for the sexual assaults commenced.

Once she was safe, Adina's therapy centered on dealing with her ambivalent and changing feelings about her father. At first, she was desperate to confront him, to ask him why he did it, and to get him to acknowledge that what he did was wrong. At the same time, Adina insisted that her father was a "good man" and that if he knew how she felt he would apologize. As time passed, Adina became angrier, distanced herself from her father psychologically, and eventually came to call him "my ex-father." Eventually, Adina was filled with rage at his betrayal and kept wondering if there was something she had done that had caused it and whether she was "bad" for having participated. Adina alternated between putting herself in the same category with him (i.e., guilty and complicit) and seeing herself as separate and blameless. As she came to accept that he was at fault for the abuse, Adina was forced to confront more directly her own helplessness, sense of victimization, and awareness that, despite his protestations, he had never loved her in the way she needed.

While dealing with the demoralization caused by this betrayal by her father, Adina was also overwhelmed with feelings of betrayal from the experiences with the various social workers and judges who throughout her six-year ordeal had refused to believe her disclosures of abuse and had repeatedly sent her back to be raped again. Adina also had to confront her anger and feeling of betrayal by her mother, who had tried to protect her daughter, but had been forced by the courts to take Adina to visit her father. Through exercises in family therapy, the two were able share their pain and frustration. Adina's mother apologized for not having been able to protect Adina. Despite all she had done to protect and heal her daughter, it would never be perceived as enough by Adina.

Adina went through much spiritual conflict. She finally came to the conclusion that the real God was the one that she believed in, not the one that her father believed in. This allowed her to preserve her faith and dissociate it from her connections with her father's religious observance. Eventually, Adina's symptoms remitted, she was able to maintain a healthy attachment to her mother, maintain a positive outlook on life, and to let go of her feelings of self-blame. Adina vowed to become a judge some day so she could help children like herself, or to become a senator so she could change laws to help abused children. While the outcome of the criminal case is unclear, the family court has continued to bar any contact between Adina and her father.

Delayed Disclosure

Adina was lucky enough to have been believed at a relatively young age and to have received therapy. Most adult survivors have not been that fortunate.

Estimates suggest that only 3 percent of all cases of child sexual abuse (Finkel-hor & Dzuiba-Leatherman, 1994; Timnick, 1985) and only 12 percent of rapes involving children are ever reported to police (Hanson, Resnick, Saunders, Kilpatrick, & Best, 1999). A nationally representative survey of over three thousand women revealed that of those raped during childhood, 47 percent did not disclose to anyone for over five years post-rape. In fact, 28 percent of the victims reported that they had *never* told anyone about their childhood rape prior to the research interview. Moreover, the women who had never told often had suffered the most serious abuse. Recent research in the Ortho-dox community found results consistent with this research; only 35 percent of sexual abuse survivors who filled out an anonymous questionnaire at the mikvah, the ritual bath, had ever disclosed the abuse to anyone before report-ing it on the anonymous survey (Yehuda et al., 2007).

It is not surprising that most children keep quiet since sex offenders, such as Adina's father, typically seek to make the victim feel as though he or she caused the offender to act inappropriately. Adina's father, for example, told her she had not dressed modestly enough, and that is what happens to "pretty girls" who do not dress appropriately. Due to these kinds of manipulations, children often have great difficulty sorting out who is responsible for the abuse and frequently blame themselves for what happened. In the end, fears of retribution and abandonment, and feelings of complicity, embarrassment, guilt, and shame conspire to silence children and inhibit their disclosures of abuse (Pipe & Goodman, 1991; Sauzier, 1989).

Boys seem to have a particularly difficult time dealing with sexual abuse and are even less likely to report it than girls. A review of five community-based studies revealed that rates of nondisclosure ranged from 42 percent to 85 percent in abused men (Lyon, 2002). Research with abused males has found that the more severe the abuse, the more likely the boy is to blame himself and the less likely he will disclose the abuse (Hunter, Goodwin, & Wilson, 1992). In addition to self-blame, reluctance of boys to disclose abuse may be traced to the social stigma attached to victimization, along with fears that they will be disbelieved. If their abuser was a male, they may also worry that they will be labeled homosexual (Watkins & Bentovim, 1992). This failure to disclose abuse does not suggest, however, that boys are less harmed by the experience. An empirical review revealed that the aftermath for abused boys may be even worse and more complex than for girls. For instance, a study of secondary school children found that sexually abused boys had considerably more emotional and behavioral problems than their female counterparts, including much higher suicidality (Garnefski & Diekstra, 1997).

Having kept the secret for years, and unable to interrupt the abuse as a child, adult survivors are often plagued with a broad range of behavioral, psychological, and physical problems. Common psychological sequelae among adults include anxiety, depression, post–traumatic stress disorder (PTSD), self-destructive behavior, dissociation, substance abuse, sexual maladjustment, feelings of isolation and stigma, poor self-esteem, and difficulty in trusting others and maintaining successful relationships (Briere, 1998; Browne & Finkelhor, 1986; Roesler & McKenzie, 1994; Waller & Smith, 1994). In addition to the well-documented adverse effects of trauma on mental health, a growing body of literature has found that experiencing childhood maltreatment has also been found to be associated with adverse effects on long-term physical health (Dallam, 2001; Kendall-Tackett, 2003).

Adult survivors of childhood abuse also report higher rates of rape or sexual assault as adults (Briere, 1998). It appears that the self-denigratory beliefs that survivors frequently hold about themselves, their roles, and their relations to others may set them on a disastrous course, where revictimization is more likely (Cloitre, Cohen, & Scarvalone, 2002). Further adding to the risk of revictimization is the increased prevalence of substance abuse problems among abuse survivors. About half of all men and two-thirds of all women in drug treatment centers report childhood sexual or physical abuse (Briere, 1998). Similarly, anecdotal reports from the Jewish survivor community in Baltimore indicate that a large percentage of residents in the community-sponsored halfway houses for addiction and recovery has had a history of sexual abuse (Giller, personal communication with Joy Silberg, October 22, 2007).

Lisa Ferentz, MSW, therapist in the Jewish community of Baltimore and national trainer on trauma and abuse, notes that, in addition to the above symptoms, Jewish survivors may feel particularly isolated within their community.[2] Those abused by priests have received tremendous validation by the widespread press coverage of their victimization. Jewish survivors, on the other hand, often feel they are suffering alone. According to Ferentz, the Jewish survivors that she works with often minimize the extent of their abuse because they lack the language to describe it or the societal validation to make sense of it. The power imbalance between victim and perpetrator often supports this minimization, as the victim takes the powerful perpetrator's point of view that the abusive events were not really "that bad."

Jewish survivors often associate their inability to disclose or be protected with aspects of their religion and identity. This can lead to spiritual crises in which survivors reject the religion that they see as having been the fertile ground on which the abuse was fostered. Sue William Silverman (2003), a Jewish survivor of sexual abuse, describes this crisis of faith and reports how objects with Christian symbolic significance became tools of comfort for her before she rediscovered her own Jewish identity. Similarly, David Clohessy, executive director of SNAP (Survivor Network of those Abused by Priests), reports that among the members of his Catholic survivor organization, the vast majority have rejected the Catholic faith as they are no longer able to find comfort from the Church they feel betrayed them (Joy Silberg's phone interview of David Clohessy, September 19, 2007). This becomes an unfortunate double bind for once-religious survivors, who often need a sense of spiritual anchoring to bolster them during the healing process.

Phil Jacobs's series of articles on survivors of rabbinic abuse in the Jewish community suggests that abandoning religious observance is also common among Jewish survivors of childhood sexual abuse. As one survivor (abused by the rabbi who tutored him for his bar mitzvah) states, "My Bar Mitzvah was the worst day of my life" (Jacobs, April 13, 2007). Another survivor abused by his bar mitzvah teacher reports that he cannot read from the Torah, the scrolls containing the five books of Moses, because of associations to the abuse.

At present, although we don't have the kind of research from the Jewish community that would allow us to generalize about whether Jews desert or adhere to their religion, anecdotal reports from the Jewish community indicate that Jewish survivors frequently do find a way back to their religion, but often at a different level of observance. The study by Rachel Yehuda et al. (2007) found that the rate of abuse in that sample of Orthodox women was higher among those who, although religious today, had not grown up in observant homes, suggesting that some survivors may seek Orthodoxy in order to find comfort away from a previous life of abuse. Against these findings is some very convincing anecdotal literature reporting on cases of abuse victims who have left, either partially or entirely, the confines of religious communities in a rebellious strike against their abusers and their community's complicity (Winston, 2005).

Lisa Ferentz observed that for many Orthodox women survivors the pre-scriptive aspect of sexual relations provides them with great relief and a sense of safety. Because of religious prohibitions against sexual relations during two weeks of the monthly cycle, the survivor may feel more empowerment about controlling her own body. Furthermore, since sexual relations can only be ini-tiated if the woman has used the mikvah, the ritual bath, the survivor may feel a further sense of control about her involvement in sexual activities. Accord-ing to Ms. Ferentz, abuse survivors also appear to take comfort in the modest requirements of dress, helping them feel less sexualized or objectified. Even when Jewish victims are not able to reconnect to their faith, Ms. Ferentz notes that finding spiritual solace in some form (sometimes in twelve-step groups) is an important healing element for survivors.

THE PENDULUM SWINGS BETWEEN AWARENESS AND DENIAL

It took many attempts and disclosures for Adina to eventually get the help she needed to deal with her tragic early history. The disbelief she faced from her community, the social workers, and the judges with whom she interacted is part of a pervasive societal pattern of denial that has complex historical and sociological origins. Contemporary society emerged from denial about child sexual abuse in the second half of the twentieth century. Yet, the academic and popular culture still struggles with an often contradictory treatment of the topic, a kind of approach-avoidance conflict when the subject of child sexual abuse is raised.

Sigmund Freud set the stage for this approach-avoidance conflict over the topic of childhood sexual abuse. In 1896, he addressed his colleagues at the Society of Psychiatry and Neurology in Vienna and attributed the symptoms of his adult women patients to the trauma of sexual experiences. Freud wrote, "It seems to me certain that our children are far more often exposed to sexual assaults than the few precautions taken by parents in this connection would lead us to expect" (pp. 275–276). Freud identified three groups of victims: those assaulted by strangers, those assaulted by trusted caregivers, and those assaults by siblings. Freud seemed to grasp that the core trauma of sexual abuse lies in the act of betrayal of the child by the adult. He wrote, "The child in his helplessness is at the mercy of this arbitrary will" (p. 284). A hundred years later, Susan Sgroi (1982), in her now-classic text, offered a similar description of the dynamics of child sexual abuse.

> The ability to lure a child into a sexual relationship is based upon the all-powerful and dominant position of the adult or older adolescent perpetrator, which is in sharp contrast to the child's age, dependency, and subordinate position. Authority and power enable the perpetrator, implicitly or directly, to coerce the child into sexual compliance. (p. 9)

Thus Freud had a perceptive understanding of the power imbalance that lies at the heart of sexual abuse. He theorized that the sexual abuse being reported by his female patients lay behind much of the distress that brought them to him for treatment. This theory, termed the "Seduction Theory," was greeted with ridicule and disbelief by Freud's colleagues (Masson, 1992). In 1905, Freud bowed to the pressure of his peers and publicly retracted the theory. He replaced it with the Oedipal theory, which attributed his patients' descriptions of childhood sexual experiences with adults to wishes and fantasies rather than real events. Of Freud's disciples, only Sandor Ferenczi viewed Freud's reversal as a mistake. While the rest of psychoanalysis began to study how women's fantasies about abuse caused them to become ill, Ferenczi continued with the original theory that some adult disorders stemmed from real experiences of sexual victimization — leading to Ferenczi's ostracism from the psychiatric community. Ferenczi made the psychiatric community even more uncomfortable by recognizing that abuse occurs even in the upper classes. In his insightful address "Confusion of Tongues between the Adult and Child," Ferenczi (1933/1949) noted, "Even children of respected, high-minded puritanical families fall victim to real rape much more frequently than one has dared to suspect" (pp. 296–297).

Early psychoanalytic writers not only rejected Ferenczi's observations, they embraced a victim-blaming stance that continues to affect social discourse on child sexual abuse to this day. Karl Abraham (1927) assumed that real sexual encounters between child and adult were rare, and attributed any actual encounters to the sexuality of the child. He wrote, "In a great number of cases the trauma was desired by the child unconsciously. . . . [W]e have to recognize it as a form of infantile sexual activity" (p. 38). Abraham further attributed the child's secrecy about these events to the child's own guilt for having caused the event or for failing to have prevented it. We now recognize that the self-blame and guilt that children often experience after child sexual abuse is often a conscious strategy of the perpetrator's. Sex offenders often hold erroneous beliefs that children enjoy sex with them, and blame their own urges on the "seductiveness" of the child (Salter, 2003). Even as late as 1962, psychoanalytic writers continued to blame victims for their abuse, even when victims complained of harm. For instance, Irving B. Weiner (1962) explained away the complaints of incest victims, saying, "It is quite likely that many incestuous daughters avoid guilt feelings by denying their enjoyment of the sexual experience" (p. 30). Lacking from these early accounts was any appreciation of the culpability of the perpetrator and the power differential between the adult and child.

Professional responses to the issue of child sexual abuse began to change in the 1970s when the women's movement found an increasingly powerful voice. The perspective of victims began to be acknowledged, first by the media and later in professional writings. In 1977, a groundbreaking article was published by *Ms* magazine, titled "Incest: Sexual Abuse Begins at Home." Ellen Weber reported firsthand accounts by incest survivors, who related how the perpetrators abused their position of authority to coerce them into a sexual relationship. The article also describes the long-term negative effects caused by such victimization. Increased awareness of the harm caused by child abuse led to the passage of the national Child Abuse Prevention and Treatment Act (CAPTA) in 1974. This act provides federal funding to states to support efforts at prevention, assessment, investigation, prosecution, and treatment of child abuse. Laws criminalizing child abuse and mandating reporting of abuse by professionals were passed in all fifty states, as the act requires such laws for states to qualify for federal funding.

Despite growing awareness of the harm caused by child sexual abuse, little was known about the extent of the problem. However, in the late 1970s and early 1980s, studies looking at prevalence began to be published. In 1979 Diana Russell conducted a groundbreaking study in which she interviewed a random sample of more than nine hundred San Francisco women. Women from every socioeconomic and ethnic population reported abuse (Russell, 1986). Thirty-eight percent of women surveyed had been sexually abused by an adult relative, acquaintance, or stranger before reaching the age of eighteen; 16 percent of the women reported that they had experienced incest. Despite the widespread nature of the abuse, only 5 percent of victims had reported the abuse to the police and only 1 percent said that their report had resulted in a conviction. Among those respondents having experienced some form of abuse, Russell found that victims traversed all religious groups.

Several years after the Russell survey of San Francisco women — disbelieving that child sexual abuse could be so prevalent and yet remain so hidden — the editors at the *Los Angeles Times* commissioned a national survey to determine the extent of child sexual abuse in the general population. Over a period of eight days in July 1985, researchers talked by telephone to a random sample of 2,627 men and women from every state in the nation. The results of this comprehensive survey were sobering. Twenty-two percent of those questioned (27 percent of the women and 16 percent of the men) reported that they had been sexually abused as a child. Abusers included relatives (23 percent), friends and acquaintances (42 percent), and strangers (27 percent). Abuse survivors were found in all ethnic and socioeconomic groups (Timnick, 1985).

The results of these two surveys have been confirmed repeatedly in studies of various populations, leading to professional consensus that child sexual abuse affects 20 to 25 percent of American women and 5 to 16 percent of American men (e.g., Briere & Elliott, 2003; Finkelhor, Hotaling, Lewis, & Smith, 1989; Gorey & Leslie, 1997). As noted previously, the first prevalence study of sexual abuse in the Jewish community has just been published. Yehuda et al. (2007) surveyed 380 women who attended a mikvah, a ritual bath that observant women use for ritual cleansing after their menstrual cycle. Twenty-six percent of the women surveyed reported sexual abuse, with 16 percent reporting abuse occurring by the age of thirteen. The perpetrator was often an acquaintance or family member. The prevalence rates for abuse were higher among the ultra-Orthodox than the Modern Orthodox, and also higher among those who had become observant later in life. Mental health sequelae in this sample included depression, anxiety disorders, eating disorders, marital problems, and other difficulties. These preliminary data will clearly need to be repeated in larger, more diverse samples of the Jewish population.

THE RECENT BACKLASH

The research explosion in the field of child sexual abuse in the 1980s was met with a backlash in the 1990s. In part, this backlash movement was spurred by the False Memory Syndrome Foundation (FMSF) established in 1991 by Pamela Freyd, whose adult child, Jennifer Freyd, a prominent researcher in the field of cognitive science, had privately confronted her father about his treatment of her as a child. Their public response to this private family tragedy steered society away from confronting the reality of the problem of sexual abuse, as the foundation began to saturate the press with sensationalistic stories of families being torn apart by false abuse accusations. Research by Lori Kondora (1998) and Mike Stanton (1997) revealed the powerful influence of the false-memory movement on public discourse. Kondora noted that with the advent of false-memory stories, "lost was any substantive concern for the women and children who had endured abuse." Instead, the media's sympathies were focused on a newly constructed victim: the accused perpetrator. This abrupt about-face by the media dramatically illustrates the approach-avoidance conflict our society continues to experience when confronted with issues relating to the sexual abuse of children.

The academic domain has also proved fertile ground for studies suggesting abuse survivors should not be believed. Academic sympathizers with the false-memory movement have published articles comparing memories of childhood sexual abuse to memories of people who believe they have been adducted by aliens (Dittburner & Persinger, 1993). Another prominent false-memory proponent, Elizabeth Loftus, published findings suggesting that older relatives could falsely convince a young person that they had been lost in a mall as a young child (Loftus, 1996; Loftus & Pickrell, 1995). Loftus has used these results as a defense expert to question the credibility of women and men claiming to have been abused. This notion of "false memories" was embraced by both media and professionals, with seemingly little appreciation for the fact that there is a considerable difference between a onetime childhood event of being lost in a mall, and the ongoing betrayal involved in repeated experiences of sexual abuse from a trusted caregiver.

As officers in a nonprofit organization that seeks to educate society about the effects of sexual abuse and other forms of interpersonal violence (the Leadership Council on Child Abuse and Interpersonal Violence; www.leadership council.org), we have worked hard to counteract the types of misinformation that have been spawned by the backlash movement (see, e.g., Whitfield, Silberg, & Fink, 2001). We have critiqued academic studies that promote misinformation on the harm of child abuse (Dallam et al., 2001) and have exposed inaccuracies in public media as well. In 2003, a documentary by Andrew Jarecki, *Capturing the Friedmans*, portrayed the story of Arnold and Jesse Friedman, a Jewish father and son who pled guilty to molesting children during computer classes in their suburban Long Island home. The film relied on myths about child sexual abuse to cast doubt on the convictions, and ultimately left viewers with the impression that the Friedmans were victims of a hysterical overreaction by the police. The film was then used to raise funds for Jesse Friedman's attempt to vacate his 1988 sex abuse convictions (Lam, 2004). The transformation of two confessed pedophiles into apparent victims of a witch hunt was accomplished through omitting reference to some of the most incriminating evidence and by reinforcing popular myths about child sexual abuse. The Leadership Council attempted to correct this misinformation by publicizing facts missing from the film, such as a previous televised confession of Jesse Friedman (see, e.g., http://www.leadershipcouncil.org/1/ctf/1.html). Yet, the wide acclaim this film received omitted mention of the inaccuracies and misinformation, and left viewers with deceitful impressions about the probability of false convictions, serving to reinforce stereotypes in the culture that inhibit children from being believed.

Silencing approaches and even legal challenges have followed professional and journalistic attempts to discuss the harm of sexual abuse. Many of our colleagues who have been at the forefront of sexual abuse research, expert witness testimony, or journalistic exposés have been subject to harassment, ethics complaints, ad hominem attacks, and public vilification. Journalists in the Jewish community who have dared to write about this topic report similar responses. Phil Jacobs, who wrote the series on abuse in the Jewish community for the *Baltimore Jewish Times*, describes receiving e-mails wishing death to him and his family, shunning from some members of the community, and rejection from some people whom he previously viewed as mentors. Jacobs struggles to understand the venom behind these types of reactions, but attributes it to the need of some to protect known abusers, along with the reflexive desire to protect against what some view as attacks on the integrity of the community's beliefs and practices.[3]

While the backlash has been hard on professionals who care for children, it has been disastrous for child victims. The backlash movement, with its promotion of myths about the rates of false conviction and the suggestibility of children, has directly affected our society's ability to protect sexually abused children from harm. Family courts have increasingly become the arena where allegations of sexual abuse are heard and adjudicated. Denial about sexual abuse, facilitated by this backlash movement, has left many judges ignorant about the signs of child sexual abuse (Neustein & Lesher, 2005). An unfortunate outcome of many court cases in which abuse allegations are raised is that children are not believed and are being placed directly in the custody of those whom they fear, the person they claim to be their abuser. This increasingly prevalent court trend has been documented in books (e.g., Bancroft & Silverman, 2002; Neustein & Lesher, 2005; Rosen & Etlin, 1996), newspaper articles (e.g., Kramer, 2001; Lombardi, 2003; O'Meara, 1999), professional articles (e.g., Dallam & Silberg, 2006; Faller & DeVoe, 1995; Neustein & Goetting, 1999), and documentaries (e.g., *Small Justice; Breaking the Silence*). The case histories described in these films, newspaper articles, and books portray the same tragic elements as the story of Adina, who was not protected from her father's abuses for six years following her first disclosure. In many cases, children are not protected from abuse until they are eighteen and able to leave the abusive homes themselves.

Contemporary denial of child sexual abuse often leads professionals like ourselves to feel we live in two worlds. In one world, there is the reality of what we know from our clients and the vast, accumulating literature on child sexual abuse and its effects; in the other, we find the topic obfuscated by denial, confusion, and misinformation. Our clients and the professionals who serve them struggle with this duality as the forces in our culture silence the victims, attack them and their supporters, and minimize the effects of their experiences.

Reasons for societal denial about child sexual abuse and the vehemence against those who seek to expose the problem are complex. Obviously people who have impulses to offend against children may cover their own interest by denying the existence of abuse. But why do we find their denials so plausible? There is an almost physical disgust and revulsion many people feel when the topic of child sexual abuse is raised. People don't want to even think that such a crime is possible. Even if we do accept that the problem exists, we do not want to believe that it could be present in our own community.

Acknowledging that normal-appearing individuals of high status would abuse a child shatters our image of our community as a source of civility and safety. The efforts of the backlash movement to promote misinformation have facilitated the defensive denial many use to protect themselves from a reality too painful to see.

Even Yehuda et al.'s 2007 study on Orthodox women surveyed at the mikvah has had its detractors. Within weeks of its publication, Rabbi Avi Shafran, director of public affairs for Agudath Israel of America, an Orthodox group, wrote in a letter to the *New York Jewish Week* that the *Jewish Week* had strongly "overstated" the results of the study.[4] Rabbi Shafran (2007) wrote that the results may not be valid since the sample was a self-selecting, non-random sample of women; that is, only women who chose to participate in the survey provided results. According to Shafran, this finding "would seem to indicate, if anything at all, that the problem is considerably less common in the Orthodox community." While it is true that a self-selecting sample is not comparable to a sample selected at random, this certainly does not suggest that the prevalence rates of abuse must therefore be inflated by this study. It is just as likely that the abuse rates reported by the women were *lower* than what would have been found in a more representative sample. One reason for this underestimate might be that married religious women are likely to be a group where the rates of abuse might be lower. This is because a history of sexual abuse is known to affect the capacity for intimacy or trust in close relationships (DiLillo, 2001; Finkelhor et al., 1989), thus leading to less likelihood of marriage as well as to a tendency to not participate in religion (Finkelhor et al., 1989).

In the end, a number of factors tend to suggest that the prevalence rates reported by Yehuda et al. may, in fact, be representative of the community at large. First, the most significant threat to the validity of prevalence studies in general is underreporting (Widom & Morris, 1997); that is, many subjects refuse to disclose abuse, even in anonymous surveys. Second, the percentage of married observant Jewish women who reported abuse is consistent with data from several national surveys, in which 25 to 27 percent of women, regardless of marital status or religious affiliation, reported sexual abuse (Finkelhor et al., 1989; Vogeltanz et al., 1999). Finally, early prevalence studies of child sexual abuse often involved self-selecting samples like this one — and later randomized studies *confirmed* rather than refuted the early data.

We will have to wait to see how further prevalence studies on the Jewish community compare with these initial findings. It is not surprising that the Jewish community has fallen prey to the cultural pressures of denial and has only reluctantly begun to discuss the reality of child sexual abuse in its midst. It is also not surprising to see resistance within the community to accepting these preliminary results.

The abuser thrives in an environment where he is confident
that his victims will not report what they have experienced
or where their reports of abuse will not be taken seriously.
— Letter to the community by Rabbinical Council
   of Greater Baltimore (Jacobs, May 21, 2007)

There are some unique aspects of Jewish belief, family life, and culture that may unwittingly serve further to promote denial and avoidance of the topic of sexual abuse. The historic effects of being a persecuted outsider living within a closely knit family unit, combined with interpretations of religious precepts, have aided the forces of denial in the Jewish community.

Both Jews and non-Jews fall prey to stereotypes about Jewish family life that serve as disincentives to believe abuse reports. As survivor Marcia Cohn Spiegel reports, "I grew up in a world where it was widely accepted that Jews don't drink, use illegal drugs, or commit acts of sexual or domestic violence. I assumed that I must have been the only Jewish woman in the world who had memories of beatings or lived with an alcoholic" (Spiegel, 2003, p. 147). While this idealistic view of Jewish family life may be a stereotype, Rachel Lev (2003) suggests that one real characteristic of many Jewish families is that they are "enmeshed," with poor differentiation of the roles and responsibilities of the family members. A parent, for example, may look toward a child as the protector, consoler, or even regulator of the parent's behavior — inverting the natural order of the relationship. In this context, a child may not know how to differentiate his/her own experiences from those of others, and may, as a result of such poorly defined boundaries, accept as reality the false "realities" presented by the abuser's distorted worldview (Lev, 2003). Sue William Silverman (2003) adds that the sacredness of the family unit in Jewish communities may make it impossible for even the adults to get help outside the family. She describes her mother's attempts to get help from her own parents when she (Silverman's mother) had problems with her husband; her mother was told she had to work it out within her own family. Many of the first author's own Jewish clients looked to the support of family and friends when they discovered that their husband was abusing their children. They reported that, instead of giving support, their parents and friends encouraged them to look the other way, to "stay with him," or to work it out.

Conservative Rabbi Elliot N. Dorff analyzed Jewish precepts that he believes have been often misinterpreted, creating barriers to disclosure and discussion of sexual abuse in the Jewish community (Dorff, 1995, 2003). For instance, *lashon hara*, a prohibition against speaking ill of others, is often referred to as the reason why abusers cannot be publicly named. Rabbi Dorff counters this argument by pointing out that the law of *pikuah nefesh*, saving a life, has precedence over *lashon hara*. It can be argued that naming one's abuser is an act of self-defense that could prevent future assaults on both current and future victims. The Rabbinical Council of Greater Baltimore, an organization of the community's Orthodox rabbis, agreed with this point of view when they stated, "Publicizing his status as an abuser — while causing enormous damage to his own family — may be the only way to truly protect the community from him" (in Jacobs, May 21, 2007). Another precept that may serve to inhibit disclosure is the commandment to honor one's parents. Dorff points out that that there are exemptions within the legal Talmudic tradition that allow rejection of parents when they have committed abusive acts against the child.

There are additional barriers within the Orthodox Jewish community that may interfere with reporting abuse. Because of a history of persecution from the outside world, Jews often seek to avoid bringing attention, shame, or undue criticism to their community. This defensive attitude about public shame extends to the private domain of family life, as well. Lisa Ferentz explains that the stigma attached to having been abused may leave an Orthodox girl with few Jewish prospects for marriage, as her worth may be diminished in the eyes of matchmakers who arrange Jewish marriages.

THE JEWISH PERPETRATOR

Within the Jewish community or outside of it, there is no single profile for sex offenders. People who sexually abuse children are diverse in terms of age, occupation, income level, religious background, marital status, and ethnic group. While sex offenders may have preferences regarding which children they are attracted to, many offend opportunistically. Thus child molesters may offend against their own children as well as children outside the family, and may target children of both genders (Becker, 1994). This type of offender appears to exist in the Jewish community as well. One rabbi, according to victims' reports, offended against boys and girls, both within the family and outside of his family (Jacobs, May 4, 2007). In turn, this rabbi's own son was later accused of similar offenses by his own students (Jacobs, July 13, 2007). It is important to keep in mind that while experiencing childhood sexual abuse can be an important risk factor for later perpetration against children (Glasser et al., 2001), the relationship is complex and most abuse survivors do not become perpetrators (Glasser et al., 2001; Lisak, Hopper, & Song, 1996). Experts agree that the availability of psychological help for abused children when they are young may provide those victims the insight to avoid repeating the cycle of abuse in the next generation.

While offenders may differ on choice of victims, the manner by which offenders ensure the victims' silence appears surprisingly similar. According to Anna Salter, a foremost expert in sex offenders, "A double life is prevalent among all types of sex offenders.... The front that offenders typically offer to the outside world is usually a 'good person' — someone who the community believes has a good character and would never do such a thing" (Salter, 2003, p. 34). In fact, Anna Salter has found that the life a child molester leads in public may be exemplary, almost surreal in its righteousness. Many have practiced and perfected their ability to charm, to be likeable, and to radiate a façade of sincerity and truthfulness. As stated by Jewish survivor Murray Levin, "I don't think they see themselves getting apprehended. They are bright people, great communicators and intellectual" (Jacobs, April 13, 2007).

Sex offenders are well aware of our propensity for making assumptions about private behavior from one's public presentation. Charles Whitfield (2001) points out that child molesters play on our doubts that an otherwise-respectable adult would ever sexually assault a child. Because we don't want to believe it, every bit of evidence that is presented to us, no matter how convincing, is filtered out through the fine mesh of our desire to find some other explanation for the child's disclosure. With this kind of internal pressure to disbelieve any and all evidence, our objectivity is impaired. We may then prematurely close our mind to the possibility of abuse, making it difficult to carefully consider and weigh the evidence before us. This causes parents to drop their guard, allowing the sex offender easy and recurring access to their children.

In fact, as recent reports of abuse by priests have shown, child molesters frequently hide behind our incorrect assumptions about what a perpetrator looks like and how we expect them to act. Rather than using force, the relationships between adult offenders and children often begin with a "grooming" process in which an adult skillfully manipulates the trusting child into participating (Salter, 2003). Usually, the process begins with a boundary violation that is small, like a back rub or long hug. According to Phil Jacobs, in Orthodox circles these small boundary violations are not noticeable since close physical contact between men and boys is the norm in a culture in which sexes are largely segregated. Thus a bar mitzvah teacher praising the child for a job well done may move subtly from a kiss on the cheek to a hand placed inappropriately on the child's thigh. Once the child has accommodated to this, the intrusions typically escalate. This confuses the child, who may not understand the perpetrator's motives, particularly when the perpetrator pretends to be the child's friend and mentor. Once the relationship becomes overtly sexual, perpetrators often continue to control their victims through a combination of bribes and threats, often suggesting the child will be blamed or punished if they are found out.

Charles Whitfield (2001) researched the defense tactics of accused and convicted child molesters and found that of all the defenses that a child molester has at his disposal, the most effective is our collective desire not to know. We all so much want the abuse *not* to have happened that when an accused person says they didn't do it, it resonates with our own personal hopes and beliefs about the incident. As a result, even the vilest of sexual offenders find it relatively easy to wrap themselves in a cloak of apparent righteous innocence.

Those who have worked in the Jewish community find these familiar patterns of denial, disbelief, and perpetrator manipulation. Lisa Ferentz reports that the perpetrators she has encountered appear to see themselves as invulnerable and entitled. They also seem able to rationalize what they are doing and thus abdicate their responsibility. She has heard of abusers in the Jewish community who even use misguided applications of Torah passages to justify their behavior. Through a misapplication of Talmudic logic, the perpetrator can convince himself that abuse is not abuse if there has been no penetration. Phil Jacobs has described that he continues to be astounded that the perpetrators he has talked to seem to have little awareness of how their own behavior can have life-changing impact on their victims. One perpetrator told him, "I can tell you I was not fully aware that I was doing something wrong" (Jacobs, July 13, 2007).

It is important to remember that while most perpetrators are men, there are women in the Jewish community who also perpetrate sexual abuse on children. While this is not as frequent, several cases have come to the attention of the first author as well as Jacobs while he was researching his series of reports. Those victimized by females feel particularly marginalized, as there is little acknowledgment of their experience, and the shame of revealing the abuse may be even more intense.

The authors have found from their vast clinical work and legal research that there are no significant differences between the methods or behaviors of Jewish perpetrators — whether pious or not — and those of the rest of the world. However, the insularity of the Orthodox world may make the Orthodox offender less aware of the full legal and psychological ramifications of his or her behavior. Based on his investigation, Jacobs suggests perpetrators must be held accountable by the state criminal justice system in order to break down the walls of insularity and self-protection present in the religious community.

A NEW ERA FOR THE JEWISH COMMUNITY

We want to end this chapter with a message of hope for Jewish survivors and for the Jewish community. In Jewish communities around the world, there are beginning efforts to discuss the problem, to document its prevalence, and to provide support and services. The Baltimore Jewish community provides a model of how to engage the public and private sector and to rally the Jewish community across denominational lines to actively address child sexual abuse. Esther Giller, executive director of the Sidran Institute, began the Shofar Coalition in 2005 to promote awareness of child maltreatment in the Jewish community and to bring together providers, agencies, schools, and community leaders to develop a network of support to assist the healing of Jewish victims of abuse.[5] Giller notes that local Jewish agencies may not be able to address these problems alone, as many survivors feel shame and prefer to get help outside of their own communities. Thus, to be effective, networks need to reach all areas of life in which the victims may interface — synagogues, schools, health providers, and families. In addition, large agencies are often weighed down by bureaucracy, making them slow to act. Institutional hierarchies coupled with the ubiquitous forces of denial may prevent issues of child sexual abuse from being prioritized when programming decisions are being made in these large agencies. For this reason, Ms. Giller advocates building broad coalitions within the community between the private and public sectors.

Working together, the Shofar Coalition and the Sidran Institute have developed several innovative programs for the Baltimore Jewish community. One of their main goals is to train frontline people in the community who are likely to come in contact with abuse survivors. These include counselors, mentors, and teachers, who can then train others in their agencies. Establishing this level of frontline knowledge creates enduring changes in the community. In addition, the Shofar Coalition offers support groups for male and female Jewish survivors and sponsors talks on sexual abuse by expert professionals for both the Orthodox community and the community at large. Spurred by the coalition efforts, the Talmudical Academy of Baltimore has prepared a curriculum on abuse for parents and educators.

Innovative programs are also under development in other Jewish communities across the country. Under the leadership of Debbie Fox, lcsw, with the Aleinu Resource Center, an Orthodox division of Jewish Family Service of Los Angeles, the Jewish community of la is breaking new ground.[6] Ms. Fox has developed a comprehensive program called the Safe School System, which seeks to train all school staff about abuse. All members of the school community must sign a detailed contract explaining what boundaries are safe with children and what to do in the event that they suspect any of these are broken. Schoolteachers also receive training on abuse prevention and identification. The children receive education appropriate to their developmental level on safe touch, using drawings that are familiar to them, with illustrations of children dressed in traditional Orthodox clothing. The preschool program uses puppets and the middle school program uses interactive PowerPoint presentations. An Internet training module is also being developed. An important component of the program is parental education about abuse. Parents are taught about how to talk to their children, how to recognize signs of abuse, and how to approach the school about these issues. This comprehensive and innovative program is now being employed in Phoenix and St. Louis as well. Efforts are also are underway to create new versions of it for schools with varying Jewish ideologies. One can imagine that someone would have intervened sooner to help Adina, had she been exposed to this kind of programming at her local Jewish day school.

Ms. Fox has not been afraid to force the community to confront its demons. In a slide show, she shows parents pictures of incarcerated members of the Orthodox Jewish community, to bring home the point that you cannot tell a perpetrator by the way he looks. She hopes that her program serves to make it almost impossible for abuse to go undetected. Ms. Fox emphasizes that the training is upbeat and enjoyable, and that all come away with a positive and energetic attitude. Because new technologies are being used to solicit children as victims, Ms. Fox has provided safety guidelines for text messages and Internet communications. Other communities can look to the energy and creativity of the Jewish communities in Baltimore and Los Angeles for models of how they can come together to solve the problem of child sexual abuse.

An important next step would be the development of a real survivor organization for Jewish men and women, such as SNAP, noted earlier. SNAP has played a powerful role in forcing the Catholic Church to be accountable to abuse survivors and has lobbied as well as provided support groups for communities. A similar model in the Jewish community would be a major step in confronting these problems. According to SNAP's David Clohessy, "It takes just a couple of brave survivors who understand the value of self-help. Together, they must promote consistent media outreach to the thousands of deeply wounded survivors who struggle in shame, silence and self-blame" (e-mail from David Clohessy to Joy Silberg, dated October 23, 2007). Clohessy adds that the most important ingredient for a successful survival movement is persistence. At some point, he suggests, the "story will break," and the momentum of the survivor movement will continue to prod journalists to investigate and ultimately bring these issues to the light of day.

As Adina stated in her last session when she had finally achieved integration and healing, "My whole brain is working together now." Similarly, it is time for the Jewish community to integrate its emerging knowledge into the full "brain" of Jewish community resources, providing a cultural context for comprehensive resources that promote healing and prevention.

NOTES

1. Authors' note: Names and family circumstances have been changed to protect the confidentiality of Adina and her family.

2. All information from Lisa Ferentz was based on a personal interview with Joy Silberg on October 23, 2007.

3. All information from Phil Jacobs in this chapter was obtained by Joy Silberg in a personal interview on November 6, 2007.

4. The *New York Jewish Week* reported the results of the study in its October 26, 2007, issue, p. 10.

5. All information from Esther Giller was obtained in a personal interview with Joy Silberg on October 23, 2007.

6. Information about Debbie Fox's programs came from a telephone interview with Joy Silberg on November 7, 2007.

REFERENCES

Abraham, K. (1927). The experiencing of sexual traumas as a form of sexual activity. In K. Abraham (Ed.), *Selected papers of Karl Abraham* (pp. 47–62). London: Hogarth Press.

Bancroft, L. R., & Silverman, J. G. (2002). *The batterer as parent: Addressing the impact of domestic violence on family dynamics*. Thousand Oaks, Calif.: Sage.

Becker, J. V. (1994). Offenders: Characteristics and treatment. *Future of Children, 4*(2), 176–197.

Briere, J. (1998). Long-term clinical correlates of childhood sexual victimization. *Annals of the New York Academy of Sciences, 528,* 327–334.

Briere, J., & Elliott, D. M. (2003). Prevalence and psychological sequelae of self–reported childhood physical and sexual abuse in a general population sample of men and women. *Child Abuse and Neglect, 27,* 1205–1222.

Browne, A., & Finklehor, D. (1986). Impact of child sexual abuse: A review of the research. *Psychological Bulletin, 99,* 66–77.

Cloitre, M., Cohen, L. R., & Scarvalone, P. (2002). Understanding revictimization among childhood sexual abuse survivors: An interpersonal schema approach. *Journal of Cognitive Psychotherapy, 16,* 91–112.

Dallam, S. J. (2001). The long-term medical consequences of childhood trauma. In K. Franey, R. Geffner, & R. Falconer (Eds.), *The cost of child maltreatment: Who pays? We all do* (pp. 1–14). San Diego: Family Violence and Sexual Assault Institute (FVSAI).

Dallam, S., Gleaves, D., Cepeda-Benito, A., Silberg, J. L., Kraemer, H., & Spiegel, D. (2001). The effects of child sexual abuse: An examination of Rind, Tromovitch and Bauserman (1998). *The Psychological Bulletin, 127,* 715–733.

Dallam, S. J., & Silberg, J. L. (2006). Myths that place children at risk during custody disputes. *Sexual Assault Report, 9*(3), 33–47.

DiLillo, D. (2001). Interpersonal functioning among women reporting a history of childhood sexual abuse: Empirical findings and methodological issues. *Clinical Psychology Review, 21,* 553–576.

Dittburner, T. L., & Persinger, M. A. (1993). Intensity of amnesia during hypnosis is positively correlated with estimated prevalence of sexual abuse and alien abductions: Implications for the false memory syndrome. *Perceptual and Motor Skills, 77* (Pt. 1), 895–898.

Dorff, E. (1995), "Family Violence," www.rabbinicalassembly.org under the link

"Contemporary Halakhah"; reprinted in Elliot N. Dorff, *Love Your Neighbor and Yourself: A Jewish Approach to Modern Personal Ethics* (Philadelphia: Jewish Publication Society, 2003), chapter 5.

———. (2003). Jewish law and tradition regarding sexual abuse and incest. In R. Lev (Ed.), *Shine the light: Sexual abuse and healing in the Jewish community* (pp. 46–60). Boston: Northeastern University Press.

Faller, K. C. (2003). *Understanding and assessing child sexual maltreatment.* Thousand Oaks, Calif.: Sage.

Faller, K. C., & DeVoe, E. (1995). Allegations of sexual abuse in divorce. *Journal of Child Sexual Abuse, 4*(4), 1–25.

Ferenczi, S. (1933/1949). Sprachverwirrung zwischen den Erwachsenen und den Kind. Translated and reprinted as "Confusion of tongues between adults and the child (the language of tenderness and of passion)" in J. Masson, *The Assault on Truth* (London: Harper Collins, 1992), 291–303.

Finkelhor, D., Hotaling, G., Lewis, I. A., & Smith, C. (1989). Sexual abuse and its relationship to later sexual satisfaction, marital status, religion and attitudes. *Journal of Interpersonal Violence, 4,* 379–399.

Finkelhor, D., & Dzuiba-Leatherman, J. (1994). Children as victims of violence: A national survey. *Pediatrics, 94,* 413–420.

Freud, S. (1896/1962). The aetiology of hysteria (translated by James Strachey). Read before the Society for Psychiatry and Neurology, April 21, 1896. Reprinted in J. Masson, *The Assault on Truth* (London: Harper Collins, 1992), 259–290.

Garnefski, N., & Diekstra, R. F. (1997). Child sexual abuse and emotional and behavioral problems in adolescence: Gender differences. *Journal of American Academy of Child and Adolescent Psychiatry, 36,* 323–329.

Glasser, M., Kolvin, I., Campbell, D., Glasser, A., Leitch, I., & Farrelly, S. (2001). Cycle of child sexual abuse: Links between being a victim and becoming a perpetrator. *British Journal of Psychiatry, 179,* 482–494.

Gorey, K. M., & Leslie, D. R. (1997). The prevalence of child sexual abuse: Integrative review, adjustment for potential response and measurement biases. *Child Abuse and Neglect, 21,* 391–398.

Hanson, R. F., Resnick, H. S., Saunders, B. E., Kilpatrick, D. G., & Best, C. (1999). Factors related to the reporting of childhood rape. *Child Abuse and Neglect, 23,* 559–569.

Hunter, J. A., Goodwin, D. W., & Wilson, R. J. (1992). Attributions of blame in child sexual abuse victims: An analysis of age and gender influences. *Journal of Child Sexual Abuse, 1,* 75–89.

Jacobs, P. (2007, April 13). Rabbi, teacher, molester: Ephraim Shapiro's mark on the Baltimore Jewish community. *Baltimore Jewish Times.* Retrieved November 1, 2007, from http://www.jewishtimes.com/scripts/edition.pl?stay=1& SubSectionID=30&ID=6531.

———. (2007, May 4). Rabbi also molested girls. *Baltimore Jewish Times.* Retrieved November 1, 2007, from http://www.jewishtimes.com/scripts/edition.pl?stay=1&SubSectionID=30&ID=6531.

———. (2007, May 21). Abuse in our community. *Baltimore Jewish Times.* Retrieved November 1, 2007, from http://www.jewishtimes.com/News/6591.stm.

———. (2007, July 13). Alleged molester investigated here. *Baltimore Jewish Times.* Retrieved November 1, 2007, from http://www.jewishtimes.com/scripts/edition.pl?&stay=1&SubSectionID=30&ID=6992.

Jarecki, A. (2003). *Capturing the Friedmans.* [Motion picture]. New York: HBO.

Kendall-Tackett, K. (2003). *Treating the lifetime health effects of childhood victimization.* Kingston, NJ: Civic Research Institute.

Kondora, L. L. (1998, March). A textual analysis of the construction of the False Memory Syndrome: Representations in popular magazines, 1990–1995. *Dissertation Abstracts,* DAI-B 58/09, p. 4721.

Kramer, J. (2001, October 24–30). Custody switch. *Pacific Sun* (San Rafael, Calif.).

Lam, C. (2004, January 9). Convicted molester wants to clear name: Cites evidence seen in film. *Newsday* (Long Island, N.Y.).

Lev, R. (Ed.). (2003). *Shine the light: Sexual abuse and healing in the Jewish community.* Boston: Northeastern University Press.

Lisak, D., Hopper, J., & Song, P. (1996). Factors in the cycle of violence: Gender, rigidity, and emotional constriction. *Journal of Traumatic Stress, 9,* 721–743.

Loftus, E. F. (1996). Memory distortion and false memory creation. *Bulletin of the American Academy of Psychiatry and the Law, 24,* 281–295.

Loftus, E. F., & Pickrell, J. E. (1995). The formation of false memories. *Psychiatric Annals, 25,* 720–725.

Lombardi, K. (2003, January). Custodians of abuse. *Boston Phoenix.*

Lyon, T. D. (2002). Scientific support for expert testimony on child sexual abuse accommodation. In J. R. Conte (Ed.), *Critical issues in child sexual abuse* (pp. 107–138). Newbury Park, Calif.: Sage.

Masson, J. (1992). *The assault on truth.* London: HarperCollins.

Moskovits, I. (Writer, producer, and director). (2007). *Narrow bridge: A film about sexual abuse* [Motion picture]. (Available from IzzyComm Motion Pictures at http://narrowbridgefilm.com).

Neustein, A., & Goetting, A. (1999). Judicial responses to protective parents. *Journal of Child Sexual Abuse, 4,* 103–122.

Neustein, A., & Lesher, M. (2005). *From madness to mutiny: Why mothers are running from family court and what can be done about it.* Boston: Northeastern University Press.

O'Meara, K. P. (1999, April 26). Has Psychiatry Gone Psycho? *Insight Magazine.* Retrieved November 7, 2007, from http://findarticles.com/p/articles/mi_m1571/is_15_15/ai_54451069.

Pipe, M. E., & Goodman, G. S. (1991). Elements of secrecy: Implications for children's testimony. *Behavioral Sciences and the Law, 9*, 33–41.

Putnam, F. W. (2003). Ten-year research update review: Child sexual abuse. *Journal of the American Academy of Child and Adolescent Psychiatry, 42*, 269–278.

Roesler, T. A., & McKenzie, N. (1994). Effects of childhood trauma on psychological functioning in adults sexually abused as children. *The Journal of Nervous and Mental Disease, 182*, 145–150.

Rosen, L. N., & Etlin, M. (1996). *The hostage child: Sex abuse allegations in custody disputes.* Bloomington: Indiana University Press.

Russell, D. E. H. (1986). *The Secret Trauma: Incest in the Lives of Girls and Women.* New York: Basic Books.

Salter, A. (2003). *Predators, pedophiles, rapists, and other sex offenders.* New York: Basic Books.

Sauzier, M. (1989). Disclosure of child sexual abuse: For better or for worse. *Psychiatric Clinics of North America, 12*, 455–469.

Sgroi, S. M. (Ed.). (1982). *Handbook of clinical intervention in child sexual abuse.* Lexington, MA: Free Press.

Shafran, A. (2007, November 7). "Sexual Abuse." Letter to the Editor, *New York Jewish Week.*

Shengold, L. (1999). *Soul murder revisited.* New Haven, Conn.: Yale University Press.

Silberg, J. L. (Ed.). (1998). *The dissociative child: Diagnosis, treatment and management* (2nd ed.). Lutherville, MD: Sidran Press.

Silverman, S. W. (2003). My Jewish journey home. In R. Lev (Ed.), *Shine the light: Sexual abuse and healing in the Jewish community* (pp. 128–134). Boston: Northeastern University Press.

Smith, D. W., Letourneau, E. J., Saunders, B. E., Kilpatrick, D. G., Resnick, H. S., & Best, C. L. (2000). Delay in disclosure of childhood rape: Results from a national survey. *Child Abuse and Neglect, 24*, 273–287.

Spiegel, M. C. (2003). Survival and recovery: Jewish women confront abuse. In R. Lev (Ed.), *Shine the light: Sexual abuse and healing in the Jewish community* (pp. 146–161). Boston: Northeastern University Press.

Stanton, M. (1997, July/August). U-turn on memory lane. *Columbia Journalism Review*, 44–49.

Teicher, M. H. (2002). Scars that won't heal: The neurobiology of child abuse. *Scientific American, 286*, 68–75.

Timnick, L. (1985, August 15). The Times Poll: Twenty-two percent in survey were child abuse victims. *Los Angeles Times*, p. 1.

Vogeltanz, N. D., Wilsnack, S. C., Harris, T. R., Wilsnack, R. W., Wonderlich, S. A., & Kristjanson, A. F. (1999). Prevalence and risk factors for childhood sexual abuse in women: National survey findings. *Child Abuse and Neglect, 23*, 579–592.

Waller, G. (Writer, Producer, and Director). (2001). *Small justice: Little justice in America's family courts* [documentary film]. (Available from Intermedia, Inc., 1818 Westlake Ave. N., Suite 408, Seattle, WA 98109).

Waller, G., & Smith, R. (1994). Sexual abuse and psychological disorders: The role of cognitive processes. *Behavioral and Cognitive Psychotherapy, 22,* 299–314.

Watkins, B., & Bentovim, A. (1992). The sexual abuse of male children and adolescents: A review of current research. *Journal of Child Psychology and Psychiatry, 33,* 197–248.

Weber, E. (1977, April). Incest: Sexual abuse begins at home, *Ms.,* 64–67.

Weiner, I. B. (1962). Father-daughter incest: A clinical report. *Psychiatric Quarterly, 36,* 607–632.

Whitfield, C. (2001). The "false memory" defense: Using disinformation and junk science in and out of court. In C. Whitfield, J. L. Silberg, & P. J. Fink (Eds.), *Misinformation concerning child sexual abuse and adult survivors* (pp. 53–78). Binghamton, N.Y.: Haworth Press.

Whitfield, C., Silberg, J. L., & Fink, P. J. (Eds.). (2001). *Misinformation on child sexual abuse and adult survivors.* Binghamton, N.Y.: Haworth Press.

Widom, C. S., & Morris, S. (1997). Accuracy of adult recollections of childhood victimization: Part 2. Childhood sexual abuse. *Psychological Assessment, 9,* 34–46.

Winston, H. (2005). *Unchosen: The hidden lives of Hasidic rebels.* Boston: Beacon Press.

Yehuda, R., Friedman, M., Rosenbaum, T. Y., Labinsky, E., & Schmeidler, J. (2007). History of past sexual abuse in married observant Jewish women. *American Journal of Psychiatry, 164,* 1700–1706.

RABBI MARK DRATCH

A Community of Co-enablers

Why Are Jews Ignoring Traditional Jewish Law
by Protecting the Abuser?

Despite many advances in the last decade, the Jewish community still suffers from denial of the incidence of child abuse and domestic violence among us, as well as of professional "improprieties." In fact, many systems, policies, and attitudes prevent innocents from receiving the protection they deserve and prevent perpetrators from being held accountable. We still lack institutional policies that promote safe practices, protocols for professional boundaries and accountability, universal background checks of employees and volunteers, prevention education, and the like. Some communal values silence or revictimize those who think of coming forward to complain or seek help, prevent the use of appropriate and meaningful safety practices, and interfere with law enforcement. In addition, certain values protect perpetrators and institutions at the expense of innocent victims.

When the members of our community fail to live up to our responsibilities to prevent abuse and to help survivors of abuse heal and find justice, our community is more than just irresponsible: we are guilty of enabling and perpetuating abuse. Consider: Rambam (Maimonides) codified the various interpersonal laws found in Leviticus 19 in the beginning of his code of law and ethics (known as Mishneh Torah) in chapters 6 and 7 of *Hilkhot De'ot*, which deal with human character and ethical behavior. However, the laws detailing the obligation to help others in distress do not appear there. Instead, they are found in the first chapter of *Hilkhot Rotzei'ah u-Shemirat ha-Nefesh* (the Laws of Murder and Self-Protection). By this placement, Rambam teaches an important lesson: whoever does not come to the aid of someone under assault is not just lacking in character, but shares in the guilt of perpetrating that assault.[1]

Truth to tell, during the last decade or two we have witnessed increasing acknowledgment, awareness, and activity across the spectrum of the Jewish community, concerning all areas of abuse. Today there are many agencies and programs to which people can turn for help and support. Educational initiatives and policy declarations have been forthcoming from rabbinical organizations and many community organizations. The Internet has been a rich resource of information and advocacy, and blogs have given voice to many who were previously silent or alone.

INDIVIDUAL RESPONSIBILITIES

But there is more to do. The Torah's attitude regarding our responsibility to help others in need differs sharply from the law in most of the United States[2] where, unless there is a special relationship — like that of parent-child, employer-employee, school-pupil, or physician-patient — there is no duty to rescue.[3] This lack of obligation is based on the common law stress on the protection of individual rights:[4] "Every individual right, in the sphere of the law, is inherently negative in character. One does not have the right to speak, work, eat, or even live; one has the right not to have these freedoms infringed by others. Similarly, one does not have a duty to protect the rights of others to speak, work, eat or live; one only has the duty not to infringe upon these freedoms."[5]

Opposed to this common law approach, Jewish law imposes a considerable number of affirmative obligations. These include such commandments as loving one's neighbor, returning found property, helping to load and unload the cargo from an animal in distress, giving charity, lending money to those in need, visiting the sick, comforting mourners, ensuring that wedding expenses are met, celebrating with a bride and groom, escorting the dead to burial, hospitality, and more.

The Obligations to Help

The Torah expresses the obligation to help those under assault or subject to abuse through both positive and negative precepts: "You shall not stand by the blood of your neighbor" (Lev. 19:16) and "And you shall restore him to himself" (Deut. 22:2).[6] The Talmud teaches that while the latter verse instructs that one must intervene personally, the former expands that responsibility; a person may not just stand idly while someone is being hurt. He is required to call others to do whatever is necessary to help those in need.[7] This obligation requires us to help others whether their lives are in mortal danger or whether they are "merely" under physical, sexual, or emotional assault.[8] The obligation obtains even if one is in doubt as to whether or not there is a clear and present danger, and even when one is not fully aware of the circumstances of the attack.[9]

These same verses are cited in the Talmud as sources for the law pertaining to a *rodef*, someone who is in pursuit of another with the intention of committing murder or sexual assault. Those who either witness this pursuit or are aware of it are obligated to intervene in order to save the life or well-being of the pursued. Due to the severity of these assaults, Jewish law authorizes this third party to do anything that is necessary in order to save the pursued, even to the point of killing the pursuer if necessary.[10] This response is modified in civilized countries that outlaw such vigilantism and that have a fair and effective system of justice. In such places, reporting perpetrators to the police, an issue that will be discussed later in this chapter, is required.

One may not ignore the cries of someone who needs help. The principle enunciated in the lost-object mandate applies here as well:[11] one who sees a lost object is warned, "You may not ignore it" (Deut. 22:3).[12] One may not close his eyes or ears, pretending as if he is unaware of the loss, thus exempting himself from getting involved.[13] Furthermore, the very language of the verse concerning the neighbor's blood warns us not "to stand" on another's blood. Standing is a passive act. And we are not permitted to remain passive. In fact, in this sense, there is no such thing in Jewish law as an "innocent bystander."[14] Unless intervention will be hazardous to the witness — in which case the witness must call others to help — he is obligated to get involved. If he doesn't, he is not innocent.

That Your Brother May Live With You

Ramban (Nachmanides) comments that the verse, "And if your brother has become poor, and his means fail with you; then you shall relieve him; though he may be a stranger, or a sojourner; that he may live with you" (Lev. 25:35), is another source for the obligation not only to give charity if another is in need, but to save his life and come to his assistance when necessary.[15]

Cruelty to Animals

Two verses in this context seem to be irrelevant, but serve as further sources that obligate Jews to come to the aid of others in need: "If you see the donkey of one who hates you lying under its burden, you shall refrain from leaving it with him, you shall help him to lift it up" (Ex. 23:5); and, "You shall not watch your brother's donkey or his ox fall down by the way, and hide yourself from them; you shall surely help him to lift them up again" (Deut. 22:4). These verses require passersby to help load and unload goods from animals that have fallen under the weight of their burdens. They are the sources for the more general concern of *tza'ar ba'alei hayyim* (the interdiction against cruelty to animals).[16]

Many authorities maintain that these verses are not limited to concerns for the well-being of animals, but include the welfare of humans as well.[17] Rabbeinu Yonah ben Abraham of Gerondi, a thirteenth-century Spanish-Jewish authority, argues that human beings who are created in the divine image certainly deserve at least the same level of protection as animals.[18]

In this connection, it is a great historical irony that the first case of child abuse in the United States was brought to court under legislation banning cruelty to animals — there were no similar laws protecting children at that time. In 1874, a case was filed in a New York State court on behalf of Mary Ellen Wilson, a nine-year-old girl who had been severely beaten and neglected by her foster parents. With the police lacking any legal means to intervene, a neighbor, Etta Wheeler, approached Henry Bergh, the founder of the American Society for the Prevention of Cruelty to Animals, seeking his help. According to some accounts, Bergh filed a petition on behalf of Mary Ellen, arguing that being human, Mary Ellen was part of the animal kingdom and entitled to "at least the same justice as the common cur." Due to the public outrage over Mary Ellen's case, the New York State legislature passed laws chartering societies for the protection of children. In 1875, the New York Society for the Prevention of Cruelty to Children, the first child-protection agency in the world, was created. It investigated three hundred cases of child abuse in its first year.[19]

What does the Torah's prohibition of "cruelty to animals" add to other biblical commandments concerned with human welfare? It has been suggested that the concern about the general well-being of animals and humans expands our involvement in relieving the pain — physical and emotional — of both.[20] In addition, the other bans on assault and battery focus on the act or threat of violence and are concerned with the perpetrator; the "cruelty to animals" injunction creates an obligation to get involved to prevent or relieve the suffering of the victim. The Torah here expresses its concern for victims[21] — no one should ever be subjected to an attack by another no matter how "trivial" that attack may seem.[22]

Preventing and Removing Danger

The Torah, in commanding "Take utmost care and guard yourself scrupulously" (Deut. 4:9), requires Jews to avoid dangerous situations. Expanding on the commandment that we enclose the roofs of our houses with fences (Deut. 22:8), the Talmud requires us also to remove various hazards from our homes and to protect against potentially hazardous conditions.[23] Some prominent authorities have applied this principle not only to life-threatening situations but to non–life-threatening ones as well.[24] Contemporary Orthodox authorities cite these sources in order to support an employer's responsibility for occupational safety at work[25] and in order to restrict reckless driving.[26] Clearly, the physical, emotional, and spiritual dangers that result from perpetrators of abuse and violence are at least as dangerous as those with which these sources are concerned, and obligate each of us to protect potential victims from them.

These obligations speak to individual responsibility. The practical outcome is that, in connection with allegations of child abuse, traditional Jewish law obligates individuals in the following ways:

\ To learn about the relevant issues; to seek out the resources available for helping those in need.

\ Not to dismiss or minimize allegations.

\ To reach out to someone you think is being abused to offer support, trying to ensure that he or she is not being isolated from family and friends.

\ Not to give up or become frustrated with the victim or with the situation.

\ For parents and school officials, to make sure that children know about abuse and with whom it is safe to speak and get help.

\ To call the police if you have reasonable suspicions of abuse.

\ To support organizations that advocate for abuse and assault survivors.

\ To advocate for policies and accountability at your schools, synagogues, camps, Jewish community centers, etc.

So far I have focused on the obligations of individuals to help others. It is also clear under traditional Jewish law that the community qua community has obligations to protect the welfare of its members. The biblical commandments to establish courts, enforce laws, and pursue justice define these obligations. "Justice, justice you shall pursue" (Deut. 16:20) is complemented by the commandment, "[J]udges and officers shall you appoint in all your gates, which the Lord your God gives you, throughout your tribes; and they shall judge the people with just judgment" (16:18). Even in the Diaspora, the Jewish community is obligated to establish these institutions in order to protect the welfare of its members.[27]

The *beth din* (rabbinic tribunal) is the traditional mechanism through which communities organized themselves and promulgated Jewish law. In early Jewish history, the beth din, as the central community authority, had the responsibility to ensure public welfare.[28] In addition to these rabbinic tribunals, community councils composed of lay people were also responsible for advancing and protecting the interests of the community. In Talmudic times there were seven-member councils (*sheva tovei ha-'ir*) that administered the public affairs of Jewish communities,[29] set and inspected weights and measures, established reasonable prices for merchandise, and enacted regulations as required.[30]

While the beth din continues to be an important institution in traditional Jewish communities, contemporary experience has shown that while some rabbinic and communal organizations have responded effectively to incidents of abuse, others have not. Denial and protectionism, as well as a lack of real authority and a corresponding inability to enforce its decisions, have compromised the beth din system and, as a result, endangered abuse victims.[31]

PROBLEMS IN UNDERSTANDING
OF TRADITIONAL JEWISH LAW

Notwithstanding the obligations imposed by traditional Jewish law, there are many who — in spite of their adherence to tradition — remain uninvolved, not because of indifference, but because of arguments that stem from their understanding of the law. The interdiction of *lashon ha-ra* (derogatory speech), they say, prohibits talking about such matters, despite clear rulings that obligate speaking out against abuse. The law against *mesirah* (informing or traducing), they say, prohibits making reports to the police, despite clear rulings that obligate them to do so. The sin of *hillul Hashem* (desecration of God's name), they say, prohibits them from making these matters public since they cast aspersions on the Jewish community, despite the fact that the greater shame is caused by systemic cover-up. Finally, the goal of protecting the integrity and welfare of "the community" or of a particular institution has too often led them to sacrifice the integrity and welfare of individuals.

These principles, and others, are indeed part of traditional Jewish law and are carefully observed by pious Jews. But, all too often, misplaced priorities and misconceived interpretations of Jewish law have trumped equally valid principles concerned with the safety and security of bodies and souls.

Lashon Ha-ra

The prohibition of *lashon ha-ra* (which includes slander, gossip, and tale-bearing) is often used as a tool to silence abuse victims and their advocates from speaking out against abusers. "You are not allowed to say derogatory things," they are told. "There's no proof!" "There are no witnesses." "You can't make this public." And so women, girls, boys, and men are silenced and are often unable to get the help that they need or appeal for the support that they deserve. By invoking *lashon ha-ra* improperly, the community to which they turn not only revictimizes them, but enables their abusers to continue abusing them and, potentially, others as well.

The truth is that under Jewish law there are times when a person is obligated to speak out, even though the information is disparaging. While *motzi shem ra* — spouting lies and spreading disinformation — is always prohibited, the law is different when a person's intent in sharing truthful but negative information is for a constructive and beneficial purpose. In such cases, the prohibition against *lashon ha-ra* does not apply.[32] Moreover, if the speech in question serves as a warning against the possibility of future harm, such communication is not only permissible, but, under certain conditions, obligatory.

This distinction — between derogatory speech that is solely detrimental and therefore prohibited, and derogatory speech that serves a helpful purpose and is required — derives from the biblical text from which the prohibition is deduced. The verse contains a significant juxtaposition of clauses: "You shall not go up and down as a slanderer among your people" and "nor you shall stand [idly] by the blood of your neighbor" (Lev. 19:16). As traditionally interpreted, this verse prohibits defamation (clause 1); however, that prohibition is overridden by the obligation to save another or to testify on his behalf (clause 2).[33] Thus, in rabbinic tradition the verse is read, "You shall not go up and down as a slanderer among your people; but, nevertheless, you shall not stand by the blood of your neighbor (and you must speak out in order to prevent harm to him)."

In his epic work on the laws of derogatory speech, R. Yisrael Meir Kagan, known by the name of his famous book *Hafetz Hayyim*, not only permits a victim to speak out, but at times *requires* a victim to speak, specifically if her aim in speaking out is not to exact revenge but to achieve a positive objective (*to'elet*). Examples of such positive objectives include:

\ protecting others from harm;[34]
\ preventing others from learning inappropriate behavior;[35]
\ shaming the subject into repenting;[36]
\ clearing one's own reputation;[37]
\ asking for advice;[38] and
\ speaking for one's own psychological benefit. This is based on the verse, "Anxiety in the heart of a man weighs him down; but a good word makes him glad" (Prov. 12:25); i.e., sharing burdens with others is therapeutic.[39]

Rabbi Kagan lists seven criteria that must be fulfilled when *lashon ha-ra* is spoken for a *to'elet* (constructive purpose). The following are those conditions, together with explanations as to how they relate to abuse victims:[40]

1. One must have firsthand knowledge of the problem and is not merely repeating hearsay, or else has verified the information. Certainly a victim has firsthand knowledge of the abuse she has suffered.

2. Careful consideration and judgment should be used to determine whether or not the act is actually a prohibited one. Every act of abuse is prohibited.[41]

3. One should first rebuke the transgressor in a private, calm, and appropriate manner in order to motivate him to change his ways. Only if one is unsuccessful in achieving her ends in a private manner may she then publicize the misdeed. However, private confrontation may be difficult for a victim who cannot bring herself emotionally or psychologically to confront her abuser. It may also be physically dangerous for her to do so.[42]

4. One should not exaggerate.
5. One's intention should be for a *to'elet* and not for any personal gain or benefit. In addition, one should not be motivated by hatred for the subject of the report.
6. One should try to achieve the constructive result without speaking *lashon ha-ra*, if possible.
7. One should not cause more harm to the subject than he would otherwise deserve by law.

Similarly, those who repeat the reports of abuse are bound by the same criteria.[43] In addition, when repeating allegations, one should not give the impression that he has personal knowledge of the situation, but should introduce his comments with, "I heard it said about So-and-so. . . ."[44]

Lashon ha-ra can be a tool of abuse, both when derogatory speech defames innocent people, destroying their reputations, and when warnings to refrain from derogatory speech are used to silence victims of abuse who cry out for help. As careful as we must be not to speak, listen to, or repeat disparaging information when it is forbidden, we must not allow the accusation of speaking *lashon ha-ra* to silence the cry of innocent victims. Victims of abuse need to speak out, for all kinds of personal reasons, in order to help themselves. Their supporters need to speak out in order to help them. And the community needs to speak out in order to hold the perpetrators responsible and in order to protect other innocents from potential harm.

Mesirah

Although not flawless, the civil authorities, through the police and courts, can go a long way toward protecting victims. Orders of protection, arrest, imprisonment, and removal of children from abusive situations are among the measures to which civil authorities may resort. The availability of such measures obligates us to report child abuse to the civil authorities and to allow victims to seek help in protecting themselves from their abusers. The judicial process can hold perpetrators responsible and accountable for their actions. Despite historic debates and arguments, the consensus of contemporary Jewish religious authorities is that such reporting is religiously mandatory.

This conclusion is not as obvious as it may appear. Despite the legitimacy granted by Jewish law to non-Jewish legal systems, there are significant problems for traditional Jews regarding the use of secular courts for adjudication.

"These are the laws which you shall place before them" (Exodus 21:1), says the Torah in its introduction to its chapters on civil law. The rabbis interpret this verse as requiring that all legal matters between Jews be submitted "before them," i.e., before rabbinic tribunals, for judgment — not to non-Jewish judges, whether religious or secular.[45] This prohibition applies even if non-Jewish laws are similar to Jewish law and even if the non-Jewish courts are honest and just.[46] If one violates this injunction, "he denies God and His Torah,"[47] "profanes the Divine Name and ascribes honor to idols,"[48] "is wicked and is as though he has reviled, blasphemed, and rebelled against the laws of Moses,"[49] and "acts as if the Torah of Moses were not true."[50] Thus, traditional Jews are enjoined not only to give place to the Jewish legal system over others, but to submit only to rabbinic courts and their judges. Under Talmudic law, all matters between Jews must be redressed exclusively in a Jewish court[51] and only according to Jewish law.[52]

Naturally, every government has the right to enforce its own laws within its own borders and to punish those who violate them.[53] However, according to Jewish law, *mesirah*, "turning over" a fellow Jew to non-Jewish authorities, is one of the most severe offenses that a Jew can commit. So grievous is this transgression that a blessing was added to the thrice-recited daily prayers to ask of God, "May there be no hope for the informers."[54] This prohibition of *mesirah* applies whether the fellow Jew is innocent or guilty, whether the informant is "turning over" the other's person or their property, and even if his fellow Jew is harassing him or harming him in any way. "Anyone who turns over a Jew, whether his person or his property, has no share in the World-To-Come."[55]

Significantly, the prohibition of *mesirah* was motivated not only by a concern for the priority of Jewish law but by anxiety over Jewish self-preservation. The vulnerability of the Jewish community, a relatively defenseless minority subject to the whims and prejudices of a discriminatory majority, was real and dangerous through most of Jewish history.

Notwithstanding the strong language quoted above, there are circumstances in which one may report a fellow Jew to the civil authorities. As early as the Early Middle Ages,[56] many rabbinic courts lacked the authority to enforce their rulings, creating the potential for lawlessness in the Jewish community. Under these circumstances, Jewish courts often granted permission to Jewish litigants to turn to the general courts for adjudication and for enforcement of their legal rights.[57] And if a person refused to attend a Jewish court or to submit himself to its authority, rabbinic tribunals granted permission to the plaintiff to tender his complaint to the general courts.[58] In such cases, there is no violation of traditional Jewish law. The prohibition obtains only when one could otherwise successfully adjudicate his concerns in a Jewish court.

Maimonides notes that the prohibition of *mesirah* restrains a *private individual* who is being harassed from making a report to the civil authorities. However, when there is a public menace, informing is permissible.[59] While this might seem to restrict an abused wife from calling the authorities on her husband, or a concerned party from reporting an abusive parent, this is not the case. First, the rate of recidivism in child abuse cases is high and therefore a child molester can be considered a "public menace."[60] Second, the legal commentary known as the *Siftei Kohen*, or *Shakh*, maintains that one is permitted to report any repeat or chronic abuser to non-Jewish authorities in order to prevent him from abusing again.[61] Third, Maimonides's proscription may be limited to situations in which the victim faces no real personal harm, and therefore would not apply in cases of actual physical or sexual abuse.[62]

In addition, there are situations in which a rabbinic court is ineffective, incapable of adjudicating, and powerless to protect victims. This may occur for any number of reasons: perhaps one of the parties refuses to appear before it; perhaps a party will not accept its decision; perhaps the beth din will be unable to protect one of the litigants from physical or financial harm. The famous medieval authority known as Rabbeinu Gershom understood that even if a defendant agrees to come to the rabbinic court, he may be doing so only because he thinks he can delay or complicate the proceedings, or because he feels that he will be able to avoid certain punishment or fines if he avoids the civil courts. Rabbeinu Gershom therefore enacted that in such cases the beth din should give the other party permission to go to the general court.[63] Rabbi David ben Solomon ibn Zimra (known as "Radbaz") confirms that "this is the practice of all rabbinic courts in every generation in order not to give the upper hand to aggressors and intimidators who do not respect the judgment [of the beth din]."[64]

In a ruling of great significance for victims of abuse, Rabbi Moshe Isserles wrote in the sixteenth century: "A person who attacks others should be punished. If the Jewish authorities do not have the power to punish him, he must be punished by the civil authorities."[65] According to Rabbi Isserles, the victim has the right to go to the civil authorities not just to prevent an attack, but to seek punishment and justice for an attack that has already taken place.[66]

One of the leading contemporary authorities in Jewish law, Rabbi Yosef

Shalom Elyashiv, has ruled that one may report a child abuser to the civil authorities in the United States if he is certain about the abuse (a false report, he adds, can destroy a person's reputation or life).[67] And Rabbi Shmuel HaLevi Wosner, author of *Teshuvot Shevet ha-Levi*, rules that a tax agent must report tax fraud committed by a fellow Jew to the government for prosecution. Rabbi Wosner argued: this is the law of the land, and the report will not cause the imposition of a dangerous sentence on the criminal.[68]

Furthermore, a child abuser can be considered a "pursuer," one intent upon inflicting physical harm; in such a case one is permitted to do anything to stop the attack.[69]

In fact, some traditional authorities maintain that the prohibition against *mesirah* and related laws do not apply to these situations at all. R. Yitzchak Weiss avers that the state has an interest in the safety and welfare of its citizens, and that one may report those who are endangering that safety.[70] Rabbi Herschel Schachter, a prominent contemporary authority on Jewish law (and *rosh kollel* [head of rabbinic studies] at Yeshiva University), has stated that the prohibition of *mesirah* applies only when testimony assists civil authorities in illegally obtaining the money of, or excessively punishing, another Jew. It does not obtain when it aids a non-Jewish government in fulfilling such rightful duties as collecting appropriate taxes or punishing criminals. In Rabbi Schachter's view, when the information concerns criminal activities — as long as the Jewish criminal has also violated Jewish law, and even if the punishment will be more severe than the sentence the Torah prescribes[71] — the ban of *mesirah* does not apply.[72]

The nineteenth-century text *Arukh ha-Shulhan* maintains that *mesirah* was prohibited because of the nature of the autocratic governments under which Jews lived throughout much of history. Informing on fellow Jews to such governments often led to dangerous persecution of the entire Jewish community. The author argues that this injunction does not apply to those societies in which the government is generally fair and nondiscriminatory.[73]

Hillul Hashem

Victims of abuse are often told by others — and, at times, even tell themselves — to keep their secrets. They are told that making their abuse public would be a *shonda* (a shame and embarrassment) for the Jewish community, for their families, and for themselves. Even worse, they are told that going public constitutes a *hillul Hashem*, or desecration of God's name. Traditional

Jewish law deems an act committed by a religious Jew that arouses public disgust (particularly on the part of non-Jewish observers) a "desecration," in effect, of God Himself, since in the eyes of the Talmud Jews are identified with God through the responsibility of observing His law. This fear of the negative judgment passed upon Jewish husbands and parents, as well as upon the Jewish community, if child abuse charges are publicized is used as a tool to enforce the victims' silence. Furthermore, there are many who are afraid to speak because of the damage it may do to their reputations, the acceptance of their families in their communities, and even the ability of their children or siblings to find desirable marriage partners.

It must be clearly stated that this is *not* the position of Jewish law. These victims are innocent and should not have to pay an extra price for the cruel and abusive things that were done to them. If anything, they are to be admired and honored for their courage in overcoming adversity.

Of course, there were reasons that Jews, a vulnerable, exposed minority, developed such self-protective attitudes. Historically, invoking *hillul Hashem* was a way of protecting a Jewish minority from retribution by an anti-Semitic majority in response to the wayward activity of one of its members. Jews were vulnerable and the majority population was often hostile. Acts of *hillul Hashem* made the Jewish community even more vulnerable.[74]

However, this concern about protecting the reputation of the Jewish community by repressing public discussion of scandalous behaviors and actions may in fact itself constitute *hillul Hashem*.

First, it is the unethical behavior in and of itself—not merely discussing it—that constitutes a desecration of God's name.[75] The abuser, not the abused, has committed *hillul Hashem*. To silence victims who have a right to speak, to oppose those who seek justice and the protection of innocent victims, is also the kind of conduct that desecrates God's name.

Second, when efforts to deny or suppress the truth about a crime are exposed, the scandal is much greater than the exposure of the crime alone. And Jewish tradition insists that scandalous behavior will always come to light despite efforts to keep it hidden:

R. Johanan b. Berokah said: Whoever profanes the Name of Heaven in secret, the penalty will be exacted from him publicly. [In this respect, it is all] one [whether one has acted] in error or with intent, in [a case where the result is] the profanation of the Name.[76]

Third, there is ample precedent not only for allowing exposure of such matters, but also for actually requiring it. For example, the Talmud rules that a garment made from a biblically prohibited blend of wool and linen fibers is to be forcibly and publicly removed from the wearer,[77] based on the example of the biblical Judah, who, despite the shame he brought on himself, publicly admitted his sin, thereby sanctifying God's Name.[78]

Finally, the essence of *hillul Hashem* is that it creates a godless vacuum in the world and in people's lives.[79] This perfectly describes the effects of child sexual abuse — particularly when the abuse is concealed and denied. When that happens, victims of abuse are doubly exploited, first by their attackers and then by the reaction of the family and community they thought would help them. In many cases, these victims lose faith in themselves, in their religious community, and in God. Such victims are disillusioned by the institutions and leaders they thought they could trust. Too many of them abandon religious observance and their connections to the Jewish community are weakened. This is exactly the sort of "desecration" the laws of *hillul Hashem* are meant to prevent.

In today's democratic countries, Jews are more secure than ever before in our history. Our rights are protected by law. In such countries, there is, generally, respect for religious and ethnic diversity. Enlightened people recognize that the failings and faults of individual Jews do not necessarily represent the community at large. In our day, if the news of a case of child sexual abuse is a *shonda*, a greater *shonda* occurs when abuse is systematically covered up by Jewish leaders and communities.

COMMUNAL RESPONSIBILITY

Already in Talmudic times the rabbis warned us about pious fools who miss the forest for the trees due to their claims of religiosity and devoutness. These fools, we are told, are represented by those who would refuse to save a woman in distress for fear that they may have to look at her or touch her,[80] or would allow a baby to drown in the river because they needed time to remove their tefillin before jumping into the water.[81] It is the responsibility of a religious Jewish community, and its leaders, to embrace healthier principles.

Here are some communal responsibilities for dealing with child sexual abuse:

\ Schools, synagogues, camps, and youth groups must regulate the activities of those who work for them, to help prevent violation of professional boundaries and to avoid circumstances in which students and members might be vulnerable.

\ Each Jewish community must have effective protocols for handling complaints about rabbis,[82] teachers, counselors, and youth leaders.

\ Jewish institutions must do all they can to protect their members from those who are known to pose dangers to children — this includes background checks, registries, and effective hiring and reporting practices.

\ Jewish institutions must train their employees to recognize signs of abuse and to respond appropriately — this includes training in the requirements of mandated reporting of child abuse.

\ Rabbis must be trained in the unique nuances of counseling abuse victims and perpetrators. Judges on rabbinic courts must be trained in these areas.

\ Systemic change that makes it safe and acceptable to report abuse is necessary.

\ Age-appropriate education for children about the dynamics of abuse is essential.

\ Abuse must be made a subject of public conversation, lectures, and programs.

\ Jewish communities must develop the resources to help victims: counseling, shelters, and other means of support.

There are no innocent bystanders — not if being a "bystander" means "standing by" silently when a crime is being committed against a child. Traditional Jewish law makes it the duty of each one of us to recognize the problem of child sexual abuse for what it is, to acknowledge it, and to correct it.

NOTES

1. See also *Issur ve-Heter ha-Arukh, kelal* 59, no. 38.

2. States that have Good Samaritan Laws, which impose a general duty to help a crime victim or injured person, or to report a witnessed crime, include Minnesota (Minn. Stat. Ann. 604A.01 [West 1997]), Rhode Island (R.I. GEN. LAWS § 11-56-1 [1997]), Vermont (Vt. Stat. Ann. tit. 12, § 519 [1997]), and Wisconsin (Wis. Stat. Ann. § 940.34 [West 1997]). Massachusetts (Mass. Gen. Laws Ann. ch. 268, § 40 [West

1998]) and Florida (Fla. Stat. Ann. § 794.027 [West 1998]) require observers to report sexual assaults to authorities. Ohio and Washington require individuals to report felonies in certain situations.

3. Ernest J. Weinrib, *The Case for a Duty to Rescue,* 90 Yale L. J. 247, 247 (1980). All fifty states have passed some form of a mandatory child abuse and neglect reporting law.

4. See *Buch v. Amory Manufacturing Co.,* 44 A. 809 (N.H. 1898):

Actionable negligence is the neglect of a legal duty. The defendants are not liable unless they owed to the plaintiff a legal duty which they neglected to perform. With purely moral obligations the law does not deal.... Suppose A, standing close by a railroad, sees a two-year-old babe on the track and a car approaching. He can easily rescue the child with entire safety to himself, and the instincts of humanity require him to do so. If he does not, he may, perhaps, justly be styled a ruthless savage and a moral monster; but he is not liable in damages for the child's injury, or indictable under the statute for its death.

See Francis H. Bohlen, *The Moral Duty to Aid Others as a Basis of Tort Liability,* 56 U. Pa. L. Rev. 217, 230–31 (1908):

There is no distinction more deeply rooted in the common law and more fundamental than that between misfeasance and non-feasance, between active misconduct working positive injury to others and passive inaction, a failure to take positive steps to benefit others, or to protect them from harm not created by any wrongful act of the defendant. This distinction is founded on that attitude of extreme individualism so typical of anglo-saxon legal thought.

5. Philip W. Romohr, *A Right/Duty Perspective on the Legal and Philosophical Foundations of the No-Duty-to-Rescue Rule,* 55 Duke L. J., 1054 (2006).

6. This verse — which speaks in the first instance of returning lost property — is extended to requiring the restoration of a person's health and life.

7. The Talmud, *Sanhedrin* 73a, states:

How do we know that if a man sees his neighbor drowning, mauled by beasts, or attacked by robbers, he is obligated to save him? [We learn this] from the verse, "You shall not stand by the blood of your neighbor" (Lev. 19:16). But is it derived from this verse? Is it not [learned] elsewhere? How do we know [that one must save his neighbor from] the loss of himself? [We learn this] from the verse, "And you shall restore him to himself" (Deut. 22:2)! [Now, the resolution:] From that verse (Deut. 22:2), I might think that it is only a personal obligation, but that he is not bound to take the trouble of hiring others [if he cannot save him personally]; therefore, this verse (Lev. 19:16) teaches that he must do so.

8. *Hafetz Hayyim, Be'er Mayyim Hayyim, Hil. Rekhilut, kelal* 9, no. 9. While all agree that one is obligated to come to the aid of someone in distress, there is a dispute as to whether the category of *rodef* (pursuer) applies in non–life-threatening attacks. Most authorities agree with Rambam, *Hil. Rotzei'ah u-Shemirat ha-Nefesh* 1:15, who

introduces the law of *rodef* by saying, "If one sees a person pursuing another *in order to slay him* or [pursuing] one forbidden to him sexually in order to have relations with her, and he is able to save [the victim] and he does not save him . . ." [emphasis added]. Rambam limits the obligation to rescue to cases of injury that may result in death. See, however, *Piskei ha-Rosh, Baba Kama*, ch. 3, no. 13: "If a person sees a Jew attack another and he cannot rescue him without hitting the attacker, *even though [the attacker's] blow is not lethal,* he may strike the attacker to prevent him from committing the crime" [emphasis added]. Similarly, see *Yam shel Shlomo, Baba Kama*, ch. 3, no. 9 and Mordekhai to *Baba Kama*, no. 38.

9. *Hiddushei ha-Ran to Sanhedrin* 73a. He derives this from the additional verse, "Do not stand by the blood of your neighbor." The lost-object source (see n. 6) applies when there is certainty of actual harm; the neighbor's blood injunction extends the obligation even to cases of uncertain danger. See *Teshuvot ha-Radbaz* 5, no. 218.

10. *Hil. Rotzei'ah* 1:10–13; *Hoshen Mishpat* 425:1. I have followed *Yad Ramah*'s reading of the Mishneh, *Sanhedrin* 73a. Rashi understands that the focus of this obligation is not on protecting the victim but on preventing the perpetrator from sinning.

11. Rabbeinu Bahye to Deut. 22:3 applies this principle to all interpersonal obligations.

12. *Minhat Hinukh, Kometz la-Minhah, Mitzvah* 237; Maharsha to *Sanhedrin* 73a; *Ha'amek Se'eilah* to *She'iltot* 38:1.

13. Rashi.

14. Of course, this does not imply guilt on the part of someone who is simply the unintended victim of an injury.

15. *Commentary on the Torah*, Lev. 25:35.

16. *Baba Metzi'a* 32a–b.

17. *Teshuvot ha-Rashba* 1, nos. 252, 256, and 257; Rambam, *Sefer ha-Mitzvot*, prohibition 270; *Birkei Yosef, Yoreh De'ah* 372:2; Rabbeinu Yonah, *Sefer hah-Yirah*, no. 266; *Sefer ha-Hinukh*, no. 540. *Sema* to *Hoshen Mishpat* 272, no. 13; *Birkei Yosef* to *Yoreh De'ah* 372 citing *Teshuvot haRashba*, 1, 252 and 257; *Teshuvot Keren L'David*, no. 18; *Teshuvot Mishneh Halakhot* 4:239 and 285; *Teshuvot Minhat Elazar* 4:61. See *Sefer Tza'ar Ba'alei Hayyim*, ch. 8 and *Sefer Nefesh Kol Chai, siman* 4. See, however, *Teshuvot Havot Ya'ir*, no. 191, who, according to some interpretations of his responsum, excludes humans as the subject of this obligation. See Yitzhak Nahman 'Eshkoli, *Tza'ar Ba'alei Hayyim ba-Halakhah u-ba-'Aggadah*, 5762 (2002), pp. 243–280.

18. *Sefer ha-Yirah*, no. 266.

19. "Children As Animals — Origins of Anti-Cruelty Laws, December 5, 2001, BBC Web site http://www.bbc.co.uk/dna/h2g2/A640810.

20. Yo'el Schwartz, *Ve-rahamav 'al Kol Ma'asav* (Jerusalem: Hotsa'at Devar, Yerushalayim, 5744 [1984]), p. 44.

21. Others do not extend the principle of cruelty to animals to humans, maintaining that the Torah's focus here is solely on the welfare of animals. See *Teshuvot*

ha-Radbaz, 2, no. 728; *Keneset ha-Gedolah, Hoshen Mishpat,* no. 272; *Teshuvot be-Tzel ha-Hokhmah,* 4, no. 125; *Pit'hei Hoshen, Nezikin,* ch. 2, note 6. Others maintain that there is a rabbinic obligation, see *Shitah Mekubetzet* to *Baba Kama* 54b. They argue that it is not necessary to prohibit the causing of harm or pain to a fellow human because other verses in the Torah already address those concerns. Furthermore, they reason, these verses are concerned with the welfare and protection of ignorant beasts that have no control over the weight or volume of cargo placed upon them. They need to be protected. Humans, however, are sentient, intelligent beings who can limit their burdens themselves and, if they take upon themselves loads that are too difficult for them to bear, they have no claim on others to help them. See *Teshuvot Havot Ya'ir,* no. 191. It has been debated whether he extends the cruelty-to-animals concept to humans or not. See Yitzhak Nahman 'Eshkoli, *Tza'ar Ba'alei Hayyim ba-Halakhah u-ba-'Aggadah,* pp. 250–253.

22. Rambam, *Hil. Rotzei'ah u-Shemirat ha-Nefesh* 13:14, summarizes the intent of this obligation: the Torah is deeply concerned about the welfare of all Jews and thus the owner of a distressed animal should not be abandoned on the road, left alone with his animals and his possessions. In such a situation he is vulnerable; he may find himself in dangerous circumstances and come to harm. Clearly, the Torah's interest is not limited only to the needs of distressed travelers but includes all those who find themselves in dangerous circumstances.

23. *Baba Kama* 15b:

R. Natan says: From what source is it derived that no one should breed a bad dog in his house, or keep a rickety ladder in his house? [We learn it] from the text, "You shall not bring blood upon your house" (Deut. 22:8).

Hil. Rotzei'ah u-Shemirat ha-Nefesh 11:4:

It is a positive commandment to remove, guard against, and warn against any life-threatening obstacle, as it says: "Take utmost care and guard yourself scrupulously." If he did not remove the item but rather left dangerous obstacles in place, he has violated a positive commandment and transgressed a negative commandment, "Do not bring blood-guilt on your house."

24. *Sefer ha-Hinukh,* mitzvah 547. See *Teshuvot Devar Avraham* 1, 37:25, and *Hazon Ish, Likutim,* chs. 18 and 19.

25. *Piskei 'Uziel,* no. 47.

26. *Teshuvot Minhat Yitzhak* 8, no. 148.

27. *Hil. Sanhedrin* 1:2.

28. It is its duty, for example, to warn property owners of the unstable conditions of their landscaping or walls in order to prevent possible damage to the public. *Hoshen Mishpat* 416. The beth din establishes the fact that the trees or walls are dangerous; otherwise, the owner can claim ignorance of its status. See Michael Wygoda, *Ahrayut la-siluk mifga ba-'etz she-anafav notim la-shetah tzibori, Misrad ha-Mishpatim, ha-Mahlakah le-Mishpat 'Ivri,* Jerusalem, May 9, 2004, *Medinat Yisrael M'shared*

ha-Mishpatim, ha-Machlakah l'Mishpat Ivri (Department of Justice, Division of Hebrew Law) http://www.justice.gov.il/NR/rdonlyres/EE04EB08-259B-4CF2-BA6B-700AD8078F74/0/etznotelershutharabim.doc.

29. *Megillah* 26a; *Baba Batra* 8b.

30. *Yevamot* 89b.

31. On the need to reestablish appropriate rabbinic courts in our days, see Rabbi Yosef Eliyahu Henkin, *"Madur ha-Halakhah," Edut beYisrael*, p. 167; J. David Bleich, "The Bet Din: An Institution Whose Time Has Returned," *Tradition* 27:1, 1992, pp. 58–67.

32. See *Hil. Lashon Hara, kelal* 10 and *Hil. Rekhilut, kelal* 9.

33. See *Ha'amek Davar*; *Ha'amek She'eilah, Parashat Vayikra* 68:2; *Or haHayyim*; *Meshekh Hokhmah*.

34. *Hafetz Hayyim, Hil. Lashon Hara, kelal* 10:4.

35. Ibid., *kelal* 4:10.

36. Ibid., *kelal* 10:31.

37. See *Berakhot* 5b, where Rav Huna speaks *lashon ha-ra* in order to clear his name.

38. *Hafetz Hayyim, Hil. Lashon Ha-ra, kelal* 10:31.

39. *Ketubot* 69a. *Hafetz Hayyim, Hil. Lashon Ha-ra, kelal* 10:13.

40. *Hafetz Hayyim, Hil. Lashon Ha-ra, kelal* 10; see also *Hafetz Hayyim, Hil. Rekhilut, kelal* 9.

41. The details of this statement are beyond the scope of this chapter. See, for example, *Sanhedrin* 56a:

> Resh Lakish said: One who lifts his hand against his neighbor, even if he did not smite him, is called a wicked man as it is written, "And he said unto the wicked man, 'Why would you smite your fellow?'" (Ex. 2:13) "Why *did* you smite?" is not said, but "Why *would* you smite," showing that though he had not yet hit him, he was termed a wicked man. Ze'iri said in R. Hanina's name: He is called a sinner, for it is written, "But if not, I will take it by force" (I Samuel 2:16); and it is further written, "And the sin of the young men was very great before the Lord" (2:17).

42. *Hafetz Hayyim, Hil. Lashon Hara, kelal* 10:8.

43. Ibid., *kelal* 10; see also *Hafetz Hayyim, Hil. Rekhilut, kelal* 9.

44. *Hafetz Hayyim, Hil. Issurei Rekhilut, Tziyyurim* 3:11.

45. *Gittin* 88b.

46. See Rabbi Norman Lamm, *"Din ha-poneh la-arka'ot ha-memshalah," Bet Yitzhak* 36, 5764, pp. 3–7. Rabbi Lamm points to the opinion of *Mordekhai* to *Gittin* 10b, who cites the position that it is only unscrupulous, dishonest, and unjust non-Jewish courts that are subject to the prohibition; Jews may avail themselves of those non-Jewish courts that have the reputation of being just and honest. Rabbi Lamm points out that this minority opinion is not normative.

47. *Tanhuma, Mishpatim* 3.

48. Rashi to Exodus 21:1.

49. *Hil. Sanhedrin* 26:7; *Hoshen Mishpat* 26:1.

50. *Netivot haMishpat* 26:4.

51. See Simcha Krauss, "Litigation in Secular Courts," *Journal of Halachah and Contemporary Society* 2, no. 1. For a modern application of this prohibition, see *Teshuvot Iggerot Moshe, Hoshen Mishpat*, no. 8.

52. Rashba to *Gittin* 10b. See *Shakh* to *Hoshen Mishpat* 73, no. 39, who allows for secular law to be applied in situations of monetary matters that are subject to conditions and stipulations set by the parties to an agreement, or in situations in which there is no explicit halakhic statement. See, however, *Hazon Ish, Hoshen Mishpat, likkutim*, no. 16, 1 who argues that there are no areas in which there are not halakhic guidelines and principles.

53. Ran to *Sanhedrin* 46a; *Teshuvot Avnei NezerYoreh De'ah*, no. 312, secs. 46–52. See also Ritva to *Baba Metzia* 83b–84a.

54. *Berakhot* 28b.

55. *Hil. Hovel u-Mazik* 8:9; *Hoshen Mishpat* 488:9.

56. Rav Paltoi Gaon, cited in *Piskei ha-Rosh* to *Baba Kamma* 8:17; *Otzar ha-Gaonim* to *Baba Kamma*, ch. 8, and *Teshuvot*, no. 227.

57. Rosh to *Baba Kama* 92b, ch. 8, no. 17; *Hil. Sanhedrin* 26:7; *Hoshen Mishpat* 26:2.

58. *Baba Kama* 92b; *Rosh* to *Baba Kama* 92b, quoting R. Paltoi Gaon; *Teshuvot Ha-Ramban*, no. 63; *Hoshen Mishpat* 26:2.

59. *Hil. Hovel u-Mazik* 8:11; this view is followed in the authoritative *Shulhan Arukh, Hoshen Mishpat* 388:12, according to the textual emendation followed by *Shakh*, no. 59, and *Gra*, no. 71.

60. Rabbi Eliezer Waldenberg, quoted in *Nishmat Avraham* 4, p. 209, maintains that for this reason, child molesters must be reported to civil authorities. See R. Asher Zelig Weiss, "*Mesirah la-shiltonot be-hashud be-hit'olelut be-yeladim*," in *Yeshurun*, 5765, p. 659; R. Yehudah Silman, "*Teshuvah le-shei'lah be-inyan divu-ah al pegiyot be-yeladim*," in *Yeshurun*, 5765, p. 661.

61. *Shakh, Hoshen Mishpat* 388, no. 45 and 60.

62. *Geresh Yerahim* to *Gittin* 7a. See his interpretation of Rashi, s.v. *ha'omdim 'alai*, in which he points to Rashi's explanation of Mar 'Ukba's complaint, "Certain men are annoying me," explaining that they were merely insulting him. But, if Mar 'Ukba had been subjected to greater injury, i.e., physical or financial harm, it would have been permissible for him to complain to the non-Jewish authorities, even though he is just an individual. Similarly, *Me'irat Einayim* adds that the distress of the private individual that one is forbidden to report is *tza'ar be-alma* (general distress). However, if one is the subject of assault or attacks, reporting is permitted.

63. Manuscript Frankfurt 123; see Rabbi H. Shlomo Sha'anan, *Hafna'at tove'a le-bet Mishpat, Tehumin* 12, p. 252. See *Piskei Ri MiKorbeil* in Sha'anan, *Ner LiShmaya, pesak* 69.

64. Radbaz to Rambam, *Hil. Hovel u-Mazik* 8.

65. *Hoshen Mishpat* 388:7 and *Shakh*, no. 45; See also gloss of Rema to *Hoshen Mishpat* 388:9; *Ba'i Hayei* and *Maharam miRiszburg* cited in *Pahad Yitzhak, Ma'arekhet Hovel be-Haveiro.*

66. See *Darkei Moshe, Hoshen Mishpat* 388 and *Teshuvot Maharam MiRizbork*, cited by *Shakh.*

67. "*She-eilah be-inyan hoda'ah la-memshalah al hit'olelut be-yeled 'o be-yaldah*" in *Yeshurun*, p. 641.

68. *Teshuvot Shevet ha-Levi* 2:58. See also *Teshuvot Iggerot Moshe*, Hoshen Mishpat 1:92, which, in a similar situation, allows the tax agent to report because even if he did not report, others would, thus relieving the Jew from being the one who is solely responsibility for the indictment of another Jew.

69. R. Moshe Halberstam, *Mesirah le-shiltonot be-mi she-mit'olel be-yeladav* in *Yeshurun* 5765, p. 646.

70. *Teshuvot Minhat Yitzhak* 8:148.

71. Ran to *Sanhedrin* 46a. See, however, *Teshuvot Rema*, no. 88, who maintains that according to *Tosafot, Baba Kama* 114a, s.v. *ve-lo*, if the punishment exceeds that prescribed by the Torah, the *mesirah* prohibition maintains.

72. Rabbi Herschel Schachter, "*Dina De-Malchuta Dina*," *Journal of Halachah and Contemporary Society*, 1:1, 1981, p. 118.

73. *Arukh haShulhan, Hoshen Mishpat* 388:7. This source is authoritatively cited by R. Gedalia Dov Schwartz in "The Abused Child: Halakhic Insights," *Ten Da'at, Sivan* 5748, p. 12.

74. Katz, *Exclusiveness and Tolerance* (New York: Schocken, 1969), pp. 101–102, 158–159.

75. See, for example, *Yoma* 86a.

76. Mishnah, *Avot* 4:4.

77. *Berakhot* 19a.

78. *Sotah* 10b.

79. According to *Nefesh haHayyim*, sha'ar 3, ch. 8, the term *hillul* comes from the Hebrew root, *HLL*, meaning "vacuum" or "empty space." Forms of the three-letter root *HLL* refer to a corpse, the desecration of sacred property and the violation of honor. By engaging in *hillul Hashem*, we diminish God's honor and void the world of His influence.

80. *Sotah* 21b

81. *Tosafot, Sotah* 21b, s.v. *heikhi dami hasid shoteh.*

82. Many of the major rabbinical organizations have such protocols.

MICHAEL LESHER

The Fugitive & the Forgotten

Cracking the Cold Case of
Rabbi Avrohom Mondrowitz

THE ADVOCATE

Late summer, 2006. In the back of a nondescript shop not far from New York City, three people are meeting to discuss a child sex abuse case more than twenty years old.

The case is officially captioned *State v. Mondrowitz*, Indictment No. 7693/84, State of New York, County of Kings. What's in that impersonal string of words and numbers can mean radically different things, depending on who you are and how the case affects you.

To the Brooklyn police, *State v. Mondrowitz* is a file shoved somewhere into the recesses of a dark shelf, unopened for two decades. A dead case — hardly worth blowing the dust off. It's about a suspect who, though indicted, lives in a foreign country, out of reach of the police. Which means, in a word, that *State v. Mondrowitz* is a failure.

To the sixteen-year incumbent Brooklyn district attorney, Charles "Joe" Hynes, *State v. Mondrowitz* is something of an embarrassment, because recent press accounts have delineated his office's quiet efforts to bury the case, even though the charges include multiple counts of sodomy and related Class B felonies — short of premeditated murder, the heaviest, grimmest sort of ink in New York's penal code.

To at least dozens of alleged crime victims — for twenty years they have been "alleged" victims of child sexual abuse, because the case has never come to trial — *Mondrowitz* is something very different: an open sore, an unhealed wound in a collective memory.

One of the people meeting in the shop-keeper's office — Mark Weiss — was, as a boy, among those "alleged" victims. It has been more then twenty years since then, but for him the details are still fresh and he repeats them unhesitatingly, for the man he has driven here to meet is a child advocate — like him, an Orthodox Jew — with a passion for steering troubled young Jews away from drugs and alcohol. In the course of his work the advocate has found that many such yarmulka-wearing youngsters were victims of sexual abuse as children. And he knows many people, dozens of them, who say they were sodomized, fondled, or otherwise sexually violated as children by the same man: Rabbi Avrohom Mondrowitz.

"I'm another one," says Weiss.

The advocate listens as the visitor tells his story. He will never forget Rabbi Mondrowitz, Weiss says: a charismatic Hasid whose charm and academic degrees (phony, it turned out) had secured him overlapping jobs as a school administrator and a child therapist in Brooklyn from the late 1970s until the end of 1984. At the age of thirteen, Mark was sent by pious Jewish parents all the way from Chicago to be "treated" by the great Rabbi Mondrowitz. "After all," says Weiss, "he was religious. A rabbi. He was one of us. Who could be the better choice to talk to a Jewish kid who was showing the rebellious streak I was?"

Young Mark had been dazzled on arrival by Mondrowitz's sports car, complete with flashy audio system. They had spent the first day on "love-bombing."[1] Mondrowitz had taken him to amusement parks, had indulged his every whim, had impressed him with an almost overabundance of "cool."

And then . . .

"At night, he somehow talked me into getting into bed with him. It was amazing how smoothly he did it. He told me I could sleep anywhere, but other beds weren't clean, and the other rooms were cold, and so on, and so on — so finally I ended up sleeping in his room. And then suddenly we were in the same bed. And then . . ."

The advocate is nodding. He has heard all this before from other alleged victims of Mondrowitz. So has the other person at the meeting, Dr. Amy Neustein, who as far back as 1986 was one of the very few Orthodox Jews to talk publicly about the case. She knows — by now, many of us know — that Brooklyn police believe Mondrowitz's victims may have numbered in the hundreds, nearly all of them Orthodox Jews, before he fled the country for Israel in December 1984.

So Dr. Neustein is not surprised by the rest of Weiss's story. Even so, it's hard to listen to him talk. Weiss tells of sexual violations, genital fondling, sodomy, a whole world of unwanted and terrifying sex that went on night after night, after days of what was supposed to be "therapy," the thirteen-year-old cowed by something worse than force — by the assurance, the authority, the utter self-confidence of the grown man whose title "Rabbi" was enough to overcome any scruples in a boy raised to obey an Orthodox Jewish clergyman without question.

For Dr. Neustein, there's something even worse about the story than what happened to the boy. It's the fact that neither he, nor the crowds of other Orthodox Jewish alleged victims of Mondrowitz, ever formally pressed charges. Their families had listened to rabbis who had urged them to keep quiet, to avoid involving their children in scandal, lest they embarrass their families, and — worst of all — the Jewish community. Now, twenty years later, it seems that the closet door is coming off its hinges. Skeletons are beating their way out, one by one, their stories as vivid as ever. Pushing them inside has healed nothing.

No one knows this better than Mark Weiss, who as an adult has decided to go public with his accusations against Rabbi Mondrowitz.

Mark's face is flushed when he has finished with his story; he needs to pause. Then he and Dr. Neustein explain why they have come. They tell the advocate they are now working with me, Michael Lesher, a writer and lawyer who wants to see Mondrowitz finally brought back from Israel to face justice. Lesher, they explain, is also an Orthodox Jew. He isn't charging any fees for his work on the case. But in the nine years he's devoted to it, he has slowly gathered a group of alleged Mondrowitz victims as his clients; on their behalf, he is filing complaints with the Brooklyn district attorney, spreading word of the case to the news media, and agitating to revive efforts to extradite Mondrowitz to stand trial on charges for which he was indicted in absentia in February 1985.

"I know," says the advocate. "I tried all that myself, when Mondrowitz first ran there. It was a failure. The law doesn't allow extradition for abusing boys."

But Lesher says things are different now, explains Dr. Neustein. The trouble with the extradition treaty between Israel and the United States is that it only applies to rape, not to sex crimes in general. A few of Mondrowitz's alleged victims — five young non-Jewish boys who lived near him in his Borough Park neighborhood — had, in contrast to the Jewish victims, made official complaints to police in November 1984, resulting in criminal charges and eventually an indictment for sodomy and first-degree child sexual abuse. Somehow alerted to the proceedings, Mondrowitz fled the country in December and surfaced in Israel in early 1985. Back then, Israeli law defined "rape" exclusively as the rape of a woman by a man, so Mondrowitz's indictment for abusing *boys* wasn't extraditable from Israel.

But Israeli law changed just about the time the current D.A., Charles Hynes, came into office. Since 1988, says Dr. Neustein, homosexual rape has been equated with heterosexual rape in Israel. Lesher insists that Hynes could seek Mondrowitz's extradition at any time. He says that influential people just don't want it done. But if enough victims were to come forward and demand justice . . .

Having discussed all this with me in advance (I'm unable to attend this particular meeting), Mark Weiss and Dr. Neustein lay out our requests. We know that the advocate knows many self-described Mondrowitz victims (one of them, in fact, is now a client of mine). He was involved in the case as long ago as 1984. Let's pool resources, they suggest, share the information we have, bring together as many victims as we can. The testimony of five abused boys — all of them non-Jews — led to Mondrowitz's indictment. Now it's time for the far more numerous Jews among his alleged victims to be heard as well.

"And then what?" The advocate's tone is sharp.

"Michael believes we can bring Mondrowitz back to stand trial for what he did," says Weiss. "Maybe he can't be tried for every child he abused. But the good news is, the D.A.'s office assures Michael the victims in the indictment are still ready to testify. The case is still legally viable. So all of us can still see justice, at least for some of what this man did."

Dr. Neustein adds, "Michael says he won't stop until Mondrowitz has to face his victims in a court of law."

The advocate must have expected these words, but they seem to stun him for a moment. Then his shoulders sag and he looks at his visitors, his face bitter.

"It will never happen," he says. "I tried. I couldn't do it. None of you will do it."

He stands up, effectively ending the meeting.

"Nobody is ever bringing Mondrowitz back," he says.

The child advocate was wrong.

On November 16, 2007, I was able to announce at a press conference in Manhattan that Rabbi Mondrowitz had been arrested at dawn in Jerusalem that very day — over twenty years after the commission of the crimes charged in his Brooklyn indictment.[2] That same day, the *New York Times* ran a prominent story on the case against Mondrowitz — its first Mondrowitz story since 1984.[3] Shortly afterward, the Israeli government ordered Mondrowitz extradited to stand trial in New York. Mondrowitz's challenge to this order in the Israeli courts was denied, and if his last-ditch appeal is rejected by Israel's Supreme Court he will be on his way, finally, to face at least some of his accusers.[4]

All that is easily written. But reaching the goal took so much labor, so many years, so many maneuvers, the overcoming of so much indifference, fear, and misunderstanding that for years I wondered myself whether the child advocate's attitude might not be the right one after all.

To bring Mondrowitz to justice, I had to challenge the entrenched bureaucracy of Brooklyn's district attorney — and those in the Jewish community leadership who apparently wanted the Mondrowitz case ignored. Not to mention government agencies that didn't want to interfere.

Again and again, I was told that the goal was beyond hope; that no one cared; that too many influential people stood between Mondrowitz and justice. Even more disturbing to me — an Orthodox Jew myself — were the Orthodox Jews who innocently asked me why *I* cared. Wasn't it better to let Mondrowitz go free? Why bother with child abuse that happened years ago? Even the brother of an alleged Mondrowitz victim whose experience had driven him to suicide was against publicizing the case, believing the exposure would interfere with his family's marriage opportunities.

Fortunately, I didn't have to face these obstacles alone. Over time, I was able to turn to a growing number of remarkable people — nearly all of whom have remained anonymous — who helped me to find things I needed, people with stories to tell, or reporters who might be receptive to the Mondrowitz story. Eventually I found myself at the center of a sort of underground: people who wanted the same things I did, though they were not willing to say so openly. This underground proved critical in cracking the Mondrowitz case.

But most of the time, the principal or fundamental effort had to be mine. Significant steps had to be made publicly to be effective — and often there was no one else to make them. Even behind-the-scenes efforts had to be focused and coordinated. And after all, I was a lawyer as well as a writer. I had taken on alleged victims as my clients. I had to be responsible for anything that might allow them, once again, to hope for some sort of justice.

I like to think I haven't let them down.

\ \ \

The only way to tell this story is to go back to 1997, when Dr. Neustein first told me about Rabbi Mondrowitz. By that time I had tried my hand at some freelance writing, in which I had made use of my legal training as well as my intimate knowledge of Jewish communities. (I embraced an Orthodox Jewish lifestyle in the 1980s and have lived in intensely religious Jewish communities ever since.) I said I was willing to take on one more such story and to do whatever I could with it. But what I originally heard about Mondrowitz wasn't especially promising.

A few facts were known. Mondrowitz had moved from Chicago to Brooklyn in the late 1970s, when he was about thirty years old — already married and with a sizable brood of children — and had quickly become a respected figure. His family included some distinguished Talmudic scholars, and no one ever doubted Avrohom Mondrowitz's own brainpower. But he was no cloistered scholar. He claimed to hold a Ph.D. in psychology. He helped to found a school for children with learning disabilities. When the school became a reality, Mondrowitz was one of its leading administrators. Meanwhile, he opened an office in the basement of his house and offered therapy for children there. He ran a local radio show. He hobnobbed with Orthodox community celebrities — rabbis, performers, writers.

That was Rabbi Mondrowitz's public persona, at least, until late 1984. Then — overnight — all that changed.

The first call to the police came on November 21, 1984. One of Rabbi Mondrowitz's neighbors, a young boy from an Italian-American family, reported having been molested by Mondrowitz.

Detectives Patricia Kehoe and Sal Catalfumo interviewed several of Mondrowitz's neighbors. Again and again they heard similar stories: the rabbi was friendly to all the children; he often gave them gifts; they used to visit him at his home; he would even take them for weekend trips.

As Detective Kehoe later told the story, the parents saw nothing alarming in this, but she herself, knowing the nature of the accusation against Rabbi Mondrowitz, worried about what they *hadn't* seen. And when at last the children were asked directly about any uncomfortable experiences with Mondrowitz, tears came — and then reports of sexual abuse. Serious abuse. Over and over.

More police interviews located more alleged child victims, some of whom had been recipients of "therapy" in Mondrowitz's basement office. Soon the police were prepared to arrest the rabbi.[5] But when officers came to his door armed with a warrant, Mondrowitz and his family were gone — and there was nothing for the *New York Times* to report in a terse two-paragraph article except that Rabbi Mondrowitz was wanted on charges of child sexual abuse, and that his whereabouts were unknown.[6]

From that point, I could piece together what was known of the story from a handful of newspaper articles and wire service dispatches. Mondrowitz appeared in Jerusalem in early 1985, just about the same time a formal indictment was handed down by a Brooklyn grand jury. He denied any sort of guilt; his Israeli lawyer called the charges against him "an ugly libel."[7] Brooklyn's district attorney at the time, Elizabeth Holtzman, took the case seriously, securing an indictment with five separate complainants — ages nine to fifteen — on thirteen counts of sodomy and first-degree child sexual abuse. She also enlisted the aid of the federal government, which issued a formal request for Mondrowitz's extradition from Israel.

The story took a frustrating turn later in 1985, when the government of Israel formally declined the U.S. extradition request. Israel's reasoning was based on the peculiarly narrow wording of the U.S.-Israel extradition treaty and the anachronistic state of Israel's law of sexual assault. The treaty listed only specific offenses as extraditable: rape was among them, but no other sort of sexual assault was, so that Mondrowitz could face extradition only if he was charged with rape. Yet Israeli law at that time recognized as rape only the forcible sexual penetration of a woman by a man. Since all the complainants listed in Mondrowitz's indictment were boys, Israeli law did not recognize what had been done to them as rape (though much of it allegedly was), which meant that the crimes were not extraditable under the language of the treaty.[8]

After that, to my surprise, the story seemed to peter out. For two years the news media had scarcely anything to say about Mondrowitz. Suddenly, in March 1987, a new administration took over in Israel, and the new interior minister, Ronni Milo, made headlines by announcing that he was about to deport Mondrowitz forthwith. (Deportation rests on a theory quite different from that of extradition, so the government was not restricted by Israel's definition of rape.) Calling the Mondrowitz case "one of the worst cases I could ever imagine," Milo promised that he would return Mondrowitz to New York to stand trial "for the terrible things he did to children."[9]

The promise was never kept. Nothing in the press explained why, but once again the case against Mondrowitz just melted away.

In 1989, Charles "Joe" Hynes was elected Brooklyn's district attorney. Hynes was not Jewish, but he clearly appreciated the political heft of Brooklyn's Orthodox Jewish constituency. He actively courted the community's support during the campaign, and immediately after his election he boasted that he had assembled an informal "Jewish Advisory Council" — virtually all of whose members were rabbis or prominent lay leaders in Orthodox Jewish communities — to advise him on all issues affecting Brooklyn's Jews.[10]

One might imagine that this council, hailing from precisely the community that had allegedly been ravaged by Rabbi Mondrowitz a few years earlier, would have seen to it that the D.A. made prosecuting the fugitive a high priority. And why not? Mondrowitz had allegedly victimized hundreds of Jewish children; his alleged crimes had undermined the success of a Jewish school he had helped to run with money raised from Jewish parents; he was said to have used the title "rabbi" — a designation of great moral prestige in a religious Jewish community — to lure still more victims; and to top it all off, he had sheltered from prosecution in the Jewish State.

Ironically, Hynes's Jewish advisers apparently took a different approach. Dr. Neustein told me that she had made a point of trying to speak personally to the members of the Jewish Advisory Council about the Mondrowitz case. Most of them avoided her entirely; the two who did speak to her both told her that "the community" did not want to see Mondrowitz prosecuted. One of those, Rabbi Herbert Bomzer, would say almost the same thing as late as 2006, when he was interviewed by ABC's Cynthia McFadden.

For these "leaders," it seemed, the alleged victims' needs were anything but paramount.

But I saw things differently. I was both confused and infuriated by what I had learned. The story as it stood made no sense; a case as grave as the one against Mondrowitz couldn't just fade into oblivion. It *had* to go farther. And if the members of the victims' own community couldn't fight for justice in a case like this, I thought, we had no business using the word "justice" at all.

Thus began the second phase of my research into Mondrowitz. Now I was determined to fill in the gaps in my knowledge of the case. I made up my mind I was going to find out exactly what had happened — and then to undo it, if that proved to be humanly possible.

THE COLD CASE

Reporters have sometimes asked me why I cared enough about the Mondrowitz case to take it up so resolutely when no other professional wanted it. Frankly, the question baffles me. I think I would have been deeply interested in Mondrowitz under any circumstances, simply because of the story's bearing on the justice system (of which, as a lawyer, I'm a small part) and on the religious community I joined as an adult, whose educational system is premised on a belief that our children are our most precious resource. I couldn't square that lofty sentiment with the idea of walking away from a case alleging multiple child rapes by a rabbi.

Actually, my commitment to the case grew stronger precisely *because* no one in similar circumstances seemed willing to take it. The great sage Hillel left behind a saying — preserved in the Talmud — that translates idiomatically as, "In a place where no one will take responsibility, try to be responsible."[11] I'm not comfortable with the role of preacher, but for me, this case underscored the wisdom of that advice. I was a published writer; I was a lawyer; and I was a Jew. If I didn't accept the challenge, who would?

It would be tedious to detail all the steps I took — the Freedom of Information Act requests I filed, then amended, the administrative appeals I wrote, the hours and hours in law libraries, the lawsuits I threatened — in order to get more of the critical facts of the Mondrowitz case. Suffice it to say that the process took over two years, and that when all that time was up, I was still missing a few pieces of the puzzle.

But I had learned a critical thing: the Mondrowitz case had not simply petered out. It had been covered up.

I don't mean just that every single government agency from which I sought documents about Mondrowitz — the Brooklyn D.A.'s office, the State Department, the Justice Department — initially (and wrongfully) withheld documents from me until threatened with legal action. (I backed up my threats with detailed legal arguments; otherwise I'm sure they would have been ignored.) I don't mean just that the Brooklyn D.A. never even acknowledged the existence of documents that, as I now know from the disclosures of other agencies, must have been in his files all along — and which his office has not produced to me to this day.

What I learned from the stack of papers I finally collected from the State and Justice Departments was more fundamental than that. People who suspected that government officials had tiptoed around the Mondrowitz case were even more right than they knew.

The file I could now read showed that Mondrowitz had initially been given high priority by Hynes's predecessor, Elizabeth Holtzman.[12] Under pressure from her, the State Department agreed to try to hunt down Mondrowitz even after Israel declined to extradite him. "Natives of Brooklyn are becoming restless," read one typical State Department memo in February 1986 — over a year after Mondrowitz had fled the United States — which went on to describe telephone calls that Holtzman's office was still placing to the department's Law Enforcement and Intelligence office. By then, Holtzman's strategy was to seek Mondrowitz's deportation from Israel, where he was not a citizen, a step that would have required him to be shipped back to New York, where he would have been arrested the moment he landed.

But all that changed after Charles Hynes, with his Jewish Advisory Council, swept the Brooklyn polls in 1989. Once Hynes was elected district attorney, there were no more State Department memos about pressure from Brooklyn; no more nervous queries about how, and how soon, the "natives" could be satisfied. The case had been shifted to a back burner.

In 1993 things went from bad to worse. In July, after years of silence from Hynes, the Justice Department notified his office that it would close the file on Mondrowitz — thus ending any efforts to either extradite or deport him — by September 15 unless they heard that Hynes still wanted to pursue the case. Amazingly, Hynes waited until that very day, and then had an employee named Andrew Calia call Justice with a bombshell: the district attorney was no longer interested in Mondrowitz so long as he remained in Israel; if Mondrowitz left that country, Hynes would "consider pursuing the case." *Consider*, mind you. And even that, only if the fugitive left Israel — which Rabbi Mondrowitz clearly had no intention of doing.

Not a word about the effect of the 1988 change in Israeli law on Mondrowitz's extradition status, even though the U.S. Embassy and its legal staff had openly, in a closely argued memo, declared this change a breakthrough in the case. Nothing about pursuing efforts to deport Mondrowitz — who, as the documents showed, had never been granted Israeli citizenship — to New York. Not even a suggestion that U.S. authorities might press for a broader extradition treaty with Israel to make cases like this one easier to handle.

Hynes's office, in effect, had quietly buried the Mondrowitz case.

To be fair, Hynes was not the only official who seemed prepared to forgive and forget vis-à-vis the alleged crimes of Avrohom Mondrowitz. A letter from the Justice Department's Office of International Affairs to the State Department had complained, as far back as October 1986, that the Israeli government appeared to be giving Mondrowitz "special treatment" by extending his visitor's visa despite the pending charges in New York and the request for his deportation by the United States. The reason for this "special treatment" was not difficult to guess: Yitzchak Peretz, of the ultra-Orthodox Shas party, was then Interior Minister, and he had openly stated his belief that a Jew should not be deported to a non-Jewish country to stand trial, unless and until he had been proved guilty. Since no one could be proved guilty without a trial, this position translated as: no Jew who fled to Israel to escape prosecution would ever be sent back, at least not if the Shas party could help it. Large blocs of Orthodox Jewish voters in Israel have always followed the lead of the religious parties, making this a serious political issue, as noted in a cable from U.S. Ambassador Thomas Pickering the following May, in which he cautioned that Mondrowitz's deportation would be strongly opposed "by those whose interests lie in areas other than his guilt or innocence."

So religious politics, the fragility of Israel's governing coalition, and a D.A. apparently afraid to counter his Jewish advisers — whose priority was the community's image, not justice for the victims — had conspired to keep Avrohom Mondrowitz a free man.

That Mondrowitz was wanted for some of the worst crimes short of murder made all this an outrage to me. That the fugitive was also a rabbi, who had allegedly used his status as clergyman as part of his criminal modus operandi, made it intolerable.

\ \ \

All this information was finally in my hands in the year 2000. It was now three years since I had begun my research into the case, and I had to admit I was no closer to bringing Mondrowitz to justice.

But I knew now what was standing between Mondrowitz and the law. And I had also studied extradition law, checked with other lawyers, and confirmed that there was no legal excuse for the case to languish: Israel's adoption of a gender-neutral sex offense code in 1988 had effectively equated homosexual and heterosexual rape and rendered Mondrowitz extraditable. (Legal experts would later confirm this to the press.) The legal staff at the U.S. Embassy in Israel had come to that conclusion twelve years earlier.

But what was I to do with what I knew? Again, it would be tedious to list all my efforts to connect with the press. But in 2003, Stephanie Saul of *Newsday* agreed to run a long feature, in installments, on the problem of child sex abuse in Orthodox Jewish communities, and she gave prominent attention to the Mondrowitz case.[13]

Her series was well researched and provocative. It did not draw much public reaction from the Jewish community, as far as I could tell, but it was the first time my efforts to bring Mondrowitz to justice were mentioned in print, and that fact alone would have important consequences three years later.[14]

Ms. Saul's determined reporting stimulated my own. While she was researching her article, I dug deeper into Mondrowitz's history. I had managed to obtain a transcript of a radio show from the 1980s in which Mondrowitz had hosted a popular Orthodox Jewish singer named Mordechai Ben-David. Now I studied it closely for clues to his character, his persona. It was a bizarre experience. I don't know how Mondrowitz conducted himself on his other broadcasts, but this transcript showed him weirdly effervescent with Ben-David, who presented himself as an old friend of the rabbi's. At one point Mondrowitz read a poem of his own, rhapsodizing about sensory pleasures as a divine gift; Ben-David pronounced it "beautiful." Then the conversation turned to the nature of the soul, with Ben-David declaring — to Mondrowitz's evident approval — that non-Jews lack a soul entirely.[15]

Besides reading that transcript, I had performed some Internet searches; as a result, I knew that as late as 1997 — while wanted as a criminal in Brooklyn — Mondrowitz (in Jerusalem) was calmly answering people's religious questions online, on such topics as when humorous comments may be classified as prohibited "mockery."

The thought of the rabbi who had allegedly sodomized Jewish and non-Jewish boys pontificating to radio listeners all over Brooklyn against the soulless Gentiles, delivering rhapsodies on the sensory pleasures of God's world, and offering instruction on details of Talmudic ethics made me almost literally sick.

I had to do more.

I found Mondrowitz's e-mail address; I wrote to him in Jerusalem.

And he wrote back.

This exchange of e-mails was the only direct communication I've ever had with the man over all these years, and I'm still not sure why I tried it. I'm also not sure what sort of response I had expected from him. I can say, though, that his answer to my query was even more outrageous than the on-the-air comments he had delivered in Brooklyn. Mondrowitz was clearly not worried about being prosecuted. Nearly twenty years after dodging arrest in New York, the fugitive did not hesitate to ridicule his accusers; in fact, he claimed the role of victim for himself:

> I was never questioned by any official representatives — civil or religious — in the United States. I admit that there was a great deal of noise from some who consider themselves self-appointed spokesmen of G-d. . . . I do have a "psak" [ruling of a Jewish court in his favor] from the Badatz of Yerushalayim [Jerusalem]; from Harav [Shlomo Zalman] Aurbach[16] . . . and from other respected rabbonim [rabbis]. . . . May the Jewish virtues of Baishonim, Rachmonim and Gmilas Chasodim — Modesty, Compassion and the doing of good deeds — continue to guide your actions.

After another e-mail query, evidently having learned a little more about me and my work, Mondrowitz was even more impudent in his complaints of mistreatment by the justice system:

> I'm sure you also know that I had officially offered to meet and speak with any qualified official, at the American Embassy. I was in Israel before any "warrant" was issued. A "warrant" was never delivered to my home, my wife (who was in residence) or to my lawyers. In fact, when my lawyers formally requested a copy of the "warrant" — a constitutional right, I believe, they were told that there was no such document. Years later someone told us that it was a "hidden warrant" — whatever that means. At the time, due to the lack of openness — that, by the way, continues to this day — I was advised . . . not to respond to any request of information whatsoever.[17]

So the indicted child rapist, in his own eyes, was a civil rights victim. The rabbi who could still take it on himself to answer questions on religious law and had unhesitatingly offered me a sermon on Jewish character could mock his alleged victims' defenders as "self-appointed spokesmen of G-d" and refuse to discuss the charges against him! Could hypocrisy go further?

Mind you, during my research I had heard from people in religious Jewish communities that Mondrowitz had probably "repented," or at least that he was under steady surveillance by rabbinic authorities in Jerusalem. Mondrowitz's e-mails to me baldly refuted both claims. Yet, as he himself said, he appeared to have significant support from rabbis in Israel, and presumably from those who followed them, too. And the rabbis I approached with my new information — though some admitted it was disturbing — denied, to a man, that there was anything they could do about it.

MY FIRST MONDROWITZ CLIENTS

In the early spring of 2006, I learned that *New York* magazine was preparing an article on sex abuse allegations against Rabbi Yehudah Kolko, who had taught in Brooklyn yeshivas for decades. A new blog called "The Unorthodox Jew" had brought together men who accused Rabbi Kolko of having sexually abused them as children; now these men were filing a lawsuit against him and against the school that had employed him.

I immediately contacted the reporter, contributing editor Robert Kolker, and then met him in Manhattan to discuss all I knew about Mondrowitz. I also referred him to Dr. Neustein and to others I knew would share important information.

By this time, my knowledge of the Brooklyn D.A.'s record on sex abuse in the Jewish community included several cases more recent than Mondrowitz's. I knew, for instance, about the way a group of rabbis had persuaded Hynes to drop serious sex abuse charges against one Rabbi Shlomo Hafner.[18] I described this, and other cases, to Kolker. I expressed my deep frustration with the way these investigations had been handled, both within the Jewish community and by the district attorney. But mostly I talked about Mondrowitz, sharing information with Kolker that I had been the first person, apart from D.A.'s staff and the relevant people in the federal government, ever to lay eyes on. My information, I argued, went a long way toward explaining why cases like Kolko's had been ignored for so long.

Kolker was impressed.

His article appeared in *New York*'s May 22, 2006, issue.[19] Although he focused on the civil lawsuit filed against Rabbi Kolko by his alleged victims, Kolker made use of material I had given him to address the general problem of prosecuting child sex abuses cases in Brooklyn's Jewish community. He also made a point of discussing the Mondrowitz story. (I was not mentioned.)

Kolker's sensitive and strongly written piece struck a nerve. Rabbi Avi Shafran, spokesman for the influential Orthodox organization Agudath Israel of America, denounced the article as "lurid" and unfair to religious Jews.[20] But a very different response issued from many members of Shafran's religious community. The editors published several passionate letters from Brooklyn Jews who had clearly had enough of the stand-pat attitude that had been the norm for twenty years on cases of child sex abuse. One wrote, "I couldn't believe someone actually put the horrible truth in writing . . . just as I have dreamed of doing. I was, and continue to be, a victim of abuse and rabbinical cover-up." Another declared, "I was abused for four years when I lived in Borough Park, and to this day, I can't come to terms with what happened. I tried telling the grand rabbi and others, but nobody listened." An Orthodox woman in Borough Park (where Mondrowitz had the basement office where he allegedly abused his young patients) wrote that, in contrast to her rabbinic leaders, "there are those like me who believe it's about time this issue was discussed."[21]

This welcome evidence of attitude shift was also reflected in the newly defensive tone in which the district attorney parried Kolker's questions about Mondrowitz. Hynes's first response to my exposure of his backpedaling on extradition attempts had been an almost offhand denial: his spokesman had insisted (falsely) to *Newsday* in 2003 that the office didn't even know the federal government had closed the Mondrowitz file ten years earlier.[22] But this time, Kolker was able to speak directly to Rhonnie Jaus, head of the Sex Crimes unit, who was clearly eager to restore her office's credibility in the case: "Our position," she said, "has always been that were Mondrowitz to return to the United States, we would prosecute him for his heinous crimes." Of course, the truth was that Jaus and her boss could have been doing much more about those "heinous crimes" — to begin with, they could have reversed their office's 1993 decision to leave Mondrowitz untouched as long as he stayed in Israel — but for the first time they sounded stung, and that was all to the good.

But much more was to come. Within days after the magazine reached the newsstands, my relation to the Mondrowitz case had changed substantially — and forever.

I had a Mondrowitz victim for a client.

\ \ \

After all the years of effort I had put into the case, the May 26 e-mail from Mordechai (not his real name) still came as a bolt from the blue.

All I knew was that there was a note in my inbox from someone whose name I didn't recognize. A complete stranger was telling me how he, a Jewish man in his thirties, had been reading Kolker's article in *New York* that week, while the descriptions given by Kolko's alleged victims stirred more and more painful memories of his own sexual abuse by a rabbi when he was a small boy . . . until, suddenly, the sight of the name "Mondrowitz" in the article had jolted him so violently he had to put the magazine down.

Rabbi Mondrowitz!

That was the man who had abused him, week after week, in the basement office of the rabbi's Borough Park home. That was the rabbi and psychologist with diplomas all over his "bragging wall," as Mordechai later called it, whose hands did terrifying things to the nine-year-old that his parents never knew about.

Startled into action, Mordechai did some Google searches on Mondrowitz's name and found mine, in the 2003 *Newsday* article, as the lawyer who was trying to hunt the rabbi down. Thank God I had been so persistent in telling the story! — Had either the *Newsday* or the *New York* article three years later not appeared in print, Mordechai would never have crashed into Mondrowitz's name as a wanted child abuser, and would never have found me.

But he did.

I'm not a particularly emotional man, but tears came to my eyes when I read Mordechai's message, especially when he confided that I was literally the first person with whom he had shared his story. For six years — ever since I first learned that extraditing Mondrowitz depended mainly on the political backbone of the Brooklyn D.A. — I had been praying for Jewish victims to come forward, dreaming that they and I could one day storm the D.A.'s office and demand a change of policy on the case.

And now it was finally happening.

As a member of an Orthodox Jewish community, Mordechai said, he still needed anonymity so as not to expose his family to the backlash that might follow a public disclosure. But anonymity was his only condition. After talking to me, he confirmed that he was ready to speak with reporters (if I vetted them first) and to make a formal complaint to the Brooklyn D.A.

We had soon done both.

I will never forget the day in June 2006 when Mordechai and I entered D.A. Hynes's office to reopen the Mondrowitz case, almost thirteen years after that same D.A. had quietly kissed it goodbye. The weather was gray, rainy, murky — the sort of day on which nothing good ever happens in fiction. We met outside the large building in uptown Brooklyn that housed the district attorney's complex. Mordechai, always taciturn, was visibly nervous. Looking up at the building, I felt the same way. What the two of us were trying to do seemed as impossible as if we'd undertaken to physically lift that massive edifice off the damp street. But I had brought him this far and I couldn't let him down.

"Look," I told him. "I don't know what's going to happen today. But I'll tell you this. Once we walk through that door" — gesturing at the steel-and-glass entrance and the security guards behind it — "nothing will be the same." I hesitated, then added, "And wherever it goes, I'll be there with you."

I had deliberately chosen not to give the office advance notice of our errand. So I wasn't surprised when the desk clerk, after calling upstairs with the nature of our visit, was told to have us wait. Wait we did — for quite some time, in fact, until we were asked to go up to the Sex Crimes Unit, where we waited some more.

Finally, some forty-five minutes after our entry into the building, we were admitted into an office with a young and rather flummoxed A.D.A. named Maria Cienava, flanked by Lisa Cohen, an apparently more experienced supervisor. They said that their chief, Rhonnie Jaus, was out of the office that day. What did we want? Taking the initiative, I asked the two A.D.A.s to take down an official complaint from my client against Rabbi Mondrowitz. This they refused to do. I asked if there was some sort of police report or similar document we could fill out. There wasn't. They did agree to take notes while Mordechai told his story, so he told it to them; what they actually wrote down I do not know, because when they were through they refused to give us a copy. All they would say to Mordechai, or me, was that because of the statute of limitations they really couldn't pursue a charge on his behalf. . . . Would he like to sign up for some sort of counseling?

I felt like strangling them with a bit of their own red tape, but I chose to be polite. I told them that Mordechai had come forward to let them know how determined he was to see Mondrowitz prosecuted and to aid them in that prosecution in any way he could. I told them I would do the same; I asked only that they talk to Ms. Jaus about the status of the Mondrowitz prosecution once she returned to the office and then to let me know, for my client's benefit, where the case stood. They said they would — but they never did, despite several follow-up calls from me.

Still, we had reopened the Mondrowitz case.

And over the next weeks, it was as though an invisible gate had swung aside. After Mordechai, one after another Mondrowitz victim found his way into my office, until I officially represented six of them, and knew specifically of at least a dozen more.

Their stories were wrenching. No matter how many of them I heard, the next one was just as searing as the first. I never got used to the sense of betrayal these men radiated when they described their experiences. One had even been sent to Mondrowitz for therapy after having been abused by another man!

"I felt like I had the word 'whore' written on my back," he told me. "I was just a kid. And already I felt like nothing, like worse than nothing. I was numb." Another — call him Abe — told me how, after his own abuse by Mondrowitz, the rabbi encouraged him to draw other young boys to Mondrowitz's house on the Sabbath. "I know for a fact what he did to some of them there," he told me. Instead of complying, Abe quietly warned fellow students to stay away from the rabbi. (This occurred during Mondrowitz's tenure as a leading administrator at a school for young Jews with learning problems.) "When he found out, he charged into class one day and beat me with his fists, right in front of the teacher and other students," Abe told me.

The details of what these men reported were bad enough, but another thing that made me grieve for them was the secrecy of their pain. All of my new clients were Orthodox Jews, grown men now, with families. Yet hardly anyone knew what sort of anguished memories they carried. The Mondrowitz story was a private wound. Not one of them felt he could trust his religious community, or its rabbis, with much of the truth. A few had tried telling rabbis about their experiences, but each time they had been disappointed by the coolness of the response. Many others who declined to become clients told me they simply couldn't risk speaking out about their abuse by Mondrowitz, even anonymously, for fear their coreligionists might connect them with the story, with the result that their children would be marked as "undesirable" marriage prospects. Even those who became clients — with the exception of Mark Weiss, whose story I described earlier — insisted that the use of their names was too high a price to pay even for justice. They were also skeptical about our chances of changing anything. "Our community never wanted him reported," said one. "This D.A. is listening to people in the community who never want this to see the light of day. Never. There are a lot of them. And they vote."

Despite all this, I felt we were a little closer to our goal with every new Mondrowitz complaint I filed. With real victims to talk to — the first Jewish victims of Mondrowitz who had ever come forward — the press began to take notice of my campaign. Suddenly, after nine years, my unflagging insistence that Mondrowitz could be extradited any time the D.A. chose to push for it, and the evidence of the way he'd avoided pushing for it before, made the Mondrowitz story news. Between July and November of 2006, the *New York Post*,[23] the *Village Voice*,[24] *Forward*,[25] the *Jewish Week*,[26] and New York's *Eyewitness News*[27] all ran prominent stories on Mondrowitz. And so did ABC's national program *Nightline*.

I was pleased that all the legal experts contacted and quoted by these reporters agreed with me; Charles Hynes was acting more as Mondrowitz's lawyer than as the district attorney for his constituents and an advocate for victims. But even knowing what I did, I was frankly astonished when Hynes's office offered a new, and patently false, rationalization for his inaction on the case. Yes, his spokesman now said, the treaty had effectively been changed by Israeli law in 1988 so as to render homosexual rape an extraditable offense; but this change could not be applied to Mondrowitz "retroactively" since Mondrowitz had fled to Israel three years before the change was accomplished. "Our position," added D.A. spokesman Jerry Schmetterer, "is that he cannot be extradited; he could not be extradited then, and he cannot be now," though the reporter on whom Schmetterer tried out this sleight of hand pointed out, correctly, that "that line of legal reasoning was explicitly rejected by the American embassy in Tel Aviv, soon after the Israeli law was changed."[28] I had provided the reporters with ample legal precedents showing that extradition treaties are not subject to ex post facto limitations. Clearly, the renewed press attention was driving Hynes into producing some kind of excuse; but, just as clearly, it would take more to make him change course.

I shall always be grateful to ABC's *Nightline*, and particularly to producer

Roxanna Sherwood, for bringing the Mondrowitz story to national television on October 11, 2006. After many lengthy discussions with Dr. Neustein,
Nightline's reporters came to me and my new Mondrowitz clients in the summer of 2006 and asked us to tell them all we knew. We did — and soon the
Mondrowitz case had been named as the national issue I had always thought
it deserved to be.

On camera, I explained to *Nightline*'s Cynthia McFadden that only public
pressure could spur a renewed effort to obtain the extradition of this indicted
felon from Israel to New York. When asked whether, after all this time, my
community might be better off forgetting about Mondrowitz, I said, "That's
not what my clients believe, and they're the victims carrying the wounds.
That's not what I believe, and I belong to the community they do." Mark Weiss
appeared on the program with me, as did Dr. Neustein — all of us Orthodox
Jews — to stress the need to see Mondrowitz prosecuted at last. Mark said it
all when he commented, "Nobody's going to look down upon the Orthodox Jewish community negatively because we're talking about this. They are
going to come to admire us for being straight about it and admitting we have
a problem and we're going to solve it."[29]

Still, there was plenty the public did *not* learn from *Nightline*'s coverage.
Nightline's audience did not know that ABC had sent a film crew to Borough
Park, Mondrowitz's old stomping grounds, and there encountered many Jews
who angrily demanded why TV news people were "attacking" Mondrowitz and
his innocent family. (Others approached the reporters to congratulate ABC
on pursuing the story, but every one of those did so quietly and off-camera.)

Also out of public view was the story behind the airing of the broadcast.
The segment was ready for television well before the actual air date of October
11. But ABC higher-ups, I learned, were unwilling to broadcast the story near
the date of the Jewish High Holy Days, feeling that the coincidence would be
"in bad taste."

As I recited the solemn prayers for Rosh ha-Shana and Yom Kippur (the
New Year and the Day of Atonement) in synagogue that year, my mind
sometimes wandered back to those network executives — many of them
Jews — with their ever-ready bromides about "the public's right to know," and
how they had decreed it was better for Jews to begin their new year without
hearing about the efforts to bring Avrohom Mondrowitz to justice. As always
during that season, the congregation was called upon to atone for its sins,
both personal and collective. But there wasn't a word about the alleged child

rapist still hiding behind Jewish politics in Jerusalem. Maybe some of the hundreds of "alleged victims," as they recited their penitential prayers, might have been consoled by the knowledge that someone finally cared about *their* suffering, that someone wanted to atone for the decades of indifference that had doubled their victimization by their alleged abuser. But ABC's bosses put the Jewish community's public image over the needs of abuse victims, just as nearly everyone else had for over twenty years.

The aftermath of the broadcast, and of investigative reporter Sarah Wallace's follow-up on ABC's *Eyewitness News* on November 8, was just as sobering. Several people took me aside and told me — quietly — to keep on with what I was doing. But other Jews were furious. An Orthodox rabbi wrote me an e-mail accusing me of "desecrating God's name," one of the gravest sins in the traditional canon. The administrator of the popular Jewish blog "Chaptzem" insisted that by speaking out for Mondrowitz's victims I had proved myself to be not only a sinner but an impostor, since no Orthodox Jew would appear on television to "publicize" child abuse.

The most common reaction from Jews was one of despair. "I fear that there's virtually nothing we can do in the Mondrowitz case," one man ultimately confessed to me. "I am very fatalistic and resigned in this case. . . . If you put 1,000 people in front of Hynes' office, it wouldn't help." Even the mother of an alleged victim (and eventual suicide), who learned of me from the broadcast and afterward e-mailed me to say, "I truly don't understand why these well RESPECTED RABBIS sat back and did nothing," later added sadly that Mondrowitz could not be prosecuted, that "only [God] could be the 'JUDGE AND JURY,'" lest news of the case reach "the 'GOISHA [Gentile] WORLD' and publicize a 'HUGE CHILLEL HASHEM' [public scandal]" (emphases in original).

But despite the opposition and the doubts, the Mondrowitz victims were becoming impossible to ignore. They gave interviews to reporters to whom I had explained the facts of the Mondrowitz case; some appeared on television (all but Mark Weiss with their faces and voices disguised to avoid recognition).

And then, in early 2007, a very peculiar windfall came my way.

\ \ \

I wouldn't, at first, have characterized it in those terms. The news that another suspected Jewish child molester, Stefan Colmer, had left Brooklyn without being charged because none of the alleged victims' families (all Orthodox Jews) was willing to come forward was depressingly familiar. And the fillip that Colmer had moved to my own community of Passaic, New Jersey, didn't make the story any sweeter.

But when the suspicions about his record circulated through town, and Colmer imitated Mondrowitz, in February 2007, by running away to Israel; when my efforts to locate victims turned up a dozen children who were likely molested by Colmer; when two of those did come forward to police and press charges; when another alleged victim, from years ago, contacted me so that I, in turn, could put him in touch with reporters — then the Colmer case joined Mondrowitz's as a focal point of my work to drag accused sexual abusers of children out of their sanctuary in Israel.

And I was fortunate. The "underground" that had gradually crystallized during my Mondrowitz investigations came again to my aid. Just as anonymous people had provided me with pictures of Mondrowitz's apartment building and an up-to-date physical description for ABC's reporters, so now they led me so close to Stefan Colmer that even though he had taken an assumed name in Israel — and withheld his exact address from his closest friends — I was able to lead police to his doorstep.

The detective in charge of the investigation, Steve Litwin, was grateful for my information. He was also grateful for the support I gave the family of a victim who had agreed to press charges, and for the information I gave him on Jewish law to share with others we both believed to have been abused by Colmer. He had not known how to talk to religious Jews about their reluctance to report other Jews to the police; the information I gave him enabled him to show anxious families that Jewish law supported them in seeking justice for their children.

I also turned to my Mondrowitz clients for help. I wanted Jewish parents of young children who had been victimized to know how it felt to grow up a victim of abuse, knowing that one's wrongs had been kept a secret, that no one had ever paid for his suffering. Several of my clients agreed to help spread that message to the families of new "alleged victims." One of them put his thoughts into writing:

a) Speaking out about the issue of Sex Abuse in the frum [ultra-Orthodox] community is the first step in acknowledging that it is a very real existing problem.

b) By bringing the spotlight on the issue, we might force schools, rabbonim to implement reporting procedures that will keep offenders away from kids vs. sweeping the issue under the rug. If we don't speak out, then we have no right to complain about things remaining status quo.

c) By showing the DA that we the Orthodox community will no longer stand for abuse cases being kept quiet & covered-up. . . .

I have found it to have a very therapeutic effect by telling the story & having this large burden lifted off my shoulders. . . . It is important to have your voice heard and get the story out, it will give you a sense of empowerment as well, that you're doing something about it & not standing by passively. We need to force changes in the system so that abusers are dealt with appropriately. The victims have done NOTHING wrong. The shame should be on the abuser, NOT the victim. [Emphases in original.]

I could not have said it better. Of course, I couldn't know how deeply the message was penetrating among Colmer's alleged victims, or others like them. But I was determined to help spread it.

In the end, I did more than that. In June 2007, armed with the up-to-date information I had provided on Colmer's whereabouts and activities, Israeli authorities arrested the wanted man in Jerusalem.[30]

The United States had already made an extradition request, and this time there would be no monkey business over the fact that Colmer was only accused of sexual abuse, not rape (whether homosexual or heterosexual). At the beginning of 2007, a new extradition treaty had taken effect between Israel and the United States, which made any crime punishable by more than a year in prison in both countries an extraditable offense. That meant that any serious sex offense — including everything Colmer had allegedly done to his victims — was clearly subject to extradition.

The extradition of Stefan Colmer under the new treaty would therefore be the next legal body blow to Hynes's indifference over the Mondrowitz case.

And Colmer *was* extradited — just months later.[31]

Of course, I had known about the new treaty, soon to take effect, even when *Nightline* aired its piece — and so, I assume, had D.A. Hynes. But his office had continued to insist that *State v. Mondrowitz* was dead regardless of any changes that might come about in the law. When Detective Litwin had informed me of the official request for Colmer's arrest and extradition, I had asked him for only one thing: "I've got a bunch of clients who want to see what's being done for Colmer's victims done, at last, with Avrohom Mondrowitz," I'd said. "Could you please talk with people in the D.A.'s office and see what can be done? I would love for all of us to be working together on this."

The message Detective Litwin brought back to me was — to put it mildly — negative. Hynes's office conveyed the same message to a reporter for the *New York Post* in the spring of 2007, after the new treaty had already become law.[32]

But I was gaining confidence that the Jewish community would no longer tolerate that answer. At least two recent cases, Kolko and Colmer, were now galvanizing public interest. To everyone who would listen, I ticked off the aspects of these cases that showed our communities had not yet learned their lesson from Mondrowitz: the alleged abuser had not been separated from children in spite of repeated accusations; the alleged abuser was able to move from community to community, unharassed by word of the accusations against him (because community leaders in the know kept the information to themselves); the accusers were exhorted to be silent. And Kolko, like Mondrowitz, was a rabbi. Both men were accused of violating a sacred trust. Yet decades had gone by, and no tangible steps had been taken to bring either of them to justice.

People simply weren't going to stand for that sort of pattern anymore.

I turned to the Jewish media. I turned to politicians, carefully climbing a ladder of contacts toward New York's governor — with eventual results.

But I knew I needed public support, and the best way to harness it seemed to be through blogs, the most democratic of today's grassroots media. Though not a keen blogger myself, I had come to appreciate what blogs can do: they had enabled me to find important contacts; and they can bring together people linked only by their interest in a common subject. Blogs are particularly valuable in the Orthodox Jewish community because the anonymity they offer protects individuals from public shaming if they broach a taboo subject — like child sex abuse.

Now I used every contact I had, including blogs, to encourage a campaign of letters, e-mails, and phone calls to the office of the district attorney. I urged a simple and strong message: it was time for justice in the Avrohom Mondrowitz case. Stefan Colmer's pending extradition proved the Israeli government would respond favorably if only U.S. authorities did their part. The redefinition of rape by Israel in 1988, and now the new extradition treaty, had removed any possible doubt. The D.A.'s stated worries about "retroactivity" were nonsense; and, perhaps most important of all, the community's attitudes had changed — the old advisers who had counseled against prosecuting Mondrowitz no longer spoke for the rank and file of Brooklyn's Orthodox Jews. To one of many Jews who wrote to the D.A., I offered thanks and encouragement by letter: "If our community speaks out publicly, in firm and unequivocal language, demanding that Mondrowitz — an indicted felon many times over — be brought back to Brooklyn for trial, it will be difficult for the D.A. to ignore us. . . . Only the old politics of looking the other way stands in our path."

I do not know how many messages and calls were generated by these efforts. I believe the number was large. At any rate, I know that the timing was right. All my efforts had finally coalesced. Alleged victims were clamoring for justice; a growing body of press coverage was increasingly critical of Hynes; the law was firmly on my side; an angry public was demanding the revival of the Mondrowitz case. All I seemed to need was one last push to set the indicted rabbi on an irrevocable path that would lead to his arrest and, eventually, his return to Brooklyn, his victims, and a criminal trial — now twenty-three years overdue.

Just one push.

In fact, I got more than one.

THE ARREST

I had not ignored New York State politicians during the long campaign. When I first learned about Mondrowitz in 1997, I had consulted Jeremiah McKenna, former chief counsel for the New York State Senate's Committee on Crime and Correction, who was highly sympathetic. Ten years later, in October 2007, Dr. Neustein and I had written to Eliot Spitzer, then New York's attorney general, urging the appointment of a special prosecutor to pursue the Mondrowitz case. Citing New York statutes and case law, we argued that the district attorney's inaction on Mondrowitz — and other, similar cases — necessitated special action to ensure that the guilty were brought to justice. Then Spitzer was elected New York's governor, and yet another strange windfall dropped into my lap.

In late January, as I was investigating the Colmer sex abuse case, and just before Colmer decided to follow Mondrowitz's escape route to Israel, I got a tip about material on a computer hard drive, one that had allegedly been copied from Mondrowitz's own, which the source of the tip thought would interest me. Through a series of maneuvers and inquiries too complicated to repeat here, I verified that this material probably was what the source said it was. And yes — I was interested. After a Sunday-night pickup of an unlabeled package from a night guard at a designated Manhattan building (the source insisted on the greatest secrecy), I was in possession of the hard drive.

Immediately afterward, I invited a team from ABC to my Passaic house to review the drive's contents with me. Based on what I had been told of the provenance of the hard drive and the contents we were able to view over the next few hours, the technical expert ABC had sent along with its reporters pronounced it "almost certainly" a genuine copy of the contents of Mondrowitz's own computer.

And what I found on the drive (in a search taped by ABC's cameraman) made all the maneuvers worthwhile. Because, together with considerable evidence that Mondrowitz had been supporting himself by selling phony diplomas, the drive contained some hard-core child pornography. This did more than refute Mondrowitz's prior claims that he had no sexual interest in children:[33] since the downloading and possession of child porn is a criminal offense in Israel, the new evidence suggested that Mondrowitz had violated Israeli law, quite apart from the charges still awaiting him in Brooklyn.

I was hesitant to publicize this, because I knew that if Mondrowitz learned about the copying of his computer drive, he was likely to destroy or abandon his computer — and with it, the best evidence police would have of the full extent of his activities. Still, I believed — and I told ABC's reporters — that this discovery brought us another step closer to bringing Mondrowitz to justice.

I had a plan.

After a series of telephone calls to federal authorities, who (as I had expected) said there was nothing they could do about evidence of a crime in Israel, I drafted with Dr. Neustein a second letter to Eliot Spitzer. As New York's attorney general, he had received our earlier letter about the gravity of the Mondrowitz case. Now, as governor, he was New York's top administrative officer. So in February 2007 we wrote to him again — this time, first turning to Judge Sam Coleman (a former state assemblyman of long standing and considerable influence in New York's Democratic Party) to act as intermediary between us and Spitzer's Albany office. Our letter described the new evidence I had reviewed, and argued that renewing the extradition request for

Mondrowitz would not only serve the victims but would be a political benefit to all concerned:

> This accomplishment [bringing Mondrowitz back for trial] would be welcomed and applauded by the citizens of New York and the hundreds of families of Mondrowitz's victims, not to mention the national and international audience of the coverage ABC News intends to give this process. It should be noted that Israel ordered (and Israel's High Court of Justice approved) the extradition of Zeev Rozenstein to the United States last year, and that Israel is not likely to wish to protect a non-citizen caught red-handed with child pornography. Therefore, this new evidence is of great importance toward achieving a significant victory for justice in this case. . . .

My hunch was that the embattled Spitzer — he was already at odds with the legislature when I drafted the letter, and things only got worse in the months that followed — would be looking for an issue that allowed him to regain the heroic aura he had worn as a prosecutor. My hopes were raised when, in April, I learned that Spitzer's office had taken the matter up with the Brooklyn district attorney. In fact, that was one of the reasons for the timing of the public campaign I encouraged that summer.

And again, the effort seemed to pay off. In September, at long last, U.S. authorities reversed their long-standing aloofness to the Mondrowitz case and presented Israel with a new formal request for Mondrowitz's extradition to stand trial in Brooklyn. The news wasn't made public until October[34] — and the exact date of Hynes's renewal of his predecessor's request for action to federal authorities remains unclear.[35]

But it was done. Irrevocably done. As I had told Mordechai when we made that first trip into the D.A.'s office, "There's no going back."

Reaction on blogs like "The Unorthodox Jew" was stunned and ecstatic. Hundreds of comments appeared on the blog before the ink was dry on the first news reports. "Tell me I'm not dreaming," one man wrote. Hundreds upon hundreds more tumbled in over the next few days. My e-mail inbox was also busy: alleged victims wrote to me, hopeful at last after decades of cynicism. Newspapers in Israel, the United States, and then around the world began carrying the story.

Even the *New York Times* got into the act. In June 2006, after presenting Mordechai's complaint, I had discussed the story at some length with a *Times* reporter, who bluntly told me the Gray Lady wouldn't print anything about Mondrowitz until there was an official change of policy on the case. At the time — despite all my determination to succeed — that had sounded like a very distant goal. But now the goal was ours, and on November 16, the *Times* weighed in with its first reference to Avrohom Mondrowitz in almost twenty-three years. Reporter Tina Kelley quoted one of my clients, who spoke about "the pain and torture" he had endured "on a daily basis . . . knowing that this monster is still out there among children"; she also quoted Rabbi Mark Dratch, who confirmed that "social pressure in the community" had allowed Mondrowitz "to continue his activities for a while and escape the jurisdiction." But I was proud to be given the last words:

> I want it [this case] to be an example of what it looks like when you do try to sweep something under the rug, and 23 years later it comes back from the dead. . . . Had we looked at this kind of case differently to begin with, and said, "Let's go to the police and stop this man as soon as we can," how many of these men wouldn't be victims at all?[36]

Still, all was not well. An extradition request had been made for Rabbi Mondrowitz; but why hadn't he been arrested? Had U.S. authorities not asked for this obvious precaution, as they had in Colmer's case? Was political pressure being brought to bear on the Israeli government to let Mondrowitz get away?

Press coverage had always driven the Mondrowitz story forward, and I knew this crucial moment was no exception. Fortunately, at this moment one of my underground contacts brought the Mondrowitz story to a sharp-witted reporter, Aviva Lori, at *Ha-aretz*, Israel's most prestigious newspaper. Ms. Lori devoured the facts. She interviewed several of my clients; one even traveled to Israel just to tell his story in person. I also shared with her the evidence of Mondrowitz's long devotion to child pornography. (Apparently, Israeli police had already raided Mondrowitz's apartment for evidence, though to this day he has not been charged with violating Israel's child pornography laws.)

Ms. Lori's feature-length article appeared as the cover story in *Ha-aretz's* magazine on November 15, and it was a blistering exposé. She quoted retired Detective Pat Kehoe as saying, "That man should have been in prison for the past 23 years," and stated that Israel's police, who had left Mondrowitz at large, nevertheless believed that he was "devoting most of his energy" to Internet porn, where "he gratifies his deviant inclinations by watching clips of sadistic activity and pedophilic material." She pointed out that Mondrowitz had actually held at least one teaching position in Israel. Finally, she stressed that while the rabbi had lived undisturbed in Jerusalem, "Mondrowitz's victims [had] organized and, through Lesher, put pressure on the DA's office" to revive the case.[37] Ms. Lori's article, I knew, would enrage Israelis and would ensure that authorities in Israel, not just Hynes, would be feeling pressure to act.

At the same time, working with my most reliable allies, including Dr. Neustein, I hastily assembled a press conference at the Manhattan office of Michael Wildes, the mayor of Englewood, New Jersey, who had taken an interest in the case. Our goal was to send an unmistakable message to all concerned that special treatment for Mondrowitz would not be tolerated. We arranged for the conference to take place on Friday, November 16, the day the *Times* article appeared.

But on the very morning of the event, I got a tip from Israel that our long wait was over. It seemed our activism and the new *Ha-aretz* story had done the job; at any rate, Israeli officials had finally acted. I confirmed with a spokesperson for the Ministry of Justice that Mondrowitz had been arrested, early that morning, in deference to the United States' pending extradition request. At long last, justice was on the way.

Even then, as if the spirit of denial that had always haunted this case couldn't help but to reassert itself, all did not go smoothly. A prominent rabbi who had promised to attend the press conference backed out at the last minute; a leading member of an Orthodox organization called Mayor Wildes the morning of the event, suggesting that he call it off. But with a little diplomacy, the other participants and I managed to keep everything on schedule.

It was all I could do to control my emotions when I announced to TV cameras and reporters (from Jewish papers and New York City tabloids alike), that Avrohom Mondrowitz was finally in custody. It was a complex moment. My happiness was edged with grief over how much the lost time had hurt my clients, and so many others. Knowing that one "alleged victim" of Mondrowitz had killed himself only a year earlier, after expressing despair that the rabbi would ever be brought to justice (God, did I move too slowly?), I said that this was not a time to celebrate. On the other hand, I had to express my gratitude, and I did it freely: to victims who had had the courage to come forward and to expose their pain . . . to all those who had supported them . . . and to the God of justice, who, I said, had never abandoned us.

I knew there was still plenty of work ahead. Already, money was being raised in Israel for Mondrowitz's legal defense; members of his Hasidic community were telling reporters that the rabbi was a victim of slander. He would fight extradition until the last possible moment. And once in New York, who knew what sort of influence he and his defenders might still have on the justice system?

But the seemingly impossible was now in our grasp. Mondrowitz was behind bars, and the legal systems of two countries were now working with methodical doggedness to bring him back to Brooklyn to face his accusers in a courtroom.

It was a Friday, the eve of the Jewish Sabbath. After the press conference I hurried home to help ready the house for the approaching holiday, and during the cooking and dusting and laundry, with the sun nearly at the horizon, the phone rang.

"Is it true?" said a hoarse, unfamiliar voice from the receiver. "He's in jail?"

"You mean Avrohom Mondrowitz? Yes, he's in jail."

I waited for the caller to identify himself, but he didn't. I wasn't surprised; I frequently got such calls from people who knew about my work on Mondrowitz. They often didn't say who they were. It didn't much matter. I knew why they called.

I heard him breathing a few seconds, and then he asked, "Are you sure they won't let him out for Shabbos?"

"They didn't. It's already Shabbos there. In fact" — I glanced at the clock — "in fact, it's close to midnight in Jerusalem." And suddenly, out of all the facts I had accumulated about Mondrowitz over the years, a strange one rose and struck me. "In an hour he'll be sixty. This Shabbos is his birthday."

"His birthday? You're kidding me."

I assured him I wasn't.

"And he's locked up?"

"Yes."

There was another brief silence. Then his voice was louder than before. "Listen, you don't know me, but I know who you are. When you get that bastard back, you tell him. All right? Tell him for all the people he ruined the lives of, how much we liked giving him this present for his birthday. And you tell him — have many, many more! You hear me? Lots more birthdays locked up in jail, Rabbi." He was shouting now. "You tell him!"

I wanted to say I would do my best. But the connection was dead.

As of this writing, Rabbi Mondrowitz remains in custody in Jerusalem. He has not yet been tried, though his actual extradition to New York and his prosecution in Brooklyn now seem all but inevitable. He has attempted to have his bail reduced; other Hasidim have offered the use of their homes for a form of house arrest. But the Israeli judges have been unmoved by their pleas. Mondrowitz's legal arguments against extradition were rejected by a Jerusalem court in February 2008; his final appeal to Israel's Supreme Court is still pending, but Israeli prosecutors appear confident that the high court will uphold the ruling below, meaning that Mondrowitz will soon be on his way to an U.S. jail and to a criminal trial.

That has not ended my work on the case. Now my greatest concern, paradoxically enough, is that Mondrowitz should not take all the blame for the harm he caused. Do not misunderstand me: if anyone deserves to be punished, it is Avrohom Mondrowitz. Granting that pedophilia is a disorder, and that Mondrowitz may suffer from a sex addiction, the fact remains that over all the years of his alleged abuse, he never took the most modest steps toward recovery. He never even admitted there was anything wrong with him, let alone separated himself from children. On the contrary, given the smallest opportunity, he went out of his way to seek out the greatest number of potential victims. And in more than two decades since being publicly charged, he has maintained his claim of innocence, mocked his alleged victims, and continued to court positions that could bring him into contact with young boys. The child rapes of which he is accused are among the most unforgivable of crimes. The rabbi who could do such things to boys entrusted to his care, without a trace of remorse, is the very worst sort of criminal; he deserves no sympathy.

But I don't believe he is the only one at fault. Many others could have stopped him long before that first call to the police in November 1984. Their refusal to do so makes them, morally at least, accessories in Mondrowitz's alleged crimes.

Evidence of this kind of guilt continues to accumulate. Let me mention one unusually dramatic instance. In 2000, among the FOIA documents I received from the federal government on the Mondrowitz case, was a copy of a police report in which the name of a child witness had been accidentally included. (Normally such information is removed for privacy reasons.) Naturally, I kept the witness's name to myself. But I also tried discreetly, in every way I could think of, to locate him with the goal of seeing if he would share any information with me. My efforts never bore fruit.

But one day in 2008, out of the blue, the man himself (for by now he was in his thirties) wrote me an e-mail and offered to see me in my office. He had read about Mondrowitz's arrest and said he had some things to share with me.

"I've been waiting to meet you for eight years," I told him, rather to his astonishment, even before we laid eyes on one another.

Like all the other "alleged victims" of Mondrowitz I have met, he was an Orthodox Jew. Yes, he had witnessed Mondrowitz sexually abusing another boy; yes, he had been a victim himself, he told me. He had not spoken to police until after Mondrowitz fled the country, and his parents had refused to allow him before a grand jury, so his complaints had not been included in the indictment.

His continuing trauma — he told me he was still in therapy for the effects of what Mondrowitz had done to him — was evident in his trembling voice, his anxious gestures as he spoke (especially when, at his request, I showed him the prosecutors' report on which his name appeared). But he had a bit of information that left me breathless with outrage. He said that he had known yet another alleged victim of Mondrowitz. And this boy had been a foster child in the care of Ohel Children's Home, the Orthodox-run foster care facility located in the heart of Borough Park. Ohel was among the Brooklyn Jewish community's most valued institutions. He said that this boy had complained publicly of being abused by Mondrowitz, but that no one had listened to him.

Years earlier, retired policeman Sal Catalfumo had said the same thing — Ohel had sent children to Mondrowitz for "therapy," Mondrowitz abused them, the children complained, the agency "swept [it] under the rug" — but Ohel's spokesman, Gerald McKelvey, and its executive director, David Mandel, had both laughed off the charge.[38] But now I had additional evidence supporting Catalfumo's accusation and, even more than that, I had a lead to someone who could confirm it firsthand.

This isn't the only such fact I've uncovered: sources have shared evidence with me that Ohel — and some prominent rabbis — had reports of Mondrowitz's abuse of children at least two years before anyone called the police. The public confirmation of such things would make an already ugly story even more abominable. Perhaps this confirmation will occur when Mondrowitz comes to trial . . . perhaps even sooner. The flow of information continues. Today, there is no suppressing the truth about Mondrowitz.

Not that no one has tried. Just weeks after Mondrowitz's arrest, I got a call from an assistant U.S. attorney named Harvey Bartle IV in Newark, New Jersey, who told me in no uncertain terms that he and the FBI wanted to take possession of the material copied from Mondrowitz's computer — the same stuff I had shown to ABC in January and had kept carefully stowed away ever since. Since Bartle was able to quote from my letter to Governor Spitzer — which had been forwarded to D.A. Hynes — it was obvious that Hynes must have spurred this new demand; and, in fact, Bartle did not deny this when I asked him about it.

I had no objection to having the FBI review the purported contents of Mondrowitz's computer — on the contrary, I was very eager to have experts determine the full extent of Mondrowitz's use of child pornography. But I thought it odd that Bartle insisted so strenuously on having my only copy, when another copy of the material I had would have served him equally well. My suspicions grew when he responded to my offer to have his agents copy "my" hard drive — which I would thereafter keep under lock and key — with bluster, vague threats, and accusations that I was interfering with the law. I pointed out that the federal government had been aware of my possession of the hard drive for nearly ten months (I had kept a detailed log of my actions and telephone contacts at the time I obtained the drive), and not one federal official I had spoken to had expressed the slightest interest in the material until *after* it had been mentioned in an Israeli newspaper. Since Bartle had clearly been unleashed by Hynes, I asked him what guarantees my clients had that he and his agents weren't simply taking this evidence out of my hands to cover up revelations that could further embarrass the D.A.

Given my experience in the Mondrowitz case, I was disappointed, but not surprised, when Bartle refused to answer that question — and when he went on, in an exchange of letters, to persistently misstate facts, to threaten me (as if *I* were the wanted fugitive), and to swear to the heavens that he was doing his level best to investigate Mondrowitz and that I was "impeding" his efforts. I finally agreed to turn over the hard drive to FBI agents — without keeping a copy — in exchange for a written promise that the hard drive would be examined promptly and thoroughly, that it would be returned to me (with any actual child pornography having been removed), and that child porn images would be retained by the government for the future use of my clients, if necessary. Two FBI agents duly came to my house on December 17, 2007, and took the hard drive with them. Since then, to the best of my knowledge after repeated inquiries, no investigation has ever been conducted, and nothing has been returned to me. I leave the reader to decide whether my suspicions of Bartle's motives, and of Hynes's, were justified.

Then there are the rabbis who pay lip service to sex abuse victims but shy away from practical steps to bring their attackers to justice. One rabbi who says he knows many alleged victims of Mondrowitz refused to put them in contact with me, fearing that if a well-publicized Mondrowitz trial actually occurs, "People will say, 'The rabbis are homosexuals.'" When he agreed to make those contacts for me on condition that a certain prominent rabbi instruct him to, I spoke to that rabbi — one of America's foremost Orthodox authorities — by telephone, more than once, and found him unwilling even to give the say-so I needed. He, too, suggested that a Mondrowitz trial would embarrass the community and would do nothing for the alleged victims. (In contrast, this same rabbi has given a passionate public interview on the evils of the Internet. How anyone can call the possible exposure of teenagers to ordinary pornography "a tragedy" and then suggest that prosecuting and jailing someone who allegedly raped little boys isn't a great idea, is more than I will ever understand.)

But whatever the continuing resistance, I no longer doubt that Mondrowitz's alleged victims — and the truth — are well on the way to victory. And, of course, that means victory not only for them but for all Jewish children who must face the reality, or the future risk, of sexual abuse by a rabbi.

To tell the truth, I've been sure of that ever since November 22, 2007. On that date — six days after Mondrowitz's arrest and almost twenty-three years to the day after the first phone call from an alleged Mondrowitz victim to the Brooklyn police — the Brooklyn-based *Jewish Press*, the largest and most influential Orthodox Jewish newspaper in America, made its first mention of Avrohom Mondrowitz.

In a prominent editorial, no less, the *Jewish Press* acknowledged that "the charges lodged against him [Mondrowitz] were of the most horrific nature, and it is inconceivable that he should not be required to answer for them in a court of law."

But even more than that, the editors called for

a new, more honest approach to the very real problem of pedophilia and abuse in the Orthodox community. We must avail ourselves of all legitimate resources — which would include intra-community counseling as well as unhesitating resort to secular law-enforcement authorities. Our children deserve no less.[39]

I, my clients, and all those who have shared in the struggle to bring justice to bear on the case of Rabbi Avrohom Mondrowitz, could only answer, "Amen."

NOTES

1. The term "love-bombing" is commonly used by cult critics to describe a manipulative practice where "love" and "affection" are deliberately and exaggeratively displayed by cults toward unsuspecting individuals for the sole pupose of recruiting them as new members of the cult.

2. See "Prosecutors Seek Extradition of Rabbi in '84 Sex Abuse Case," reported by N. J. Burkett, ABC's *Eyewitness News* (New York), November 16, 2007; Anthony Weiss, "Alleged Pedophile Held in Israeli Prison after Extradition Request from Brooklyn," *Forward*, November 21, 2007; Robert Wiener, "Activists Welcome Suspect's Extradition," *New Jersey Jewish News*, November 22, 2007.

3. Tina Kelley, "After 22 Years, a Child Abuse Suspect's Extradition is Sought," *New York Times*, November 16, 2007, p. B4.

4. As this book goes to press, Mondrowitz is still awaiting a ruling by Israel's Supreme Court on his final challenge to his extradition. See Matthew Kalman and Dave Goldiner, "Accused Perv Rabbi Loses Extradition Battle," Daily News, February 11, 2008, p. 22.

5. See Mike McAlary, "Community Cover-ups again Lead to Tragedy," *New York Post*, November 14, 1990, pp. 5, 25. The same facts were repeated later: "Conspiracy of Silence: Child Sex Abuse Case Still Haunts," reported by Cynthia McFadden, *Nightline*, October 11, 2006.

6. Staff Report, "Child Counselor in Brooklyn Is Charged with Abusing Boy," *New York Times*, December 10, 1984.

7. See Lea Levavi, "Sexual Assault Suspect Doesn't Have AIDS Virus," *Jerusalem Post*, March 22, 1987; Dan Izenberg, "Israel Orders Extradition of Self-Styled U.S. Rabbi," Associated Press, March 18, 1987. These articles contain some errors: for example, Israel did not order Mondrowitz's extradition (or deportation) in 1987, and would not for another twenty years. Mondrowitz did test negative for AIDS in 1987; he and his lawyer used that test as if it proved his innocence of sexual abuse, which of course it did not.

8. Izenberg, "Israel Orders Extradition of Self-Styled U.S. Rabbi."

9. Ibid.; staff report, "The World," *Los Angeles Times*, March 20, 1987.

10. See Gitelle Rapoport, "Advisory Council Gives Brooklyn Communities Clout,"

Jewish Week, June 8, 1990, p. 7; statement by Jewish Advisory Council of D.A. Charles Hynes, *Jewish Press,* May 25, 1990, p. 18B; Steve K. Walz, "B'klyn D.A. Hynes Makes an Effort to 'Humanize' the Legal Process: Reaching Out to Jews is Key Element," *Jewish Press,* March 29, 1991, p. 38.

11. Mishnah, *Aboth* 2:6.

12. Copies of all documents referred to here, unless otherwise specified, were obtained by the author from requests made under the Freedom of Information Act and New York's Freedom of Information Law, and are in the author's possession.

13. Stephanie Saul, "Tripping Up the Prosecution," *Newsday,* May 29, 2003, p. A6.

14. My work on behalf of child sex abuse victims and my criticism of the Brooklyn district attorney for his handling of such cases in the Jewish community had already been mentioned in the press. See Karen Matthews, "Orthodox Jews Have Faced Abuse Scandals As Well," Associated Press, April 16, 2002. Soon after its publication over the wires, Matthews' AP story was published in a host of local papers in cities such as Dallas, Seattle, Indianapolis, Sacramento, and London, England.

15. Transcript labeled, "Conference Inv #11558," of "Life is for Living," WEVD, a copy of which is in the author's possession.

16. Rabbi Auerbach (as the name is usually spelled) died in 1995. A letter from him, generally confirming Mondrowitz's claim, has allegedly been reviewed by two sources, who in turn communicated the contents to me. I am still attempting to obtain the documentation myself.

17. E-mails from Avrohom Mondrowitz to the author, February 20, 2003.

18. See chapter 8.

19. Robert Kolker, "On the Rabbi's Knee: Do the Orthodox Jews Have a Catholic-Priest Problem?" *New York,* May 22, 2006, pp. 28–33, 102–103.

20. Avi Shafran, "A Matter of Orthodox Abuse," *Jewish Week,* June 23, 2006.

21. *New York,* May 29, 2006, letters.

22. Saul, "Tripping Up the Prosecution."

23. Philip Messing, "'Rabbi' Rousers: '80s victims want 'perv' extradited," *New York Post,* July 25, 2006, p. 20.

24. Kristen Lombardi, "Silence of the Lam," *Village Voice,* July 25, 2006, pp. 26–34.

25. Nathaniel Popper, "Victims Press Brooklyn D.A. to Seek Abuse Suspect's Extradition from Israel," *Forward,* July 28, 2006, pp. 1, 7.

26. Jennifer Friedlin, "Hynes Mum on Mondrowitz," *Jewish Week,* October 20, 2006, p. 3.

27. "Did an Alleged Sex Abuser Escape Justice?" reported by Sarah Wallace, Channel 7 Eyewitness News at 11 P.M. (WABC-TV New York), November 8, 2006.

28. Popper, "Victims Press Brooklyn D.A."

29. "Conspiracy of Silence," reported by McFadden.

30. See Philip Messing, "Israel nabs B'klyn sex 'predator,'" *New York Post,* June 15, 2007, p. 24.

31. Matthew Kalman (with Nancie L. Katz), "Israel OKs Extradition of Brooklyn Pedophile Suspect," *Daily News*, November 12, 2007, p. 14.

32. Personal communications with the author from April–May 2007.

33. David Mould, [no title], United Press International, March 19, 1987. The UPI story was immediately picked up by the *New York Post* and several Israeli newspapers.

34. Nancie L. Katz, "Israel Asked to Extradite Fugitive Rabbi," *Daily News*, October 11, 2007, p. 30 (note that this first report of the renewed extradition request came one year, to the day, after the *Nightline* broadcast); Matthew Wagner, "US Wants Extradition of Prominent Ger Hassid Accused of Sodomy," *Jerusalem Post*, October 23, 2007.

35. The author has sought this information by means of formal requests addressed to the district attorney, the Justice Department, and the State Department. So far all three agencies have refused to release any of the documents requested, though at least some of the documents — including those comprised in the formal extradition process — are clearly matters of public record. Administrative appeals are now in process.

36. Kelley, "22 Years Later."

37. Aviva Lori, "In the Basement, Behind a Closed Door," *Ha-aretz* (magazine), November 15, 2007.

38. Douglas Montero, "Victims Learn Kid-Sex Fiend Served No Time," *New York Post*, September 21, 1999, pp. 2–3. The article, prominent enough to be mentioned on the issue's front-page banner, describes another case in which Ohel allegedly failed to protect children from a sex abuser.

39. Editorial Staff, "Justice Delayed — and Possibly Denied," *Jewish Press*, November 22, 2007.

BARBARA BLAINE

My Cross to Bear

How I Challenged the Catholic Church
Hierarchy to Atone for Their Sins against
Me and Other Abuse Victims

*Whoso shall offend one of these little ones which believe
in me, it were better for him that a millstone were hanged
about his neck, and that he were drowned in the depth
of the sea. . . . It must needs be that offences come; but
woe to that man by whom the offence cometh!*
— Matthew 18:6–7

THE BEGINNINGS OF SNAP

SNAP — the Survivors Network of those Abused by Priests
— is the nation's largest, oldest and most active self-help group for clergy sex
abuse victims, whether assaulted by ministers, priests, nuns or rabbis. For
nineteen years, we have been an independent, confidential, safe place for
wounded men and women to be listened to, supported and healed. Our group
works tirelessly to achieve two goals: to heal the wounded and to protect the
vulnerable. We have more than nine thousand members. Support groups
meet in over sixty cities.

But it all began with one person, twenty years ago.

I founded SNAP in 1988, after years of pain, depression and shame, followed by more years of therapy and support groups. Even today my personal
story is hard for me to tell.

I was sexually abused as a child in Toledo, Ohio, by a priest who taught in
the Catholic school I attended and officiated at the church I prayed in. Father
Chet Warren began abusing me during the summer between my seventh and

eighth grades. Father Warren had chosen me as one of about a dozen girls (he called us "deaconettes") to help with church functions. One evening, when I had helped clean up after a ceremony, he invited me to the rectory for dinner, where he ate with other priests. When the other priests left and we were alone, he closed the curtains and began telling me about "feelings" he claimed I had for him. I had no idea what he was talking about. I was confused and scared when he began kissing and fondling me, reaching into my dress. While he did this, Father Warren pointed to his groin and said, "Look, this is what you do to me." I was so naïve I didn't understand that he was pointing to his erection. Still, I felt ashamed and dirty. He said that I shouldn't tell anyone because no one else would understand. He said he knew that I was closer to Jesus than the other kids. That was why he had chosen me.

After that, he abused me three or four times a week — probably hundreds of times in all. I knew that what was happening was bad. But I assumed it was something that I had caused. I was a bad girl. Father Warren insisted I go to confession to tell of my sins — including what happened between him and me — and seek forgiveness. He led me to believe that somehow it was all my fault. At the same time (and adding to my horrible confusion and pain) he claimed his treatment of me was a "sacrament" blessed by God, that it would be wrong for other people but not for the two of us, because we were so "close to God." (On the other hand, he cautioned me to confess only to a priest who didn't know either of us.) I couldn't question or challenge him: he was a priest. I had been taught that priests were closer to God than the rest of us. As for me — I didn't believe that God could ever forgive me for tempting a good priest and making him sin.

I was not able to speak about the abuse until I was well into adulthood. In 1985, at the age of twenty-nine, I went to Toledo's bishop, and to the provincial of Father Warren's own religious community, seeking their help. I asked them to help me find healing, and to ensure that Father Warren didn't abuse any more children, but my pleas for help fell upon deaf ears. I became frustrated by the lack of help from church officials and their lack of understanding of the lifelong damage caused by sexual abuse. They had made so many empty promises and I tired of trying to get them to do anything to help me or to protect others from Warren.

At the same time, I was attending a self-help support group for women abused as children. The group gave me both a much-needed sense of hope and practical suggestions on coping with the awful pain that engulfed my world. Still, while the women's support group was helpful, I felt as though I didn't quite fit in. No one else in the group had been abused by a clergyman. I realized then that if these women could help each other heal, survivors of abuse by priests could help each other, too.

SNAP was born of this idea.

It was the best way I knew to lighten the burden of the debilitating pain crushing my life.

I figured that it would not be difficult to find all the survivors of abuse by priests. I reasoned that all Catholics read Catholic periodicals and would see an ad placed in one of them. I also believed, back then, that there couldn't be too many survivors to find.

So I began by contacting the attorneys representing victims, the reporters writing about victims and the prosecutors pursuing cases against clergy. Each time I saw an article about sexual abuse committed by a priest, I contacted the reporter who wrote the story as well as any attorney mentioned in the article. I asked to be put in contact with the victims. Many ignored my requests, but just as many responded. I spoke to other victims on the phone. We found encouragement in the knowledge that we were not alone. That was the beginning of SNAP.

By the middle of 1988, I knew of about two dozen victims. We communicated mostly by phone. Some victims wished to remain anonymous, but everyone wanted support and information. It wasn't long before I found myself linking survivors with others who had similar stories. Some of those stories were amazing. I can recall my shock when a victim told me a priest first molested him in the confessional. A few months later, a second person told about being abused in confession. Not knowing what to do to help, I merely told the second survivor that he wasn't alone and asked if he wanted me to give his name and number to the first survivor who had told me about similar abuse. He said yes, and that was the beginning of networking among survivors that continues to this day.

Jason Berry, the gentle and persistent journalist and author, generously responded to my requests to be connected with other victims. He gave my name and contact information to several victims; they became the first members of SNAP. Berry was the first reporter to cover sexual abuse by priests. His family lived in the town where a few courageous parents of victims brought civil lawsuits against a predatory priest who hurt their children and the hierarchy who covered up for him. Berry was extremely sensitive and seemed to understand why victims like me waited so long to come forward and report our abuse. He was shocked by what he had uncovered in Lafayette, Louisiana. Church officials had knowingly, repeatedly transferred predator priest Gilbert Gauthe, who had abused dozens of children, to new parish assignments, thus giving him access to more children.[1]

To help enable more survivors to find one another, Jason Berry kindly gave my name to TV talk-show producers who were doing segments about sexual abuse by priests. Berry told them I was articulate and credible. It was at his recommendation that several shows invited me to participate.

The first talk show I appeared on was *Geraldo*. The producers arranged for me to fly to New York, but didn't offer to put me up at a hotel. During the filming, I exposed all my vulnerabilities and was then attacked by an insensitive, ignorant audience and a host who clearly did not intend to honor or respect my story. Afterward, to make matters worse, he thanked me for being his guest with a kiss. I went outside and stood alone on a street corner in Manhattan and sobbed.

The other guests were picked up in limousines and shuttled to a hotel. I took a subway across town to a convent in the Bronx, because a sympathetic nun had agreed to let me spend the night. As I rode on the subway, tears wouldn't stop running down my cheeks. I decided I would never appear on a talk show again. I would never allow myself to be as humiliated and misjudged as I had been on that show.

When the show aired two weeks later, the producers, as they had promised, posted SNAP's mailing address on-screen so that people could write to us. In the following week I received a dozen letters, most from new survivors. I was moved by the stories in those letters, and spoke on the phone with the survivors and family members who had written them. I realized then that the emotional price I had paid to get SNAP's name and address to a larger public was well worth it. I made a new commitment never to turn down a chance to promote our organization.

As I reached out to other survivors, the movement grew. I exchanged many letters and had countless telephone conversations with survivors across the country. We were surprised that our stories were so similar. We were surprised that we were each experiencing so much pain as a result of our childhood abuse. We were surprised at the power the pain still had over our lives. We were each living separate lives and most of us had never told anyone about our abuse. Over time, we gained trust in each other and began to share our vulnerabilities. It was remarkable how each of us felt so dirty, guilty and ashamed. We each wanted, more than anything, to find a way to stop the pain in our lives. We wanted quick and miraculous healing. We were too naïve to realize how many hard lessons lay ahead.

SNAP SUPPORT GROUPS

By early 1989, several survivors had struck up friendships and held regular telephone conversations and exchanged letters. For most of us, discussing our abuse and the problems we had faced as adults became a lifeline. We found it safe to tell secrets and to share hurts that most of us had kept buried for decades. Most of us had planned to take these things to our graves, never telling anyone. It was liberating to talk with other survivors over the phone. We felt it would be even more helpful for us to do so in person. We thought that if we could hold a weekend-long gathering, that would allow enough time to sort everything out.

A few were fearful of losing anonymity by attending such a meeting, but the hope of healing enabled everyone to overcome that fear. A survivor from New Mexico, Alice McCormick, agreed to help organize that first meeting. We decided we didn't need experts and would follow a self-help model for our meeting. Since McCormick was a therapist and I was a social worker, we would couple our knowledge with our experience of surviving sexual abuse by priests. We decided to hold the event in Chicago, picked a hotel and set the date. We invited everyone on our mailing list, about fifty people in all. Jean Hughes, a Dominican nun who worked at Eighth Day Center for Justice, agreed to help with the legwork. Jean helped to design a small ad and paid for running it a few times in a national weekly Catholic paper. Jean also helped organize a news conference to announce the gathering.

About twenty people showed up that Friday evening at the Holiday Inn in Chicago for the very first SNAP gathering. It was fall 1991. We were all nervous. Several people apologized for not dressing up; others apologized for dressing too formally. We all agreed that had we been attending a funeral or a sports event we would have known how to dress. We laughed. None of us knew the dress code for a support group for victims of abuse by priests. Something like this had never existed before!

That evening we met for over three hours without a break. We spent the time introducing ourselves, telling where we were from and sharing our stories of abuse. As each person spoke, we experienced both consolation and affirmation. I thought it amazing that someone from a different state, and from such a different background, could so eloquently articulate my own experience and pain. Many of our stories were similar. By the time the evening was over, most of us felt we truly belonged in the group. For many of us, it was the first time since childhood we had had such a feeling of belonging. In spite of the tears that most participants shed and the gripping pain expressed by several, we were all grateful we had attended.

When we gathered on Saturday morning more victims arrived, having seen the news reports Friday evening. Each was given the opportunity to share his or her story. Bonds of support and friendship were formed. That weekend we heard speakers discuss the psychological impact of abuse and different coping mechanisms. We engaged in art therapy and learned about our legal rights. It became obvious we were all committed to working toward healing. By Sunday morning, when we began our discussions about the future, it was clear that our healing would not be found in one weekend. This was the beginning, not the end.

Before we left Chicago we had commitments to hold gatherings in San Francisco, Philadelphia and Boston. We recognized that we were beginning an important movement. I made the commitment to create a newsletter for our members and to start working on it as soon as I could recover from the emotionally taxing weekend. Although I was exhausted, I was exhilarated as well. The gathering had created feelings of affirmation and friendship.

I wasn't the only one with such feelings. Participants reported that it was "earthshaking," "revolutionary." "The first time in my life I felt like I belonged," someone said; and, "It gave me hope"; "I am amazed that others experienced the same things I did, I always thought I was the only one"; "I never imagined there were others, too." Movingly, one woman promised not to commit suicide because of the friendships she'd formed with members of the group.

The next gathering took place on February 21, 1992, at a Holiday Inn in San Francisco. Many commitments for organizing the event had fallen through. I was frustrated because we didn't have the guest speakers I had hoped for, and a great deal of the preparations weren't done. I feared that the participants would be sorely disappointed. I was mistaken.

In fact, everyone who attended thought that second gathering was a great success. It became clear to me then that what survivors really needed was each other. The speeches were not nearly as important as the opportunity for survivors to meet other survivors. Listening to each other was more important than listening to an expert.

I was concerned about one participant at the gathering, David Clohessy, who spoke very little and could not stop crying. Eventually, he convinced me that he was all right and insisted the gathering was "terrific." I had no inkling at the time that he would become so significant to SNAP and the survivor movement, as well as a lifelong colleague and friend.

David was raised in the diocese of Jefferson City, Missouri, one of six children in a large Catholic family. Like many survivors, he was raised by devout parents. They were thrilled when Father John Whitely took a special interest in their boys. According to David, John Whitely molested David and three of his brothers, taking them on trips across the country and bribing them with presents and expensive meals in restaurants.

Like many survivors, Clohessy repressed the memory of his abuse for years, moving on with his life and eventually settling in Saint Louis. On a date with his future wife, he watched the movie *Nuts*, in which Barbra Streisand's character, a prostitute, regains repressed memories of her childhood sexual abuse. Immediately, memories of his own abuse came flooding back. When David learned about SNAP, he joined right away.

The whole Clohessy family has suffered from the affects of the abuse. One of David's brothers, Kevin, went on to become a priest and a molester himself. David has tried to be supportive of his brother while helping his brother's victims seek the justice they deserve.

In the early '90s, Clohessy started a local SNAP support group in Saint Louis and began working with me on building the national organization. We networked with other survivors and attempted to draw media attention to our cause. Clohessy's background in public relations and political organizing provided necessary expertise for developing local support groups in cities across the country. While working to build SNAP, Clohessy also kept focused on the need to support the individuals who were leading SNAP groups. He asked his wife, Laura Barrett, who had a master's degree in social work and experience in leadership development, to assist in training and supporting local SNAP leaders.

Clohessy, Barrett and I arranged events to educate, support and build leadership within SNAP. We tried to ensure that we held events in every region of the country so as many survivors as possible could join in. It was amazing how wounded, vulnerable victims reached beyond themselves to help others.

Our goal had been for the leaders to help other survivors, but over time all of us realized and acknowledged that we, the leaders, gained far more than we gave.

THE FIRST MEETINGS WITH BISHOPS

By 1992, we were a growing and well-established organization. We felt we had done much for our members, who were trying to understand and remove the pain from their lives while supporting each other. But from the stories we shared, we also began to notice specific patterns in the way Church officials had responded when abuse was disclosed to them. The patterns were troubling.

We noticed that many survivors were describing Church officials who said that they had never before received a report of abuse by a clergyman. Rarely, if ever, did a Church official admit knowing about other abuse survivors. Yet we couldn't all have been the first. It was only after sharing many such stories that we began to realize that the Church officials were not being honest with us.

We also recognized, painfully, that Church officials had made many empty promises. Some of us were promised simple things, like a phone call from a bishop to our mother or a written apology. Others were promised more significant things, like having our counseling paid for or no longer permitting our predators to work in ministry. But it was our common experience that these promises were not kept. Many excuses were given. But the bottom line was that we were being hurt by the Church officials who were supposed to be helping us.

As we worked on issues related to emotional survival, such as dealing with feelings of shame and guilt, we also shared our experiences of interacting with Church leaders. It quickly became clear that most of us felt hurt and betrayed by bishops and leaders from religious congregations. The same experience seemed to characterize many different dioceses.

We theorized that this had happened because Church officials just didn't know any better. We decided to meet with some of them and explain to them how they were hurting victims whom they should have been helping. We naïvely assumed that they would welcome our input. We learned that one of the twice-annual meetings of the National Conference of Catholic Bishops was to take place in Washington, D.C., in November 1992, and, after sending advance word to the bishops of our intentions, a handful of us traveled there with the hope of meeting those bishops and offering our help. I was one of them.

At first the bishops refused to see us. In fact, when we walked through the halls of Washington's luxurious Omni Shoreham Hotel, where the bishops' conference was taking place, we found that special security guards had been hired to monitor us. They didn't allow us to talk to any bishops who attended the conference; we were even prevented from using the public restrooms. This was yet another painful experience of betrayal by Church officials. We had paid our own way to travel to Washington in order to meet with the bishops; we genuinely thought we could help. We were treated with absolute disdain.

Eventually we managed to confront the conference spokesperson, who told us that the bishops would not have time to meet with us. So we stood on a rainswept sidewalk in front of the hotel and told reporters that the bishops were unable or unwilling to meet with us. We also told our stories of abuse and how poorly we had been treated by bishops.

After a while, the bishops sent a spokesperson outside to tell us that they would now meet with us. Apparently, the risk of negative publicity from their petty and insensitive actions had finally led them to agree to meet with us. But even as we reentered the building to approach the bishops, their security guards followed our every movement.

Only three bishops were present for our meeting. Cardinal Mahony from Los Angeles acted as moderator. We painfully told our stories. Many of us cried and raised our voices, expressing our anger at the empty promises made by Church officials. The bishops listened and offered apologies. They said that this meeting had opened their eyes. They said they would take our input into consideration and make changes to their policies. They expressed a desire to begin a dialogue with us.

We felt gratified and consoled. We felt that we had been heard and believed. We thought they would finally make changes that were so desperately needed.

Our good feelings did not last long.

When we watched reports of the session on the TV news that evening, we saw that we had been used by the bishops. After our meeting, they had told reporters how moved they were by what they had heard, but that they had the correct policies in place and the problems were all in the past.

Our first meeting with the bishops had been nothing but a publicity stunt.

The following day, Cardinal Mahony was quoted in the *Dallas Morning News* claiming that the meeting with us "was one of the most moving experiences in [his] 17 years as a bishop."[2] NCCB president Archbishop Daniel E. Pilarczyk was quoted several months earlier in the *Detroit News* for his declaration: "Clergy sexual abuse just can't be tolerated. . . . But it's there and we've got to deal with it."[3] Like Archbishop Pilarczyk, the bishops tried to give the impression that they were aware of the problem and planning to take action. But they did not commit to any substantive change. They did not commit to any new policies or any tangible mechanisms to ensure improvements for the future.

The *Dallas Morning News* quoted Dave Clohessy and me as saying, "As survivors of sexual abuse by priests, we are grateful to the NCCB for meeting with survivors early this week and for the concern and care they have expressed. . . . We are disappointed in the [bishops'] statement, though, because it does not offer any change."[4]

The following spring, when the bishops held their semiannual meeting in New Orleans, we again tried to speak to them. We reserved a large meeting room at the hotel where the bishops were meeting. We signed a contract and paid the rental fee, but the day before the meeting was scheduled to begin, the hotel manager called and said they had made an error and SNAP would not be permitted to hold our meeting at their site. With less than twenty-four hours' notice, we scrambled to find another meeting room for our group that was also close to the bishops' meeting.

Having secured a location just down the street, we invited all the bishops and the prelates of each diocese to meet with us. Six months earlier, we had only met with three bishops; this time, we hoped to reach the majority of the NCCB members. We gave two different time options for bishops to meet with survivors. We wanted to help them understand how they were hurting us. We still believed that they just didn't know any better when they treated victims so poorly.

Not one bishop came to either of the designated listening sessions. We were surprised and hurt. We had thought that at least a few would want to meet us.

However, several reporters did come to our sessions and listened to our stories. Several wrote articles about what they heard, and we were invited to appear on a local daily talk show for a major network. A spokesperson from the NCCB appeared with us. He was a priest who claimed bishops were responding appropriately and helping victims. He also claimed that predatory priests had been removed from ministry. The handful of us on the show told our experiences of having our stories denied by Church officials. We told of the misinformation that we had been given and instances of perpetrators still in ministry. We directly refuted the priest's claims, and as he was questioned he began to hesitate and fumble and couldn't respond.

That morning in New Orleans was almost the last time any priest or bishop appeared together with a SNAP spokesperson on a talk or news show. After that event, the bishops changed their public relations strategy. They would no longer allow bishops or spokespersons to appear on the same show or in the same televised segment with members of SNAP.

WARNING VICTIMS — ABOUT THE CHURCH

I still have a hard time believing how naïve we were in those early years. We went to bishops and Church leaders assuming they would help us. We thought they would prevent our assailants from abusing anyone else. Little by little, we began to recognize that Church officials had all the necessary information but still didn't respond appropriately.

Realizing the Church officials were not going to take action, we felt compelled to warn other victims. We struggled with our decision, but eventually determined that we had to issue a warning. We had to protect other victims from being hurt by Church officials as so many of us had been.

In November 1993, SNAP leaders from several cities traveled to Chicago to hold our first-ever national press conference. A reputable public relations firm did the legwork for us at no charge. We spent a long, painstaking weekend working to get our message exactly right and preparing our leaders to speak. The decision to make such a statement was not made lightly. It was agonizing for many of us.

We issued the following warning: *Victims of abuse by priests should not go to Church officials.* Victims should look for healing and support from therapists, trusted friends and family members. Going to the Church officials could cause more hurt and pain to victims.

Our statement brought an avalanche of responses. Dozens of new victims heard the message and contacted us for the first time. On the other hand, many Catholics criticized our message and even questioned our integrity. The backlash was hurtful, but we knew we had made the right decision in warning others.

The NCCB continued its new PR campaign. Soon most bishops were using the same tight sound bites:

1. Predatory priests were no longer in ministry.
2. They had not known any better in previous decades when they returned predators to ministry. It wouldn't happen again.
3. They had studied the problem, set up committees and adopted new policies.
4. They were reaching out to assist victims.
5. The problem was solved.

SNAP support groups kept meeting. New survivors came and shared stories. It was clear that the bishops weren't doing what they said they were. Victims continued to report they had gone to Bishop So-and-So, and that he had made promises but didn't keep them. Victims had already been raped, sodomized and sexually assaulted by trusted priests and now were being revictimized by callous, dishonest bishops and Church leaders. While we shared the pain and betrayal each victim reported, we became even more certain that we had been right to issue our warning.

Almost every victim who reported poor treatment from a bishop, diocese or religious community also reported being shocked by how they were treated. Most victims who had heard our warning not to go to the Church officials ignored it. They all thought that their bishop would surely respond appropriately. They wrongly assumed that the poor treatment was a response to angry, extreme victims. Some had even been told as much by Church officials.

For some, it took months or even years to realize the value of our warning. Once they discovered the truth, they joined us and committed themselves to spreading the message. They, too, wanted to prevent others from being hurt as they had been.

THE STORY OF ABUSE BY PRIESTS BURSTS INTO NATIONAL MEDIA

The amount of publicity given to clergy sexual abuse waned during the later 1990s. But that began to change in early 2002. On January 6, 2002, the *Boston Globe* ran the first of what would ultimately become 850 stories about pedophile priests. The articles sparked the exposure and suspension of a large number of proven, admitted or credibly accused child-molesting clerics still working across the United States.

In its January 6, 2002, article, the *Globe* revealed that predatory priests had abused dozens of children and that the local bishops had known and failed to report the abuse to police. As the *Globe*'s Spotlight Team investigated, uncovered and reported more abuse, more victims came forward. Survivors were speaking up in city after city as the news spread. At the beginning of 2002, we had active support groups in fewer than a dozen cities. Now, survivors from all over the country were asking for information on the nearest SNAP support group meeting. If their city didn't have a group yet, we asked if they themselves would start one. Many did. By the end of the year, the number of cities with active SNAP support groups had more than doubled. We scrambled to train and support the new SNAP leaders.

The sheer number of victims coming forward at this time was overwhelming. Dozens of new victims and family members surfaced daily, and they were seeking help and support from us. We had been an all-volunteer organization up until this point, but we recognized that we had an urgent need to hire a staff. To meet this need we began raising funds; later that year David Clohessy in St. Louis and Mary Grant in Los Angeles became SNAP's first employees. In early 2003, I officially joined the staff and opened the SNAP national office in Chicago. In 2004, Barbara Dorris, who had become a full-time volunteer, joined the staff and became SNAP's outreach director. Today, SNAP also has a full-time administrative assistant and a part-time bookkeeper, fundraiser and Web master.

JUNE 2002: THE BISHOPS TALK,
BUT DON'T SAY ANYTHING NEW

In June 2002, after five months of almost daily exposés in major newspapers across the nation, U.S. bishops gathered in Dallas for their semiannual meeting. This time they were under the glare of public scrutiny from around the world. Over 750 reporters received press credentials for the event. On the very first day of the conference, the bishops were greeted with headlines in the *Dallas Morning News* announcing that two-thirds of the bishops in attendance had knowingly transferred a predator priest to a new ministry. Since January 6, hardly a day had passed without some news agency reporting about the abuse of children or a cover-up of abuse. Dozens of our members went to

Dallas with the hope that, after so much media exposure, the bishops would finally do the right thing.

We came to this conference armed with an important piece of information. Several years earlier, we had learned that in 1985 an important document had been given to every bishop. It was a report titled "The Problem of Sexual Molestation by Roman Catholic Clergy: Meeting the Problem in a Comprehensive and Responsible Manner" (May 14, 1985), written by Father Thomas Doyle, Father Michael Peterson and Ray Mouton. The report warned bishops to remove predatory priests from ministry. The report even went so far as to predict the immense cost to the Church if they failed to act. This gave us added hope that the bishops simply could not continue to ignore the problem.

The day before the official conference began, SNAP members and other survivors met with a group of cardinals and, later, with a group of bishops. We also met with the U.S. Conference of Catholic Bishops' Ad Hoc Committee on Sexual Abuse, headed by Archbishop Harry Flynn. The bishops who sat on this committee had significant influence over other U.S. bishops. In all these meetings, we asked the prelates to consider three objectives:

1. Removal of abusive priests from ministry.
2. Elimination of secrecy clauses (or "gag orders") in legal settlements.
3. Accountability from bishops. (For instance, bishops should be subject to discipline when they knowingly transfer predator priests to new parishes without any warnings, as has often happened.)[5]

On the first day of the formal proceedings, David Clohessy — by then SNAP's national director — addressed the entire assembly. CNN televised his speech live during its national news broadcast. Clohessy asked the bishops to do what Jesus would do in a similar situation. He asked the bishops to work for prevention by setting up "safe touch" programs in every Catholic school. He asked them to lobby to extend or eliminate the statutes of limitation for the claims of sexually abused children, so that survivors could still seek justice and perpetrators could be identified and confined.

Other survivors spoke as well. We told of the horrors of losing our innocence, as children, to Catholic priests. We also told how horribly we had been treated by Church officials when we had reported our abuse.

Many of the Church officials who heard us speak on that occasion in Dallas promised that we would meet again. Archbishop Flynn claimed that we had begun a dialogue that would continue.

It didn't.

In all the years since we left the Dallas meeting with the bishops, not one bishop, not one cardinal has ever met with us or made any effort to continue the "dialogue."

Nor did the conference produce any of the results we had hoped for. Even under the glare of publicity from every major news outlet in the world, the bishops failed to make substantial changes. When the dust settled, it became clear that they had adopted a weak, watered-down set of policies in their new Charter for the Protection of Children.

CHURCH "INITIATIVES"

The National Review Board

The only glimmer of hope came from the fact that the bishops called for the creation of a National Review Board to monitor their compliance with the newly enacted Charter. This was to be a blue-ribbon panel staffed by volunteers and loyal Catholics. Some of the members were: former White House chief of staff Leon Panetta; Robert Bennett, best known as President Clinton's personal attorney during his impeachment proceedings; Frank Keating, the governor of Oklahoma; and Illinois appellate (now Supreme Court) judge Ann Burke. All were successful in their fields — law, psychology, education or medicine — and all were lay Catholics committed to ensuring the success of the Church's apparent initiative. Maybe, we thought, the people assigned to the new board would use their position to hold bishops accountable.

That hope didn't last long.

The NRB's work did not go smoothly. Some bishops openly refused to cooperate with the NRB and failed to provide information vital for its work. Others quietly tried to undercut the NRB. The result was that, before long, the experienced and outspoken members were forced out and replaced with more docile and quiet ones.

Within a year or two, Panetta, Bennett, Governor Keating and Judge Burke had all left the board. So had a child welfare expert and a CEO of a major newspaper chain. When Keating resigned from the NRB, he had blunt words: In a June 16, 2003, letter to Wilton D. Gregory, president of the U.S. Conference of Catholic Bishops, he remonstrated that the church must serve as a "home to Christ's people," and declared that it is not "a criminal enterprise."

He added, "I make no apology. To resist grand jury subpoenas, to suppress the names of offending clerics, to deny, to obfuscate, to explain away: that is the model of a criminal organization, not my church."[6]

Other ousted or resigning members of the NRB spoke similarly about their frustrations at being stonewalled by Church leaders. Justice Anne Burke, in a March 30, 2004, letter to Gregory, said, "[W]e were manipulated." Delays of this kind, wrote Burke, will only serve to vindicate "those who said bishops were never serious about breaking free from the sins, crimes, and bad judgments of the past."

As members like Justice Burke left the board, new members took their place. One of the newly appointed members was attorney Joseph Russoniello of San Francisco, who has made many derogatory comments regarding publicly naming known, admitted and suspected abusive clerics. There has also been a troubling shift in the chairmanship of the board. Initially, it was headed by Governor Keating, a truly independent, outspoken, high-profile former prosecutor. Then the position was held temporarily by Justice Burke, who — apart from being a respected and well-known judge — had adopted a child who had been addicted to cocaine at birth. Next, it was headed by a less independent, low-profile defense lawyer. Today the NRB leader is an extremely quiet and low-profile federal judge from Ohio, Michael Merz. Since the replacement of outspoken members like Burke, there has been no tough talk and even less real action. We worry that the supposed watchdog seems to be more of a lapdog. Virtually every day, ten to twelve newspaper stories report on criminal charges, civil lawsuits, suspensions of and allegations against allegedly abusive clerics or complicit chancery officials of various dioceses. Yet NRB members are apparently not paying attention or apparently feel no obligation or inclination to speak out.

While this has been going on, we at SNAP have spoken out about our concerns and told how we were troubled by the composition, leadership and apparent direction of the National Review Board. We even wrote a letter to the president of the USCCB asking him to toughen the membership of the NRB and encourage their speaking out. Over time, we had hoped the NRB would gradually raise the bar and prod bishops toward more vigorous enforcement of the Dallas charter. Instead, there was backsliding by bishops and a lack of assertiveness by the NRB. We still feel that our complaints are not with the NRB members themselves. But we believe the goals of the board are not being met, and there seems little hope that they will be.

Lessons Learned from the National Review Board
and Its John Jay College "Study"

Early on, while the National Review Board was conducting its investigation of the extent of the problem of sexually abusive clergy, it hired the John Jay College to perform a "study." The board sent teams of investigators to every one of the dioceses and archdioceses in the United States. However, under the board's approach, each diocese or prelate determined which documents and files the investigators from John Jay College would see. Consequently, the study was really more of a self-survey, since all that could be studied was what was handed over by the bureaucrats of each diocese. There were no third-party checks and balances. It was not objective.

In February 2004, hours before the official release of the results of John Jay College's study at the National Press Club in Washington, D.C., SNAP held a news conference in the same building. It was carried live across the United States on C-span. We wanted to point out the deficiencies of the study. Catholics, and the American people, needed information about how widespread the problem of clergy abuse really was. They needed to know the names of the predators in order to protect children. They needed real answers. But the information released that day didn't provide it. We pointed out that the results of the study yielded merely partial numbers. Even the information that was released was not a sign of greater openness; it had been forced on the bishops by years of seemingly endless revelations, removals, prosecutions, admissions, exposés, verdicts, lawsuits and excuses.

We could already see that things hadn't changed since 1993 when, following the horrific Father James Porter case, Church PR people, defense lawyers and insurance companies insisted that virtually every diocese adopt a written sexual abuse policy.[7] Many dioceses established review boards. The bishops set up a national committee. Thick documents were produced. And the mantra became, "We've got a committee. We've got policies. We're moving on." Now, in 2004, the mantra was largely the same, but with one new twist: it ran, "We've got policies. We've got numbers. We're moving on." The bishops were still claiming that they didn't know any better, saying, "Our understanding of abuse has evolved." They tried to minimize the problem by insisting, "Priests abuse at the same rate as others and more abuse occurs in the home." They tried distancing the problem by claiming that most cases dated back to the '70s and '80s. They praised themselves; they insisted that no other institution was doing such self-examination. But their excuses didn't provide perspective.

We acknowledge — and the facts bear out — that in ten years there *had* been activity in the Church regarding sex abuse, there had been motion. But action doesn't necessarily mean progress and motion doesn't necessarily mean forward motion. In spite of the paperwork, policies, procedures and press releases, there has been little substantive reform. The numbers mean nothing if kids are at risk.

And they are. One simple figure proves it. The bishops have admitted that there are about five thousand priests who have abused children.[8] Some of these priests have died and a few others are behind bars. But many more are out there — they are still at large, and they are not being monitored. These child-molesting priests were shielded from law enforcement by our bishops and, even today, they are not required by any law to list their names and addresses on sex offender registries. Employers and neighbors need to know the history of these men in order to keep kids away from them, today and in the future. In our view, the bishops have a moral and civic responsibility to release the names of these child-molesting priests. A database should be established so that law enforcement officials, employers and parents can know the truth about these men before they allow them access to more children, as tutors, coaches, scout leaders, counselors and teachers. But none of this is being done.

We were also concerned that many bishops seemed to backtrack from their earlier commitment to "zero tolerance." Bishop Wilton Gregory, president of the U.S. Conference of Catholic Bishops, had said: "Bishops will not tolerate even one act of sexual abuse of a minor. No free passes. No second chances. No free strike. . . . An abuser . . . can indeed be forgiven for his sins. He just doesn't get a second chance to do it again. Period." We wanted bishops to hold on to that commitment. But examples of predator priests who *were* tolerated by the Church kept coming to light.

After we made our televised statements, some of our members remained in the hallways, answering reporters' questions and talking among themselves. Apparently at the request of the bishops, who were about to make their own presentation, the building's security guards attempted to remove us all from the corridors, claiming we had not paid for their use. Reporters from the *New York Times* and USA *Today* pointed out that they were members of the club and could not be forced out. The guards told them that they could stay, but that we had to leave. Evidently, the bishops thought they could silence us by forcing us out to the sidewalk.

As we gained confidence in ourselves and in our cause, it became clear that exposing predators was an essential part of protecting others and healing ourselves. We had to stop the cycle of violence. We needed to work to ensure that more children (and vulnerable adults) were not abused. We researched and tried different tactics. We found that the most effective mechanism to prevent further abuse by known sexual predators is the courts. The U.S. justice system allows for the fairest process of seeking and exposing the truth. However, most victims never got their day in court because of archaic, arbitrary and dangerously restrictive statutes of limitation.

Every state has its own statute of limitation on crimes of sexual abuse, but almost all such statutes require victims to come forward by the time they reach twenty years of age. Since most victims of child sexual abuse aren't able to understand or report the abuse until well into adulthood, the period in which the crime had to be charged expired long before most of the victims could speak up. This meant that hardly any victims of child sex abuse could bring about the prosecution of their abusers.[9] Ironically, the psychological damage the abusers have caused usually ensures our silence until it is too late.

Since the statutes of limitation effectively prevent us from exposing our abusers, many of us have asked lawmakers to change these laws. Ideally, we want to eliminate all statutes of limitation for sexual abuse, just as they have been eliminated for murder, or to expand them, as they have been expanded in some states for such crimes as forgery and other offenses. Lawmakers in many states have begun efforts to extend or eliminate the relevant statutes of limitation for child sexual abuse; the list includes Illinois, Delaware, California, Colorado, Missouri, Kentucky, Connecticut, Maine, Massachusetts, Louisiana, Pennsylvania and Idaho. Many other states have such bills pending before their legislatures (or plan to have them), including Michigan, Ohio, Wisconsin, Minnesota, Florida and the District of Columbia.

Two states have created a "window" that allows victims whose limitations period has already expired to bring civil suits against their abusers during a specified period of time. In 2002, California passed a window bill that allowed anyone who had been abused as a child — at any time — to file a lawsuit between January 1 and December 31, 2003. The governor of Delaware signed into law a bill in July 2007 that created a two-year window, allowing anyone abused in Delaware to file a civil complaint, regardless of when they had been abused.

We would like to see the other forty-eight states join California and Delaware. We believe that even with a more liberal statute of limitations, a window during which any abuse victim may sue his or her abuser is essential to protect the rights of victims and to prevent future abuse of children. Here are the benefits of such a window:

1. *Exposing predators.* The window enables victims to expose publicly the predators who hurt them, through the open, impartial, time-tested U.S. judicial system. It means that parents, neighbors and employers will know about potentially dangerous individuals.

2. *Exposing enablers.* Through the balanced judicial process — depositions, document production, interrogatories and sworn testimony — anyone who ignored a sex crime, shielded a molester, destroyed a document or deceived a victim's family may also be exposed. Families deserve to know whether their pastor, day-care center director or athletic association harbored a sex offender, stonewalled a prosecutor or lied to a parent. Citizens deserve to know whether a diocese or a summer camp director knowingly hired child molesters.

3. *Instilling fear of litigation.* Without the window, a supervisor who has been lax about child safety has no incentive to change bad habits or work harder. With the window, decision makers will know that if they insensitively shun a victim or recklessly endanger a child, they may be exposed in court and face consequences.

4. *Fear of financial consequences.* The window will prod defense lawyers, public relations staff and others to ensure a beefed-up child sex abuse prevention and education policy. Smart organizations will start or expand efforts to train adults about reporting abuse and teach kids about "safe touch," knowing that victims are less inclined to sue an institution that seems to take abuse seriously, and that judges and juries are more lenient with institutions that are already addressing the problems that led to a lawsuit.

There is very little opposition to such legislation — except from each state's Catholic Conference. It is saddening that Church officials work so hard to protect child molesters instead of children. Obviously, the vast majority of predators are not Catholic priests, yet Catholic officials use Church resources to defeat window legislation that could offer protection to dozens, even hundreds of children.

To justify their opposition to such legislation, Church officials predict horrific consequences if it passes. That's nonsense. We always ask for proof of such dire effects. They haven't provided it. California adopted this window five years ago. It worked there. It will work anywhere.

Those opposed to window legislation ask, "Why make institutions pay today for something that happened decades ago?" Our opponents claim that Catholics today shouldn't have to pay for past mistakes. The truth is that they already have paid, long ago. First they paid with the innocence of their children who were raped, sodomized and sexually abused by priests. On top of that, for decades, Catholics through their regular contributions to the church unknowingly paid for defense lawyers, public relations firms, secret settlements and, most of all, for expensive insurance policies to cover the legal liability of abuse.

The opposition wants to know how a dead accused molester can defend himself. But the truth is that he doesn't have to. The burden is always on the victims to prove their cases. The window doesn't lighten the burden of proof nor relax the rules of evidence. The window merely provides more time in which to sue. If there is no proof, there is no case. Since mental health professionals agree that most child victims are not ready to come forward until well into adulthood, window legislation, far from being unfair to the accused, is the only way most child victims will ever see justice.

Some in the opposition want lawmakers to focus on the individual predators instead of on the employers. We believe we should go after both. Police go after both when they pursue drug trafficking: the low-level street-corner dealer *and* the big supplier or kingpin. Pursuing those who hire and shield predators will deter others from similar recklessness.

The opposition claims that a window will make it difficult for nonprofit organizations to get insurance. Again, in California — where the window expired almost five years ago — no one has offered a shred of evidence suggesting that nonprofits couldn't get insured. Opponents also claim that a window will "break" the Church. Again, there is no evidence that it has broken the Church in California, where a window has come and gone. We believe that when Church officials make such gloomy predictions, they should have their finances evaluated by a third party to prove their claims. They won't do it — not voluntarily, that is. In one case, a San Diego judge forced them to do so after the diocese there filed for reorganization under the federal bankruptcy code. After reviewing their financial disclosures, the judge determined that officials had been less than honest. (This will be discussed in more detail below.)

Another argument Church officials make against the window is that it will force the Church to cut back on social and charitable services. But please remember that almost 85 percent of the funding for those services comes from government — i.e., taxpayers.

The opposition frequently points to Ohio's civil registry as an alternative to the window. The registry — which is supposed to list offenders whose crimes were committed outside the statute of limitations, but which provides no punishment for the offender, no compensation for the victim and no accountability for those who enabled or covered up for the offender — was devised by Church officials precisely in order to defeat window legislation in Ohio. Ohio's attorney general has publicly called it "a sham."[10] Again, experience is the best guide, and if we look at experience in this instance, it is clear that a registry doesn't work. Two years after Ohio approved the civil registry bill, not one molester is on that registry. Kids there are no safer.

Another argument frequently made is that a window bill unfairly targets private institutions and that kids abused in public schools and institutions won't have the same rights as those abused in the private sector. That is just not true. To begin with, the special protections from suit enjoyed by public institutions (a complicated issue that derives from the principle of sovereign immunity) have nothing do with statutes of limitations, so using that as an argument against window legislation is comparing apples to broccoli. (When window legislation was proposed in Colorado that would have specifically allowed suits against public as well as private institutions, Church officials still opposed the measure.) Besides, victims abused in public institutions have access to civil rights protections not available to victims abused in the private sector. Further, there is transparency in the public sector that doesn't exist in private organizations. The Freedom of Information Act allows citizens to access documents about public figures and institutions and requires that meetings generally be conducted in public. In private institutions, personnel files remain secret, and it is extremely easy to transfer predators to new locations, even across state and international boundaries, because there is no mechanism to ensure accountability or public scrutiny.

Finally, the opposition claims its goal is to protect kids, but believes the window isn't the right way to do it. I challenge them to find something better. Many options have been considered and tried over several years. There just isn't any better solution. Kids need protection *now*, and victims are willing and ready to protect those kids by exposing their perpetrators. Window legislation would allow the truth to be exposed and victims to be healed.

FILING FOR BANKRUPTCY

In addition to fighting window legislation, bishops have consistently used hardball legal tactics to keep from having to expose the truth about how much they knew and how little they did to protect children. In court, they fight victims on every conceivable technicality. A few years ago, they devised a scheme to prevent cases from going to court: filing for bankruptcy. Six dioceses have filed so far, though not one of them has submitted evidence showing the need to declare bankruptcy.

What the dioceses are calling "bankruptcy" really involves the use of the bankruptcy code to file for reorganization. No diocese is actually going bankrupt. In the four dioceses where the bankruptcy cases have been settled, the prelate of each diocese has made it clear that the diocese continues all the services it performed before the filing. The bishops admit they are continuing to do business as usual. It seems that the real goal of the bankruptcy filing is to keep the bishops' and dioceses' dirty secrets hidden. In each case in which a bankruptcy declaration was filed, it was done on the day or the eve of a trial that would have exposed shocking secrets about how much Church officials knew about and covered up for the sexual misconduct of its priests. Because a bankruptcy filing generally halts all other litigation against the debtor, which in this instance would be the Church, such a legal maneuver proved to well serve the Church. In fact, in each case, the bishop himself who might have been forced to take the witness stand and explain under oath why he had allowed a sexual predator access to children and why he hadn't called police or warned parents, was spared this ordeal.

We hope that, regarding the diocese of San Diego, which, according to the judge, "failed to disclose all of its assets and . . . [did not] report the fair market value of other property,"[11] the truth may still be exposed and the victims may get their day in court. Victims point out that this recent ruling bolsters what they have been saying all along: the bankruptcy filing was merely an attempt to avoid a trial and to keep Bishop Brom from having to take the witness stand.

A very different approach has characterized the Boston archdiocese, where Archbishop O'Malley replaced Cardinal Law in July 2003 (after Law's resignation the previous December). Instead of arguing that statutes of limitation had run and that victims had filed too late, O'Malley fired the defense attorneys who had worked for Cardinal Law. He spoke out, saying that victims need help and healing. He promised to do whatever it takes to help the victims and made it clear he will not use statutes of limitation to evade the diocese's responsibility to the victims. There are victims from Boston who aren't happy with how the Church there has treated them, but O'Malley's response is far more genuinely pastoral than most, and it has facilitated healing for many survivors.

SETTLEMENT OF CASES

Most victims of sex abuse by priests have not come forward to report that they were victimized. Of those who have reported abuse, most have not received any compensation. Many victims have received reimbursement for counseling costs for a set period of time (usually six months to one year, which arguably is not sufficient for recovery from child sexual abuse). Most dioceses give victims the bare minimum, with the argument that the victims took too long to come forward. The news media devotes widespread coverage to those *rare* instances when large settlements are given, which creates the false impression that most victims receive hefty amounts of money from the Church. The reality is that, in most states, as discussed above, the statutes of limitation prevent most victims from having their day in court, ensuring that the Church will not be held accountable financially or otherwise. Most victims don't receive any compensation from Church officials.

This raises the question of the moral responsibility of the diocese or Church to the victims. Church officials argue that they are not legally responsible because of the technicality of the statute of limitations, and they usually win that argument. But a deeper question is whether they are morally responsible to care for the victims. One SNAP leader frequently asks the question, "What would Jesus do?" Would Jesus be hiring expensive law firms to fight victims in court? Would Jesus ignore victims and their family members? Would Jesus make empty promises? Would Jesus have allowed one of his disciples to be close to children if he knew that the disciple was a sexual predator?

A very large settlement was recently announced in Los Angeles, involving the payment of $660 million to 506 victims. The settlement was announced on the night before trials were to begin. The trials would have revealed shocking secrets. Cardinal Mahony would have been required to take the witness stand and explain, among other things, how he had transferred a known predator to eight different parishes after the priest admitted to Mahony that he had abused children. The archdiocese had threatened that it might also file for bankruptcy, like so many other dioceses. But, at the last minute, it agreed to the payout. Relief that the cases had been settled was expressed by those on both sides. Some have attempted to make Cardinal Mahony a hero for prodding religious congregations to agree to the terms. It is important to recognize, though, that the credit for this settlement goes first to the brave victims; then to compassionate lawmakers who made the lawsuits possible; and, finally, to victims' attorneys, who took difficult cases and overcame endless hardball legal maneuvers by bishops. The Church hierarchy deserves none of the credit.

This settlement was made possible by the 2003 civil window in California, which opened courthouse doors to victims of child sexual abuse. Cardinal Mahony and his brother California bishops had fought long and hard to have virtually all of these cases tossed out, by repeatedly claiming, in court after court, that the law that enabled these cases to be filed was unconstitutional. They took these cases all the way to the U.S. Supreme Court. (And finally lost.)

As the 2003 civil window period began, Church officials across California launched a carefully orchestrated public relations campaign. They began ominously predicting financial hardship if child molestation lawsuits were filed against their dioceses. It is now clear that this was pure posturing, intended to discourage lawsuits and promote smaller settlements. California Church officials quietly began working even harder to keep victims away from lawyers and advocates, to pay off victims quietly and to discourage victims from bringing lawsuits. Yet financially compensating victims of devastating child rape is the absolute bare minimum step that guilty parties should take.

Under these circumstances, the much-publicized settlement was a smart business move for Cardinal Mahony, nothing more. For decades, Church officials have settled abuse cases. This is nothing new. Settlements in no way signify reform or change by the Church. When bishops settle child sex abuse cases, it is almost always to spare themselves court appearances, tough questions and the risk of perjury charges.

Most of the predators involved in the Los Angeles settlement are still priests on the archdiocesan payroll. Most have been suspended but not defrocked. Few, we believe, have been "cured" or no longer present a risk to kids.

It's tempting to think that settlements will deter deceit and recklessness by Catholic bishops in the future. They won't. The Church always has been and still is a rigid, secretive, all-male, hierarchical monarchy. That hasn't changed. Until it does, bishops will continue to protect themselves first, even above protecting kids. The truth is that settlements can and usually do lead to more healing and prevention — but only if victims and decision-makers realize this is just the first step.

Many victims of sex abuse by clergymen desperately need in-patient drug rehabilitation, alcohol treatment or addictions programs. They have waited years for therapy to cope with eating disorders, depression and suicidal tendencies. Settlements help these deeply wounded individuals begin to piece their lives together and move forward. However, no settlement will ever magically restore stolen childhoods, betrayed psyches, shattered self-esteem and damaged relationships. After the settlement checks clear, abuse victims will continue to experience nightmares, sleeplessness, isolation and self-destructive behaviors. It's crucial that these brave victims stay in therapy, keep attending support groups and remain in treatment programs. It's essential that they understand that no amount of money can produce an instant cure or bring about effortless healing. For years, often for decades, victims were made to feel that the abuse didn't happen, was their fault, wasn't severe and didn't cause their continuing suffering. A settlement cannot cure everything, but it can be healthy validation of the victim's innocence and injury.

PAPAL RESPONSE

In April of 2002, under tremendous public pressure, Pope John Paul II said that there "is no place in the priesthood . . . for those who would harm the young."[12] Sadly, however, Vatican officials have failed to take decisive action to protect kids. In repeated public comments, Vatican officials continue to minimize the crimes, the cover-ups and the devastating impact all this has had on Catholics and victims everywhere.

In spite of worldwide publicity about this issue, the Vatican seems not to understand the magnitude of the problem. Only a few years ago, Vatican officials promoted a predator priest from Cincinnati, Monsignor Daniel Pater;[13] the Vatican also ordered Cardinal Maida of Detroit to reinstate Father Brian Bjorklund, who had been removed for alleged sexual abuse of a seventeen-year-old boy. The Vatican reasoned that the Code of Canon Law in effect at the time of the abuse, which provided that children reached the age of consent at age sixteen, applied to the case and, accordingly, Bjorklund should be reinstated.[14]

When Pope John Paul II died in April 2005, many of our members were shocked to learn that Cardinal Bernard Law was playing a prominent role in the funeral and memorial services and masses. He also maintained significant influence in choosing the new pope and served on eight key committees in Rome, including the one that picks new bishops. While Catholics were grieving over a pontiff's death, it seemed inappropriate that Cardinal Law — who was so deeply implicated in sex abuse cover-ups in Boston that the Vatican forced him to resign in December 2002 — would seize the opportunity to seek the limelight. Victims and Catholics resented being reminded of the sex abuse scandal at such a solemn moment. It felt like salt being rubbed into our open wounds.

Not everyone understood our position. Some of the foreign press asked us, "Isn't it enough that Cardinal Law apologized and stepped down in Boston? Why won't you leave him alone, and move on?"

In answer, we tried to stress that the issue is neither forgiving nor punishing Cardinal Law. It's about stopping the pain and helping victims come forward. Far too many victims, their families and other Catholics are still suffering, largely because of Cardinal Law. His presence in the Church is still very painful to many. And it's tough to encourage victims to come forward, expose predators and get help when the Church hierarchy remains so insensitive. (Victims often ask us: "Why bother speaking out? Nothing will change anyway.") When a wrongdoer like Law is honored and stays in power, it adds to the victims' sense of helplessness and depression, which for so many is already overwhelming.

Alan Cooperman of the *Washington Post*, who was covering events in Rome, did some historical investigation into who had said funeral masses for previous popes. On April 12, 2005, he reported, "Vatican officials have said Law was chosen automatically for the Mass [for John Paul II] because he is head priest of a major church in Rome, the Basilica of Santa Maria Maggiore." But, Cooperman continued, "documents obtained Monday by the *Washing-*

ton Post from the church's archives show that Law's predecessor as archpriest of Santa Maria Maggiore was not given the same role after the death of the previous pope, John Paul I, in 1978." The Vatican's defense of Law's role in the papal funeral simply wasn't true.

Learning this only left survivors more confused and hurt. It raised more questions. While we can't speculate on the motives of Vatican officials, we do know that their actions at the time of the death of John Paul II and their silence at others times have been a continual source of disappointment and confusion for survivors.

Since many of us were in Rome for the funeral, we decided to use the opportunity to expose U.S. predators who were hiding out in the Vatican and Rome. We held news conferences and passed out flyers warning parishioners and neighbors about a predator living in their neighborhood. We exposed three different charged or convicted sexual predator priests from the United States. We received coverage in the United States, England, Australia, Canada and other English-speaking countries.

But the Vatican still seems to be slow in getting the message. The most recent example of hurtful comments by Vatican officials came in August 2007. Cardinal Tarcisio Bertone, the Vatican's secretary of state, told reporters that the Church has "acted with dignity and courage." He accused victims of coming forward only for financial gain, and claimed that no other institution has done better on child sexual abuse than the Catholic Church. He repeated the old canard that somehow the Catholic Church has been "singled out" for criticism.

We do not believe that the Catholic Church hierarchy has been singled out by anyone. It is, however, the institution with the most widely documented history of repeatedly protecting predators, shunning victims, deceiving parishioners, stonewalling prosecutors and stiff-arming journalists, all so that the reputations of top Church officials can be protected. Vatican officials have done virtually nothing to protect the vulnerable. We had hoped that, at least, the Vatican would stop revictimizing those already wounded by the Church.

It has not escaped out attention that in April 2008 the new Pope, during his visit to the United States, admonished Catholics to "do everything possible" to heal the wounds caused by the Catholic priest child-abuse crisis. Whether the pontiff's words will have a demonstrable effect on the behavior of over five thousand bishops worldwide remains to be seen. One reason for skepticism is that the presence of a "hierarchy" within the Catholic Church does not automatically require that admonitions that come from the top will be heeded by bishops and archbishops, even though they are technically lower on the totem pole. Contrary to what one may assume, bishops by and large are *not* tightly controlled by the Vatican, although the Vatican does in fact appoint them to their prelate positions. Given the relatively "loose" hierarchy within the Catholic Church, it remains to be seen whether the Pope's critical words of warning during his visit to the United States will filter down to all the bishops, who by virtue of their power are truly the ones in a position to purge the Catholic Church, and its educational and recreational institutions, of the evils of child sexual abuse.

PREDATORS CROSS INTERNATIONAL BORDERS

The Vatican and Rome are not the only places where predatory priests hide. In June 2004, the *Dallas Morning News* reported the results of its year-long investigation into predatory priests who had eluded authorities by crossing international boundaries.[15] They found that Church officials have knowingly helped fugitives, not only providing room and board for these priests, but even allowing them to work in ministry. Dozens of predators convicted of sexual offenses in the United States, and no longer permitted to work in this country, were openly working in other countries as pastors, teachers, administrators and counselors. Parishioners haven't been notified of the predators' history. Altogether, counting U.S. priests convicted in other countries as well, the paper had found more than two hundred predator priests working in foreign countries.

Some SNAP members in California learned that the man they accuse of abusing them had left the United States and was working in ministry in Mexico. Father Nicolas Aguilar-Rivera, as a visiting priest in 1987 in the Archdiocese of Los Angeles, allegedly abused at least thirteen children. In 1988, a warrant was issued for his arrest. Church officials allowed him to flee the United States and to continue ministry work in Mexico. In 2006, alleged victims of Aguilar-Rivera were contacted by another man — ten years younger than they — who reported having been abused in Mexico. That young person, Joaquin Aguilar (no relation to the priest) mustered the courage to speak up and expose his alleged abuser in Mexico. He later founded SNAP Mexico and is working now with other survivors to reach out and provide support, healing, information and consolation to victims in Mexico.

Early in SNAP's history, we decided to document what we learned and to pass it on, so that others wouldn't have to make the same mistakes we did. We compiled much of what we learned into an instructive guide we called "Survivors Wisdom" and passed out copies of this guide at every SNAP event. Over the years we've updated it, and we keep it posted on our Web site, *snapnetwork.org*. It is easy to find on the right side of the home page. I will quote the brief version here:

1. Acknowledge your courage and strength.
2. Know that you are not alone.
3. Don't go to the Church.
4. If you decide to go to the Church, don't do it alone!
5. Seek alternative help.
6. Learn your legal rights.
7. Take care of yourself; no one else will.
8. Face your issues; even if painful, they are part of your life.
9. Everybody is unique and has a unique journey of healing.
10. You, the victims, are innocent and are not to be blamed.

NOTES

1. Gauthe later served ten years in prison for his sexual crimes against children. Rachel Martin, "Abuse Scandal Still Echoes through Catholic Church," National Public Radio, January 11, 2007.

2. Daniel Cattau, "Catholic Bishops Urge Swiftness in Handling Sex Abuse Charges: Concern for Victims' Cooperation during Inquiries Stressed," *Dallas Morning News*, November 20, 1992, p. 1A.

3. Kim Kozlowski, "Victims Add Voice to Bishops' Meeting: Survivors' Pleas May Lead to Tougher Policy for Predatory Priests," *Detroit News*, June 13, 2002, p. 1A.

4. Cattau, *Dallas Morning News*, p. 1A.

5. In my own case, Bishop James R. Hoffman of Toledo assured me that no one before me had ever reported abuse by Father Warren (the priest who abused me) and that Father Warren was being carefully monitored in his current ministry. I have since learned that both statements were false. But Bishop Hoffman has never been held accountable for his lies or for endangering children.

6. Daniel J. Wakin, "Refusing to Recant, Keating Resigns as Church Panel Chief," *New York Times*, June 17, 2003.

7. Father Porter pleaded guilty in 1993 to sexually abusing twenty-eight children and was sentenced to eighteen to twenty years in prison.

8. See Alan Cooperman, "Church Sex Abuse Costs Rise Despite Drop in New Allegations," *Washington Post*, March 31, 2006.

9. Even when a prosecution does take place, less than two percent of the predators identified by bishops ever serve a day in jail.

10. Todd Jarrett, "Ohio's Victims of Clerical Sexual Abuse Left Frustrated by Bill 17," *Toledo City Paper*, February 28, 2007.

11. Richard Marosi, "Church Told to Defend Bankruptcy," *Los Angeles Times*, August 11, 2007.

12. Charles M. Sennott, "Pope Calls Sex Abuse Crime," *Boston Globe*, April 24, 2002, p. A1.

13. Reese Dunklin, "Vatican Elevated Abusive Priest," *Dallas Morning News*, August 31, 2003.

14. Tim Sheehan, "Victims Group Puts Spotlight on Priest," *Fresno Bee*, September 1, 2004.

15. "Runaway Priests Hiding in Plain Sight," *Dallas Morning News*, June 21, 2004, p. 1A.

Let Me Know the Way

AMY NEUSTEIN & MICHAEL LESHER

Justice Interrupted

How Rabbis Can Interfere with the
Prosecution of Sex Offenders — And
Strategies for How to Stop Them

THE HAFNER CASE

In the spring of 2000, plastered on telephone poles and synagogue message boards in the time warp that is Brooklyn's ultra-Orthodox Jewish Borough Park, notices containing the Hebrew-language verdict of a rabbinic court informed the faithful that Rabbi Solomon Hafner, a popular tutor and camp administrator of the Bobov Hasidic sect, had been "cleared" of abusing one of his former pupils, a young hearing-impaired boy.

The rabbis who announced that decision had plenty of reason to publicize it among the Hasidim. Opposing the factoid of their own verdict, as they well knew, was a ninety-six-count child abuse complaint filed against Rabbi Hafner by the Brooklyn district attorney earlier that year — a complaint supported by strong medical evidence and a police detective, before it abruptly fizzled after a group of ultra-Orthodox rabbis worked their way into the case in the midst of a grand jury investigation. Experts, including Orthodox Jewish therapists who interviewed the alleged victim, believed the boy was telling the truth. The boy's family flatly refused to back down, despite rabbinic pressure to recant the accusations against Hafner. The child sex abuse specialist who had recommended a criminal charge openly complained that supporters of the Bobov Hasidim — a tightly knit voting bloc numbering about twenty thousand in Brooklyn alone — had worked behind the scenes to suppress the charges against the alleged abuser. As for the D.A., who was supposed to be responsible for prosecuting Hafner, his staff kept their comments to a minimum, insisting the office had dropped the charges against Hafner in response to "overwhelming" evidence of his innocence, while refusing to say what any of that evidence was. (Hafner's lawyer, the redoubtable and controversial Jack Litwin, did argue publicly for his client's innocence, but, as we shall see, his claims were open to serious question.)

What had really happened? And if, as we will argue, a rabbinic court palpably interfered with justice in this case, what can be done to discourage similar abuses in the future?

Certainly, from the standpoint of the alleged victim — who never received his bravely demanded day in court — the result was neither new nor exceptional. By 2000, the year of the aborted Hafner prosecution, the tendency of Orthodox rabbis to stifle child sex abuse cases had grown so notorious that not even the Orthodox press could ignore it. In February of that year, a letter from a prominent Orthodox Jewish psychologist, Dr. Mordechai Glick, appeared in the ultra-Orthodox weekly, the *Jewish Press*, expressing dismay over what happened to Orthodox sex abuse victims. Glick complained that they were generally barred by their rabbis from going to the police in the first place. And the cover-ups did not end there:

> [I]f the police do get involved [wrote Glick], a massive cover-up and pressure campaign usually ensures that the case will either not get to trial or if it does, will be dropped because potential witnesses are pressured (code for threatened) to refuse to testify or outright lie.[1]

As a practicing psychologist and an officer of Nefesh, an international organization of Orthodox Jewish health care professionals, Dr. Glick had ample reason to know whereof he spoke. Nor, as a devoutly Orthodox Jew himself, could he be accused of invidious bias. How much Glick knew about the Hafner case is a matter of conjecture, but its details (discussed below) would not have surprised him: the invention of new "evidence" by rabbis and their efforts to silence the alleged victim and his family fit all too neatly into Glick's description of a "massive coverup and pressure campaign," which in Hafner's case did, in fact, ensure that the case would not go to trial.

Nor was there anything unusual in the attitude of the caftaned, widehatted Bobov Hasidim toward the deep-sixing of the complaint against Hafner. When Hafner was arrested in January 2000 on child abuse charges (reportedly twisting and tugging his student's genitals over eighteen months of religious tutoring), the alleged victim's mother was "harassed" and "persecuted," according to acquaintances, for exposing the matter to non-Jewish authorities. Later, at a holiday ceremony in the enormous main community synagogue, the Hasidim boisterously congratulated Hafner on the dropping of the charges against him, and derided his accusers — who later moved out of Brooklyn to protect their reputations from further attacks.

Business as usual? Alas, probably so. As Rabbi Yosef Blau of Yeshiva University asked, rhetorically, in a public Internet posting over six years later:

> What is being done to protect the young and the vulnerable? . . . [W]ill they [the Orthodox rabbinic "establishment"] acknowledge that our community is not immune to a scourge that exists in all societies. . . . Anyone in contact with survivors of abuse is aware that they rarely get any support when they complain to rabbis. How many teachers have been fired from one school only to be hired by another[?] The true reason that they were let go was not revealed because the fellow needs to make a living and the scandal will hurt his family. Proper considerations but where is the concern for new victims and their families?[2]

So if the Hafner case was unusual in any way, it differed from the norm not because of what was done in it, and not because of the priorities reflected by the rabbis' defense of the accused, but because so many of the people involved told their stories directly to the authors of this chapter.[3] That they spoke so freely means that what the rabbis apparently did to the victim — and to the justice system — can be studied in detail, whereas most such cases must be dismissed with generalities about "pressure on the witnesses" and "community unwillingness to see the charges brought to a secular court." It also means that the gap between reality and the official rabbinic account of the case against Rabbi Hafner can be demonstrated with unusual clarity. Finally, and perhaps most significantly, it gives us an opportunity to explore methods of preventing stories like this one from representing the norm in the future.[4]

If anyone harbors doubts about the urgency of such reform for all of us, not just for Orthodox Jews, these should be put to rest by this case's example of the degree to which Orthodox rabbis can intervene in the secular criminal justice system, an institution which is, after all, meant to serve citizens of all religions and ethnicities. In the Hafner case, it was after a visit from a panel of rabbis, fresh from conducting their own "trial," that the office of Brooklyn District Attorney Charles "Joe" Hynes suddenly decided to drop the charges against the accused child abuser. And just in case anyone missed the point, the rabbis frankly boasted, afterward, that they were the ones whose "evidence" had saved Rabbi Hafner from prosecution. "We educated the D.A. on how to properly conduct a sex abuse trial," Rabbi Chaim Rottenberg, one of the rabbinic judges whose court cleared Hafner, told the authors. Years later, Rabbi Rottenberg was even more emphatic. "If we didn't convince the D.A.," he asked the *Jewish Voice and Opinion* rhetorically in July 2006, "then why did Hynes drop the case so suddenly?"[5]

Why, indeed? As we will see, the facts do not support the rabbis' claim of Hafner's innocence. As "new evidence" in Hafner's favor, the rabbis told prosecutors that the site of the alleged abuse (a mostly empty house used as a synagogue on the Sabbath) was too public for such acts to have gone unnoticed — yet this was contradicted by every unbiased person who had seen the place, including Rabbi Hafner's own wife, who told the authors that Hafner taught the boy alone, on weekday mornings, in a "secluded" building.

In the end, it wasn't the evidence that mattered — neither to the rabbis nor to the prosecutors they pressed to drop the charges. "This [the Bobov Hasidim and their supporters] is a very powerful, political community," said a frustrated Katherine Grimm, the pediatrician and child abuse expert who examined the alleged victim and then turned the case over to the police. "The community [rank and file] was told not to talk to the police. . . . [And] there were definitely things said about [the boy and his family] that weren't true." In the end, said Dr. Grimm, "justice was obstructed."

A Commandment to Kill the Informer

This chapter aims at a consideration of strategies for containing rabbinic interference with the criminal justice system, of which the Hafner case presents a painfully lucid example. But why assume such strategies are necessary in the first place? Why not simply appeal to the good judgment of the rabbinate itself, and call for a more just application of the principles of Jewish law to what is, after all, equally a crime under U.S. and Jewish statutes?[6]

Alas, such an approach would be doomed to failure; it assumes that most rabbis prefer cooperation with a non-Jewish justice system (the only course that leads to actual confinement and punishment for violent criminals) to the unhampered activities of child molesters within Orthodox communities. Yet the stubborn fact remains that most ultra-Orthodox rabbis appear to be less disturbed by child abuse, even when the victim belongs to their own communities, than by the victim's decision to resort to non-Jewish authorities. Just months after a panel of ultra-Orthodox rabbis did away with the charges against Hafner (and cast aspersions on his accusers), a full-page notice was published in a Yiddish-language Brooklyn newspaper to remind all readers of the "severe prohibition" against making police reports against any Jew who abuses children. Written in the formal Hebrew of traditional religious texts, the declaration was signed by fifty prominent rabbis, and stated in part:

> A Jewish man or woman who informs [to non-Jewish authorities], saying, "I shall go and inform upon another Jew," with respect to either his property or person, and [such person] was warned not to inform and he demurs and insists, "I shall inform!" — regarding him, it is a *mitzvah* [positive commandment] to kill him and whoever has the first opportunity to kill him is entitled to do so. . . .[7]

Strange as it may seem, this incitement to murder — aimed, as clearly stated, not at the perpetrator of a violent crime but at the victim who "informs" on him — was by no means without precedent. In rough outline, it was based on a seminal sixteenth-century source of practical Jewish law, the *Shulhan Arukh*, and the authority of the ruling in question has been largely unchallenged for centuries.[8]

True, neither the Talmud nor the traditional law codes actually define a police report about a suspected criminal as "informing" within the meaning of the prohibition.[9] But this fact is overshadowed by a long Jewish tradition of deferring to rabbinic authority, as opposed to secular officials, in nearly all things — particularly where the community's public image is at stake. Historically, as a leading scholar reminds us, rabbis have "exerted full and unchallenged authority" over Jewish communal life in such areas as "trade, real estate dealings, torts and damages, marriage and divorce" since as long ago as third-century Babylonia.[10] To this day, ultra-Orthodox Jews regard it as a sin, except under clearly defined circumstances, to take their disputes to a non-Jewish court in preference to a rabbinic tribunal, or *beth din*. A sin on a large scale: for to resolve Jewish grievances in a secular court is not only to demonstrate contempt for Jewish law, but to degrade the religious community by publicly airing its quarrels among outsiders. Against such a background, it comes as no surprise that most ultra-Orthodox Jews — and certainly most Orthodox rabbis — unhesitatingly apply the same principles to an allegation of sexual abuse made by one Orthodox Jew against another.

The scandal attendant upon such an accusation is probably enough, in itself, to ensure a preference for "internal" resolution.

Not that the cases are truly parallel, of course. The enormous prestige enjoyed by rabbinic courts can blind traditional communities to the severe limitations under which such tribunals necessarily labor when they try to adjudicate a violent crime, like child abuse. Rabbinic courts, in fact, are largely impotent to stop a criminal. Lacking a police force, they necessarily rely on cooperation; they cannot arrest suspects, compel the production of information or evidence, detain a suspect pending the outcome of a trial, or even punish an offender in the event he is found guilty. Paradoxically, these courts wield much more power when their "verdicts" favor the accused. For, in that case, victims and potential witnesses alike may be threatened, on re-ligious grounds, with ostracism — or worse — if they subsequently take their grievances to the police or testify in a criminal trial. On the other hand, a real offender, if found guilty, can usually evade the verdict simply by moving to another community, a course a criminal is likely to prefer to the chance of incarceration if he stays put.

This lopsided balance of power between accuser and accused is a large enough flaw to rule out the regulation of child sex abuse by means of the beth din. But there is a more serious one. Unfortunately for the victims of abuse, the bitter historical experience of Jews at the hands of many non-Jewish gov-ernments has led most rabbis to rank "informing" above criminal sexual as-sault as an unforgivable offense, so that it is the accuser who really ends up on trial. As in the published announcement quoted above, rabbis openly speak of "informing" as a capital crime, while even the most severe cases of child sex abuse do not involve a death penalty.[11] How seldom this priority of values is challenged in Orthodox circles may be seen from a book written less than fif-teen years ago for the specific purpose of lionizing certain Hasidic rebbes, in which one reads (without any editorial comment) that a Jew who was merely suspected of passing information to the Soviet NKVD was threatened with death in order to protect other Hasidim from military service during World War II.[12]

The traditional Jewish mistrust for secular authorities is by no means re-stricted to sex abuse investigations. In February 1993, as reported in the *New York Times*, the Department of Education investigated widespread Pell grant fraud in the New York metropolitan area, much of which involved Ortho-dox Jewish yeshivas. As part of the investigation, officials issued subpoenas to principals and other school officers who were suspected of running sham postsecondary programs with federal money. For months, full-page advertisements adorned prominent Jewish newspapers, signed by eminent rabbis, urging special "sensitivity" on the part of government officials when serving those subpoenas on Orthodox Jews. The rabbis, supported by several of the region's U.S. senators, wanted the Jewish schools to receive advance notice before federal agents arrived with subpoenas to seize their records, arguing that an unannounced visit would remind Jews of "ambush" searches that characterized Jewish life in Eastern Europe.[13] The rabbis and their political escorts simply assumed that Orthodox Jews would make *no* distinction between U.S. federal officials in the late twentieth century and the Nazi storm troopers who invaded Jewish homes and businesses or the anti-Semitic Czarist goons who roughed up Jews for fun and profit. If that was really so — and plenty of evidence supports the assumption — it is hardly surprising that Orthodox sex-abuse victims who turn to U.S. police instead of rabbis find little sympathy among their coreligionists.

Not every Orthodox rabbi accepts this state of affairs. Rabbi Mark Dratch, a leading authority on Jewish clerical abuse, has publicly rejected the invocation of the prohibition of "informing" (*m'sirah* in Hebrew) to shield a rabbi accused of child abuse from being reported to secular authorities.[14] But Rabbi Dratch himself admits that more than legal issues are involved. According to him, Orthodox Jews have worried aloud that a suspected rabbi, if jailed, may be attacked in prison. (Why this makes him more deserving of sympathy than a child who was already sexually assaulted — by that rabbi — is not clear.) Another commonly expressed fear is that the convicted rabbi's family name will be so badly tarnished that his children and relatives will have difficulty finding suitable marriage partners. And then there are rabbis who fear that a publicly pressed charge of child abuse will stigmatize the entire community and encourage anti-Semitism.

These considerations certainly help to explain why, whatever authorities like Rabbi Dratch may say, most Orthodox rabbis, and in fact most Orthodox Jews, are still prepared to shield abusers from secular authorities — to "publicly defend [a religious Jew] just to keep him out of the criminal justice system," despite strong evidence of his guilt, as one well-placed insider explained to the authors.

But what happens when a victim of child sexual abuse, or his family, finally becomes convinced that only the criminal justice system can punish the abuser or protect the community from more abuse? What happens when that family is no longer satisfied with the justice dispensed by Orthodox rabbis?

Simply this: once across that Rubicon, such a victim often discovers that religious authorities not only work against him (or her), but literally against the law. In one recent case of suspected spousal abuse by an Orthodox Jew known to the authors, the man's wife (who had made a police report) was required by rabbis, as a condition of obtaining a religious divorce, to sign an agreement promising not to cooperate with police or other authorities who might investigate the charges — in other words, to obstruct justice. She was even forbidden to obey a subpoena or court order requiring her to testify unless given permission by certain Orthodox rabbis. (Strangely enough, this blatantly illegal agreement was drafted with the assistance of an Orthodox lawyer!) Similar cases have occurred with depressing frequency. To mention only one: a Hasidic woman who alleged having been raped by her husband (an assault that, she believed, had caused a miscarriage) was warned by rabbis that she would receive neither a divorce nor any monetary settlement from her (wealthy) husband unless she agreed in writing not to press charges and to leave the country immediately. (She did; she did not receive the promised settlement.) As a rule, a rabbinic threat to an Orthodox woman to withhold a religious divorce (which renders the woman unable to remarry within the religious community), or a threat to stigmatize the victim or the victim's siblings, is sufficient to ensure the victim's compliance and silence.[15]

But suppose even that fails? Suppose the victim remains determined to see his or her abuse vindicated in the criminal justice system? In that case, the victim's obstinacy brings on the final stage: the "massive cover-up and pressure campaign" described by Dr. Glick. This may take the form of a half-baked "trial" before a rabbinic court, like the one in which Rabbi Baruch Lanner, convicted in 2002 of sex abuse and sentenced to seven years in a New Jersey prison, was "exonerated" thirteen years earlier by three Orthodox rabbis after he challenged both the honesty and the emotional health of the young man who accused him. The rabbis ordered the victim, Elie Hiller, to write a public letter of apology to Rabbi Lanner, and looked aside as his name was publicly smeared; meanwhile, the rabbi, despite mounting allegations of abuse and sexual misconduct, held increasingly prestigious positions until the *Jewish Week* in June 2000 broke the silence surrounding his story.[16]

Or the cover-up may involve a rabbinic court of the kind that defended indicted child abuser Avrohom Mondrowitz in Jerusalem, several years after

Mondrowitz fled the United States to escape prosecution for first-degree sodomy and sexual abuse against several young boys. The Israeli rabbis stated that Mondrowitz — against whom they had heard no evidence from his alleged victims — could not be reported to police because of the "anguish" this could cause his aging parents. (Why the "anguish" of his victims was less important was not stated.) Even more, the rabbis allowed Mondrowitz to claim publicly that, on the strength of their ruling, he had been exonerated. This was untrue, of course, since the rabbis, not bothering with evidence of guilt, had forbidden victims to make a police report against Mondrowitz, irrespective of the crimes of which he was accused. Yet as late as 2003, Mondrowitz boasted of this rabbinic ruling as proof of his innocence.[17] The Israeli rabbis had never said a word to contradict him.

Or, again, the "massive cover-up and pressure campaign" may come as an assortment of all of the above: threats, fabrication of evidence, political maneuvers with prosecutors, blame-the-victim tactics — all of this carried out by rabbis, and aimed not only at the Orthodox community but also at the secular justice system. That is what happened in the Hafner case.

"Her Ethical Duty"

The story of the charges against Rabbi Solomon ("Shlomo") Hafner began in 1997. David Abraham (not his real name) was, by that time, a boy of nine. Due to a serious hearing deficiency, he required special tutoring in order to be "mainstreamed" into the Bobov yeshiva, or religious school. Rabbi Hafner seemed a natural choice for the job. The thirty-eight-year-old Hafner, with nine children of his own, had tutored "hundreds" of other children in the Bobov community over eighteen years, according to his wife, and he was well known to the Abraham family.

"I never fought with [the Abrahams]," a soft-spoken, earnest Chaya Hafner, Rabbi Hafner's wife, told the authors. She was shocked, she said, when her husband was charged with abuse. "[We were] friendly, good friends, knew each other for years."

The time and location of the boy's tutoring sessions with Hafner were a matter of great importance in the outcome of this case, so let these be stated clearly at once. The lessons took place from eight to nine on weekday mornings, in a converted house known as the Voydislaver Synagogue. This was, in fact, an old house, now empty and used for prayer services on the Sabbath. Indeed, according to Mrs. Hafner, its emptiness was exactly why it was chosen: because the boy's hearing aid picked up excessive background noise, he needed a "quiet" place for tutoring, and the Voydislaver building was "secluded."

Despite a year and a half of intensive tutoring from Hafner, the boy's performance, to his parents' surprise, seemed rather to stagnate than to improve. "He was daydreaming, distracted," says his speech pathologist, Adele Markwitz. This was particularly puzzling since the boy, notwithstanding his hearing problem, was described by Markwitz as "very intelligent and hardworking." In late 1998, "worried about his behavior and performance," according to Dr. Katherine Grimm, the parents fired Rabbi Hafner as their son's tutor. But no one yet suspected abuse.

Months later, the boy began to disclose bizarre details of his eighteen months with Rabbi Hafner. "They were sadistic things," said Grimm, audibly balancing outrage and professional detachment. "Pulling of his genitals . . . hitting the ear with the hearing aid." The child also said he was threatened with worse than this if he told anyone about the abuse.

Grimm confirmed that Mrs. Abraham, like so many other Hasidim, was so reluctant to allow charges like these into general view that she spent over eight months seeking a solution "within the community." "The mother's concern [was] for other children who may be at risk," Grimm told the authors. "She felt it was her ethical duty."

But, finally, after eight months of what the mother later called "nothing," she had had enough with "internal" solutions. Now she felt that intervention from "outside" was necessary. Armed with the support of two Orthodox Jewish therapists — social worker Meir Wikler and psychologist Moshe Wangrofsky, both of whom reportedly believed the boy was telling the truth — Mrs. Abraham had her son examined by Dr. Grimm, who works with the Manhattan Children's Advocacy Center and, as an assistant professor at Mount Sinai Medical Center, not only chairs a child abuse clinical evaluation program but teaches other doctors throughout the state about child abuse prevention and detection. Grimm was impressed: "The boy's story was consistent to everyone he spoke to and in all the details."

Detective Brenda Vincent Springer of the New York Police Department's (NYPD) Special Victims Squad, described by Dr. Grimm as an experienced professional with specific experience in the Hasidic Jewish community, interviewed the child after Grimm made an official report of suspected abuse. "She [Springer] found the [boy's] story to be very credible," said Grimm.

"She was so encouraging, and she was so helpful," said Mrs. Abraham of Detective Springer. "My son felt so secure with her, like she really understood him, and he wasn't scared to tell her what actually happened, like he told her things that he hadn't even told us happened."

The Abrahams might have felt secure in the course they had taken, but after Rabbi Hafner's arrest on January 13, 2000, the reaction of other Bobover Hasidim was swift and angry. Kevin Davitt, the Brooklyn D.A.'s director of public information, acknowledged that some members of the Bobov community complained to his office that the D.A. was on a "witch hunt" against Hasidim. Henna White, the D.A.'s official liaison to Orthodox Jews, went farther than that: she told the authors that after Rabbi Hafner was formally charged, she heard from "sources" that even Dovid Cohen, a prominent Brooklyn rabbi who, according to Mrs. Abraham, had approved the Abrahams' resort to secular authorities, had been "threatened."

Rabbi Cohen presumably could have responded to the threats in a number of ways — one of which would have been the issuance of a police report of his own — to bring his tormentors to justice. But, significantly, he chose not to do that. Instead he did what, as we have seen, Orthodox rabbis have generally done when they find themselves in conflict with other Orthodox Jews: he agreed to take the issue to a Jewish court. In other words, the rabbi, under attack from other rabbis, took what had been a criminal matter involving a rabbi and the Abraham boy and submitted it to still more rabbis for adjudication. And he did this even before the prosecutors had presented their case in court. As a result, the Abrahams, as pious Orthodox Jews, had to go before the new rabbinic court as well. Thus was born, in February 2000, the next stage of the suppression of the Hafner case.

Intervention of a Jewish Court

The Jewish court that was now supposed to weigh the criminal charges against Rabbi Hafner was composed of five rabbis, all of them drawn from ultra-Orthodox communities throughout New York City and its surroundings. At its head was Manhattan's Rabbi Dovid Feinstein, the son of one of the United States' most famous Orthodox rabbis, the late Moshe Feinstein. Two other members were Brooklyn rabbis; a fourth was a Yiddish-speaking rabbi from Rockland County; the remaining judge was Rabbi Chaim Rottenberg, chief rabbi of a Hasidic enclave in Monsey, a heavily ultra-Orthodox community thirty-five miles from Manhattan.

Later, Rabbi Rottenberg would be particularly explicit about the role of this rabbinic court and its relation to the official proceedings then beginning to unfold before a grand jury. The purpose of the beth din was, simply put, to persuade the D.A. to decide the case without the benefit of legal process. Rabbi Rottenberg told the authors that even as he approached other rabbis to urge them to join the panel, he warned them that if the rabbis did not intervene, "this [case] is going to stay by the D.A. until the D.A.'s decision." Rottenberg considered such a result unacceptable, and apparently the other rabbis agreed; they worked at a pace Rottenberg later described as "emergency," and by the first week in March, even before the rabbinic court had officially handed down its judgment, they were prepared to visit the D.A.'s office, together with Hafner's attorney, Jack Litman, with "new evidence" of Hafner's innocence. Assembly Speaker Sheldon Silver (an Orthodox Jew himself) weighed in with political support: "Shelly Silver said he's not taking sides," Rottenberg said, "but he does want the doors opened [at the D.A.'s office] to listen to what we have to say."

The critical meeting with prosecutors took place in mid-March. A few days later, on March 21, the D.A.'s office issued a terse statement unequivocally exonerating Rabbi Hafner.

The statement of the D.A.'s office offered no specifics to explain its action, and its officials, then and now, have not divulged details of the evidence of Hafner's innocence they are supposed to have received. In fact, it seems doubtful that they received any real evidence at all. It is axiomatic among lawyers that secondhand, or hearsay, evidence is of no legal weight, yet, amazingly, according to the members of the rabbinic court themselves, no actual witnesses to any of the "evidence" in Hafner's favor ever met with the prosecutors. Rabbi Moshe Farkas, a Brooklyn rabbi and the most active member of the court in its evidence-gathering stages, told the authors that he alone presented Bobov's case (necessarily secondhand) aided only by Hafner's lawyer, to Chief Assistant District Attorney (A.D.A.) Albert Teichman, Sex Crimes Unit head Rhonnie Jaus, and A.D.A. Deanne Puccio. Rabbi Rottenberg seconded Farkas's claim that no witnesses spoke to D.A. officials. He said that he and another member of the rabbinic panel had tried to introduce community witnesses to prosecutors before Farkas's visit (and Silver's call), but "they didn't let us in the door"—so that, after the rabbis profited from Silver's introduction, they approached prosecutors on their own. Attorney Litman insisted that witnesses were "presented" to D.A. officials, though he would not say who, or even how many, they were.

But how is a man proved innocent without the presentation of evidence from people who can vouch for it personally? The rabbis would have been barred from presenting hearsay testimony in court. If no witnesses were actually interviewed by prosecutors, the D.A.'s office should at least have required "independent confirmation" of what Farkas said, according to the opinion a former judge, Karen Burstein, gave the authors. Otherwise the prosecutors could not have discharged their duty as public guardians, because they never determined what real evidence in Hafner's defense, if any, might have been presented in a real trial. "I think if I were the D.A.," said Burstein, who called the facts of the Hafner case "troubling," "I would be chary of acting solely on their [the rabbis'] representation."

Not Interested in Pursuing the Case

Maybe Burstein would have been "chary" of taking some rabbis' word for the proper course to follow in a criminal case — especially one the New York police force's own detective had believed in so unhesitatingly less than three months earlier — but, unfortunately, the Brooklyn D.A.'s office could not be expected to share her view. Under Charles "Joe" Hynes, who was elected to the office with considerable Orthodox Jewish support in 1989, Brooklyn prosecutors have been known to take a less than zealous approach to child sex abuse cases when they arise in the Hasidic or ultra-Orthodox community.

Take the case of Avrohom Mondrowitz (mentioned above), who, with the title "rabbi" and a purported degree in psychology, won the trust of Orthodox Jewish families all over Brooklyn in the late 1970s and early 1980s. During those years, Mondrowitz ran a school for troubled children and offered one-on-one "counseling" for hundreds more, specializing in referrals from Brooklyn's Orthodox private schools. By 1984, he was popular with the community, local yeshivas, and the Brooklyn-based, Orthodox-run Ohel foster care agency. He was described as "friendly," "smiling," and "sensitive," and his image was enhanced by a local radio program on which he hosted and interviewed such popular Orthodox personalities as Shlomo Carlebach and Mordechai Ben-David. Obviously pious, with a growing family of his own, the bearded, thirty-seven-year-old Mondrowitz must have seemed the perfect choice to counsel Orthodox Jewish boys who were experiencing problems in school or trouble within the family.[18]

What the children's families did not know was that Mondrowitz, according to Brooklyn police, was also an out-of-control pedophile whose alleged activities with the young boys he counseled ranged from fondling their genitals to oral and anal sodomy. Sal Catalfumo, the detective who helped break the case in November 1984, estimated that by then Mondrowitz's victims may have numbered in the hundreds. But even as a few of them began to make hair-raising statements to the police, Mondrowitz, somehow alerted that a warrant had been issued for his arrest, fled the country and reappeared in Israel early in 1985.

The most disturbing fact about the Mondrowitz story, however, is the way the new Brooklyn D.A., who put together a virtually all-Orthodox Jewish Advisory Council to help him decide how to handle criminal cases within the Hasidic community,[19] first ignored and then tried to close the case against Mondrowitz altogether.[20] In 1993, D.A. Charles "Joe" Hynes informed federal officials responsible for seeking the fugitive's extradition that he "would not be pursuing the case any further at this time," and would "consider pursuing the case" only if Mondrowitz were to return to the United States.[21]

Nor was the Mondrowitz case the only such failure occurring on Hynes's watch. In 1990, prominent rabbis apparently threw their weight behind Mordechai Ehrman, a Hasidic operator of a Brooklyn day care center, after he was accused by parents of having molested children in his care. A beth din was convened, ostensibly for the purpose of taking relevant evidence, but which in fact referred potential witnesses to a politically influential rabbi who discouraged them from testifying. A friend of one of the parents complained openly to the *Jewish Week* that "they [the rabbis] have an 'in' with the District Attorney's office and hold weight as to whether a case is pressed or not. They want this one shoved under the carpet . . . so it is going to be hushed up." In the end, Ehrman's case was not even presented to a grand jury.[22]

More recently, in April 2008, the *New York Jewish Week* featured two articles that raised doubts about a plea bargain Hynes's office arranged with Rabbi Yehuda Kolko, who had been charged with sexually abusing two children and an adult former student. A yeshiva teacher, Rabbi Kolko had been dogged by allegations of sexually abusing children for decades; a precedent-setting civil lawsuit against him by several men who said they had been abused by Kolko as children was the focus of a feature-length article in *New York* magazine in May 2006.

Given the charges against Rabbi Kolko, many professionals — and some in the Orthodox community — were openly dismayed when Brooklyn prosecutors agreed to accept a guilty plea to two counts of child endangerment, a misdemeanor, and to drop all other charges. The deal allowed Kolko to walk out of court without serving a single day of prison time, receiving only three years of probation, and involved no admission that he had committed any sort of sexual offense.

One of this chapter's authors, Michael Lesher, was quoted by the *Jewish Week* as he assailed the Kolko deal as part of "a pattern of inaction by Charles Hynes' office in cases of this kind." The newspaper quoted Lesher further as saying that he had "hard evidence in specific cases," and that "I must at this point consider it to be a politically motivated pattern [for the prosecutor's office to abandon credible charges of abuse]." Marci Hamilton, a professor of constitutional law at Yeshiva University's Cardozo School of Law, echoed Lesher's disappointment, calling the outcome of the Kolko case "the worst of all possible worlds."[23]

Two weeks later, the same newspaper reported that the Kolko plea deal had "attracted censure both in Brooklyn's Orthodox community and from legal experts," and detailed Hynes's contradictory explanations of the result. The *Jewish Week* also reported that the families of the alleged child victims disputed Hynes's account of the facts leading up to the deal. The reporters quoted a letter written by the father of one of the boys the day after signing a form consenting to the plea deal, "indicat[ing] he had been pressured into signing his consent statement":

> "I feel justice was not served because I see the damage Kolko caused to our son," [the father continued]. "My son was ready to go to trial and we feel he would have done an excellent job and I am sorry to hear that [the case against] Joel Kolko will not proceed further."[24]

In short, there is a considerable record of the Brooklyn D.A.'s kowtowing to rabbinic influence. With such a history, should it surprise us that his office was willing to drop child abuse charges against Solomon Hafner on the say-so of five prominent Orthodox rabbis from all over the metropolis, whether they presented valid evidence or not?

"The Kid Was Bragging On and On"
It is now time to examine the specific arguments offered by Rabbi Hafner's defenders in favor of the D.A.'s abrupt decision to pull the Hafner case from

the grand jury on March 21. Even a cursory inspection shows that the case the rabbis presented in Hafner's defense was the opposite of "overwhelming" — though that is how D.A. spokesperson Kevin Davitt characterized it to the authors in an interview given some time after the fact. Davitt would not even give details of the evidence he claimed to find "overwhelming."

Hafner's lawyer, Jack Litman, was predictably less timid, but no more convincing, than Davitt. Years before the Hafner case, Litman had built his public profile as a defense attorney by attacking the character of the victim of a sex-related homicide committed by his client, Robert Chambers, in 1986. Now Litman blamed Hafner's alleged victim for "making up" the sex abuse charges. As for the evidence that proved the boy's alleged fraud, Litman told the authors that the rabbis had "discovered" the boy claimed to have been sexually abused in a place "observable by dozens and dozens of people every single day." Rabbi Rottenberg elaborated on Litman's claim, explaining that the small synagogue had "big, huge half-wall windows . . . open to the street," and insisted, "There are close to a hundred people who have the combination if it would be locked. There are twenty, thirty in and out daily. . . . There's a side door which everybody knows, it's open always."

But Rabbi Hafner's wife presented a very different picture of the place where her husband tutored — and, allegedly, abused — the Abraham boy. She said, "[The Abrahams] had asked him to learn *privately* [with the boy] *in a very secluded place* because he has a hearing aid and his hearing aid will pick up any outside noise, so he must have a quiet place. . . . He [Rabbi Hafner] tutored the child for eighteen months, once a day, in the mornings between eight and nine, *there was nobody there.* . . ."[25] This was a far cry from the crowded, open-to-the-public setting described by Litman and Rabbi Rottenberg.

A weekday morning visit to the site by the authors confirmed Mrs. Hafner's description. The aging Voydislaver Synagogue, a converted house, had no windows of any kind on the street level. All doors were locked; as for seeing inside, only someone standing on a ladder could have peered into the synagogue on the main floor. Through a small, diamond-shaped pane in one of its three weather-beaten doors (not the main one), nothing but a staircase, leading up, was dimly visible. When a buzzer next to the door was pressed, a woman's voice confirmed that the synagogue was closed and that there were no prayers inside except on the Sabbath. No one entered or left the building between eight and nine o'clock, the time period when Hafner had tutored the Abraham boy.

When asked, Mrs. Abraham maintained that some of Hafner's defenders simply fabricated the rabbis' details. "They had somebody go to the yeshiva down the block," she told the authors, "and tell the kids the combination [to the front door lock], so they could say a hundred people had the combination."

Against this background, Karen Burstein, the former judge, challenged the evidentiary worth of the rabbis' claim to the D.A. that the synagogue was wide open to the public. " 'Everybody could see,' " she said, "requires you to show that somebody did see" what transpired between Hafner and the boy. The rabbis had only made half an argument; the evidentiary value of claiming that the setting of the alleged abuse was wide open to the public lay in the implication that any criminal acts would have been immediately apparent to the "dozens and dozens of people" supposedly watching. Yet no one, including the rabbis and attorney Litman, ever claimed that even one specific witness actually observed Hafner tutoring the child. Without a witness, the rabbis had proved nothing at all, even granting their highly dubious premise that there *might have been* a witness.

Besides this, the rabbis seem to have made only perfunctory efforts to ascertain the mental or emotional state of the alleged child victim, the only inquiry that might conceivably have led to doubts concerning the credibility of an otherwise persuasive witness. Two mental health professionals were consulted by the rabbis, but neither of them interviewed the child. Toward the end of the trial, the rabbis engaged the services of Sylvan Schaffer, an Orthodox psychologist and lawyer, who was the clinical coordinator and director of education of the forensic psychiatry program at North Shore University Hospital. But, remarkably, even Dr. Schaffer was not asked to interview the boy. Instead, Rottenberg claimed the rabbis merely had Dr. Schaffer interview Rabbi Hafner, plus a "random" sample of six of Hafner's other students, for any evidence that *they* had been abused.

The sketchiness of this evidence did not prevent some members of the rabbinic court from casting aspersions on the boy's mind and character. "Because he's hearing impaired," said Rabbi Farkas, "he always wants to get attention." As usual, Rottenberg elucidated, as he dismissed the child's detailed testimony, "The kid was bragging on and on," sneered the rabbi, " 'I want to talk more, I have more to say, I want to talk.' The child spoke for a couple of hours, begging us to listen to him more and more . . . just eating the attention with such appetite." It does not seem to have occurred to Rottenberg that the boy's insistence on being heard could have been triggered by the rabbis' skepticism, or indeed from any psychological motive other than "wanting attention."

Nor did the rabbis pay much regard to the professionals who had supported his charges. Dr. Grimm, the child abuse expert, was not even invited to testify. "It was too dangerous a game, couldn't afford to lose, if you know what I mean," explained a friend of Rabbi Rottenberg's, who was himself a rabbi in Monsey, and who made a point of referring to the Abraham boy as "the rascal." "They [the rabbis] felt a goy would not have the perception . . . that's the reason why this lady wasn't called."

Rottenberg himself — a thin, boyish forty-eight-year-old behind a full beard — boasted to the authors that he "cornered" one of the social workers who supported the boy, by confronting him with the boy's claim that Rabbi Hafner had pulled his pubic hairs: "I said to him [the social worker], 'How stupid could you be?'" he remembered afterward. "A boy that age, either he doesn't have, or it's not big enough [to pull]." But Dr. Grimm told the authors that a physical examination showed the boy did indeed have pubic hair and added, reasonably, "[Y]ou don't need much" to pull it painfully. Detective Springer, though interviewed by a rabbinic court member, was, like Dr. Grimm, not invited to testify. "There seem to be real deficiencies," said Burstein of the rabbis' handling of the case. "Not hearing testimony from a forensic specialist who examined the child . . . is troubling."

The rabbis' priorities may perhaps be gauged by Rottenberg's statement that the rabbinic court started to make tape recordings of its sessions — but stopped midway "because they [D.A. officials] were going to subpoena it" and the rabbis did not believe details of child abuse allegations among Hasidim should be heard by non-Jewish authorities.[26] And then there is Rottenberg's claim that speech pathologist Adele Markwitz, though she visited the site of the trial to offer her testimony, was kept out because she had talked about the case on WNBC television news: "Making a statement in public about a private, innocent person," he told the authors, "that's being low." Markwitz, who is Jewish, claimed the rabbis also said that her willingness to discuss the case publicly proved "she hates Jews."

By the time of Farkas's meeting with prosecutors, the rabbinic court had already reached its verdict. According to Rottenberg, prosecutors asked the rabbis "unofficially" not to publish their verdict before the D.A.'s office announced its own decision to drop charges, because "they didn't want it to look like they bent under pressure." Mrs. Abraham, by contrast, had no advance warning of the outcome and was distraught when she heard it.

"'How am I gonna tell my son now that the rabbis feel he's lying?'" Rabbi Rottenberg recalled her saying. Raising his voice an octave to imitate the mother, he quoted her, "'I told him, "The rabbis are going to take care of Rabbi Hafner. They're going to put him into jail, punish him," and now what?' She started to go wild, claiming the beth din was biased, the beth din was all one sided.... [She said,] 'Now our name is going to be ruined.'"

Then it was the boy's turn to get the news. Rottenberg told him, "Are you aware that we can't buy this?" He told the authors, but without any apparent concern, that the child answered, "But that's how it happened. It's true.'"

"We Don't Have the Word 'Coincidence'"

There were no questions in Bobov about the rightness of the D.A.'s decision to drop the charges. Indeed, as the news spread through the Brooklyn community on March 21, 2000, a date that coincided that year with the Jewish holiday of Purim, when Jews celebrate their deliverance from threatened annihilation under ancient Persian rule, the Hasidim saw the timing of Hafner's exoneration as the work of divine providence. "By us *yidden* [Jews], we don't have the word 'coincidence' in our language," said Rottenberg. "We knew two or three days beforehand [that the charges would be dropped].... In Bobov, they sang all of Purim, and Shabbos after, a *niggun* [special song] to his favor and against the [Abrahams] in a shul of three thousand people, the main Bobov shul.... Everybody knew who they meant."

Mrs. Abraham still believes Hafner is a danger to other children—and has been for years. "The only people I don't forgive in this whole story is the [other] mothers," she told the authors bitterly, "who... hid their heads under the rug and they kept quiet about it... and that's why my son got hurt, because they were selfish." She herself, of course, did not make the same error; but in the end she was left alone. Even her erstwhile supporters in the Orthodox community proved unwilling to speak publicly about the case. Rabbi Dovid Cohen, a well-known Brooklyn authority who reportedly approved the use of secular authorities, was described to the authors by a close acquaintance of his as "shell-shocked" by the fierceness of the community criticism of his support of the Abrahams. Mrs. Abraham said that Cohen told her, "Let's let it die down.... They have a lot more political clout than we do.... You have to cut your losses at a certain point." Under pressure from the rabbis on the court, Cohen even wrote an open letter, which appeared on community bulletin boards, apologizing to Hafner for causing him "distress and humiliation," while nevertheless stressing his own "good intentions."

And the Abrahams? According to a close relative, they were pressured by the rabbinic court to sign a letter recanting the charges against Rabbi Hafner — which they refused to do.[27] For their commitment to the truth, they encountered so much hostility that they found they could not remain in Brooklyn, where their son had lived all his life, and, shortly after the Hafner case was dropped, they moved to a different Orthodox Jewish community.

ENDING THE COVER-UPS

To turn from the story of a scandal to recommendations for the prevention of a recurrence is, perhaps, to invite tedium. But the risk must be taken; otherwise, the story of the Hafner case stands only for the proposition that child sex abuse allegations can be mishandled by rabbis and prosecutors, and we scarcely need the detailed reporting presented here to tell us that much. The question is: now that we know exactly what happened and the means by which two institutions theoretically dedicated to justice (a rabbinic court and the Brooklyn district attorney's office) intersected to frustrate the prosecution of a crime, what can we do to both institutions to make them less vulnerable to such abuse in the future? The authors have addressed this very question in a special issue of the *Journal of Child Sexual Abuse*, devoted specifically to sex abuse committed by clergymen.[28] In this chapter, we will expand substantially on the suggestions offered there.

There can be no doubt that religious Jewish communities must shoulder a good deal of the responsibility. Child sex abuse cover-ups will not completely cease until the Jewish community comes to regard them as abhorrent and conveys this message, unmistakably, to its rabbis and lay leaders. That they occur is certainly not a recent discovery. As long ago as 1990, Rabbi Irving Greenberg recognized both the gravity and the pervasiveness of the problem:

> Rabbinic tradition repeatedly makes clear that mental anguish and moral degradation are the equivalent of physical murder. In a way, mental anguish and moral degradation are worse. The murder victim is released from further pain, whereas the incest and [sex] abuse victim is continually tortured

by the memory and its residual effects. To be silent then is to incur the grave guilt of accessory after the fact. Spiritual leaders who ignore or even cover up the presence of sexual abuse . . . , those who cut off or isolate victims who dare speak out, bring upon themselves the judgment that the Torah places on the accessory and bystander: "Do not stand idly by the blood of your neighbor." (Leviticus 19:16).[29]

So far, Rabbi Greenberg's appeal has had little appreciable effect on the rabbinate — although, happily, this has not been true of Orthodox Jews in general. In recent years, several Internet blogs devoted to Jewish subjects have begun to resound with complaints from disgruntled Jews. Many contributors (usually anonymous) describe their own abuse by a rabbi, or recount the details of cases they have witnessed, and condemn other rabbis for concealing the crimes involved. That the Orthodox rabbinate is aware of, and stung by, these accusations is evident from two recent and strongly worded attacks on blog reading, published in the same month, one written by the official spokesman for Agudath Israel of America (the most prominent organization of right-wing Orthodoxy in America)[30] and the other appearing in the *Jewish Observer*, a periodical published by the same organization.[31] Significantly, neither philippic actually denied the key charges made by the blog posters: namely, (1) that Orthodox rabbis have sexually abused children; (2) that many actual victims and witnesses exist; and (3) that the facts of these cases have, by and large, been concealed, suppressed, or ignored. In both of the antiblog articles, the authors contented themselves with execrating the medium in which the charges were conveyed; they did not touch the content of the charges. This suggests that the process of demanding change from the Orthodox rabbinate has already begun, though it clearly has a good way yet to go.

While we wait for the rabbinate to react more seriously to the problem, however, there are still ways of minimizing the damage that unrestricted child abusers have done to our communities. In fact, some such steps are already being taken. Elliot Pasik, an Orthodox Jewish attorney, recently pressed successfully for a New York state law requiring routine background checks of employees of religious schools, including yeshivas. Such checks have been commonplace for years in public schools, but were rarely carried out in New York's Orthodox institutions before the change in the law, so that even someone convicted of a sex offense could well have had unsupervised access to young children.

Pasik's accomplishment, modest as it may sound to an outsider, earned him some harsh attacks in some Orthodox quarters. Forced to justify having invited increased non-Jewish oversight of Jewish schools, Pasik pointed out that Jews had failed to regulate their own schools for far too long:

> [Our children] are entitled to the fullest protection that secular law and halacha [Jewish law] can give them. That should mean the establishment of an impartial panel of rabbis and frum [religious] experts adjudicating an abuse case ... involv[ing] cross examination of witnesses, medical and psychological testimony, medical records, and physical evidence.... It was not done.... Increased government oversight over the nonpublic schools is the only answer. Public safety and health for the benefit of our children's bodies supersede everything else.

Pasik noted with indignation that, for years, yeshivas had made no attempt to determine whether prospective employees could safely be allowed access to children, even when he and others had informally urged them to, and asked rhetorically:

> Does what I describe inspire any confidence ... that our yeshivas are capable of adjudicating abuse cases without the input of doctors and lawyers, and without accountability and transparency? Or doing background checks without the parents and the Government demanding it? I hope not....
>
> ... [Abusers] need to be forever banished from our system, and that our community has not done this, after everything that has occurred, is a great shame and stain on all [of] us.... [32]

Clearly, Orthodox activists like Pasik are not about to give up the fight. On the other hand, they are waging an uphill battle. One cannot quickly rid a community of mores formed over centuries by a complex mix of religion, sociopolitical history, and deeply ingrained memories of oppression.

That is why measures are needed from outside the Jewish community as well. If reform is to be possible at all, the valuable efforts being undertaken within religious communities must be supplemented by resources within the sphere of secular law enforcement. Both religious and secular institutions, as we have seen, are involved in the perversions of justice that too often result when an Orthodox Jew charges a rabbi with child sex abuse. Both must be included in a cure.

Who Will Judge the Judges?

To begin with the simplest but most fundamental reform, Jewish communities cannot defer educating children — and adults — about the reality of the sex abuse problem. Here and there, a few Orthodox communities, with rabbinic support, have begun to encourage such education in schools and special forums. It is axiomatic that education is irreversible; "[I]gnorance," as Oscar Wilde reminds us, "is a like a delicate exotic fruit: touch it and the bloom is gone."[33] Thus, the good news in this instance is that the process has begun, if so far only barely. No amount of blog banning will reverse it. On the other hand, how rapidly it will advance depends on the commitment of teachers and parents to demand action from their children's schools.

Rabbi Mark Dratch, whose work is mentioned above, urges rabbis to lecture on abuse-related issues. If nothing else, he says, doing this breaks the communal norm of silence and empowers victims to begin speaking out.[34] Silence, in Orthodox communities as elsewhere, undermines public confidence in the institutions of the community, which by its inaction (or worse) seems to take the side of the criminal against the innocent. Perhaps even more devastating, the tacit toleration of child sexual abuse makes Orthodox Jewish communities easy prey for pedophiles who know that, even if their activities are discovered, they are very unlikely to be reported to police.

The beth din itself should be subject to reform. Why should not concerned Orthodox Jews create an oversight tribunal for rabbinic courts that deal with child abuse cases — a board composed of rabbis, educators, social workers, marriage counselors, and psychologists? Those who set religious store by the institution of the beth din have every reason to make it functional. Rabbis are ill trained to take on sexual abuse cases and, as we have seen, all too often fail to look to the right sort of evidence or to assess accurately the kind of evidence they do consider. For this and other reasons it is doubtful whether rabbis should ever take on sexual abuse cases per se — ideally, these should be reported directly to police — but what if such issues arise in the course of a religious divorce, for example? Why not create a special structure for the handling of such allegations, to ensure that when such issues do arise before a beth din, they are not stifled? A committee charged with the oversight of rabbinic courts should report its findings regularly and in writing, and its members should be limited to a fixed tenure of office, so that cronyism and patronage do not become part of the oversight mechanism.

Under Jewish law, no one who knows of the commission of a crime can be considered innocent. Each individual has a positive duty to bear witness against injustice.[35] This principle affects different Jews in different ways, but no one is exempt from it. Concerned rabbis and Jewish communal leaders, for instance, must be acquainted with, and must help to circulate, the growing literature on Jewish law that supports the needs of abuse victims. This can be done by insisting on the duty to report abuse to police or other authorities, defending the right of victims to speak the truth, and placing the blame for any resulting scandal squarely on the abusers, where it belongs. The authors' experience suggests that few religious Jews are aware that authoritative rabbinic rulings exist that support the obligation to report sex abuse crimes to police. If local rabbis were to include these rulings in some of their classes and lectures, the effects could be significant. And, of course, lay people in the Orthodox community must play their part by studying these laws themselves and by demanding more fairness and openness on the part of their rabbinic courts. If we empower ourselves, we empower others against abuse.

The need for this has never been more evident. In October 2007, graduate students in psychology at three universities — the University of Chicago, Loyola University, and DePaul University — undertook to study the prevalence and effects of molestation in the Chicago Orthodox Jewish community. The study, called the Moral Responsibility Research Project, is focusing particularly on the rate at which victims report sex abuse to others, and, in cases in which reports are not made, the reasons for the omission. Though the study has yet to be published, some preliminary results have been disclosed.

These figures are sobering indeed. Of the Orthodox subjects who reported to researchers that they had been victims of sexual abuse as children, *not one* had disclosed this to police. Fifty-four percent of the self-reported victims explained their failure to involve the police by saying that their rabbi did not approve of informing on another Jew; another 21 percent said they feared for their family's safety, financial stability, or prestige had they come forward to secular authorities. Even reporting the abuse to their parents, to rabbis, or to other members of the Orthodox community seems to have had disappointing results; only half of those who disclosed their abuse in such a limited fashion reported receiving sympathy. Sixty-three percent of the male victims told the researchers that such disclosure had been harder for them than being victimized.[36] These statistics make it clear that rabbinic discouragement of child sex abuse reports is very much a reality, and that religious Jewish communities are far from properly educated about the sexual abuse of children and about Jewish law regarding the reporting of such abuse.

Orthodox Issues — Seen from Without

As Elliot Pasik's experience shows, reform cannot be pursued entirely from inside the affected religious communities. Important issues must be seriously considered by lawmakers and prosecutors to prevent yet another Hafner fiasco. Surely those directly involved in the criminal justice system can and should speak out forcefully about any mechanism that facilitates cover-ups of clerical sexual abuse. Ironically, to some extent, this may not require any new laws, but rather simply following existing law and policy directives that, up to now, have not been sufficiently enforced. For example, New York's Executive Law, Section 642(1) specifically requires that the "victim of a violent felony offense" (including child sexual abuse) or, where the victim is a minor, "the family of the victim . . . shall be consulted by the district attorney in order to obtain the views of the victim regarding disposition of the criminal case by dismissal."

This was clearly *not* done in the Hafner case, though the offense in question was certainly a violent felony and the alleged child victim was a minor. Why not? Perhaps the D.A.'s office is simply not accustomed to following this procedure in cases involving the Orthodox community. But the Brooklyn D.A. has a liaison specifically assigned to Orthodox Jews, and there is no excuse for not using that office to maintain communication in both directions: helping victims and witnesses understand the secular criminal process and listening to what the victims have to say when, as in this case, the prosecution hits a rabbinic snag. This is not only good policy, it is also state law. And if the law had been followed, perhaps prosecutors would have given the rabbinic court's pro-Hafner "evidence" the second look it deserved, at a minimum.

Another — and somewhat more creative — approach to reining in the overreaching of rabbinic courts is to apply to them the same standards and methods already used when witnesses are intimidated by gangs or organized crime members. This, too, is already provided for in the law of New York (as in many other states), where Section 641(2) of the Executive Law requires "notification of a victim or a witness as to steps that law enforcement officers or district attorneys can take to protect victims and witnesses from intimidation." The problem is not the absence of such a law, but the fact that the law has seldom been invoked in Jewish sex abuse cases. Obviously, rabbinic courts are not to be thought of as composed of violent criminals, and their methods are not likely to be the same as those of criminal gangs. Still, within the communities they serve, rabbinic tactics can be just as intimidating and can undermine justice just as effectively. A potential witness, told that if he testifies he will be ostracized from his community, that his children will never marry, and that he will be punished in the afterlife, may be as effectively silenced as if he had been threatened with a gun. No one denies this — so there is no denying the applicability of the statute to Orthodox Jewish sex abuse cases. Police and prosecutors had better be educated about the potential of rabbinic courts to interfere with victims and witnesses in child sex abuse investigations — and must act accordingly, even if this means finding new applications for old laws. In the Hafner case, no steps of any kind were taken to protect the witnesses, several of whom (as we have seen) were shunned or insulted by the rabbis.

The legal system is an integral part of a society's web of governing institutions; obviously, it is crippled if it fails to enforce the laws against child sexual abuse everywhere, including inside religious Jewish communities. Perhaps no prosecutor can completely ignore the significance of large voting blocs. But district attorneys can establish policies that, for example, bar prosecutors from relying on religious courts to take over their function — as in the Hafner case — a practice that raises serious constitutional questions and can only erode the credibility of the legal system as a whole. The general public can and should demand that all abused children be given the same sort of treatment in the criminal justice system.

So far we have discussed state legislation as a basis for reform. Yet some additional legal resources, though never before used to combat child abuse cover-ups, may be found in federal civil rights law. This is an area ripe for exploration and application. For example, under Section 241 of Title 18 of the U.S. Code, a conspiracy of two or more people "to injure, oppress, threaten, or intimidate any person in any State . . . in the free exercise or enjoyment of any right or privilege secured to him by the Constitution or laws of the United States" is a crime punishable by a fine and/or up to ten years' imprisonment. Since access to the court system is defined by courts as just such a "right or privilege" protected by the Constitution,[37] this means that what the rabbis allegedly did in attempting to prevent the Abrahams from pursuing the criminal charges against Hafner may have been a federal crime. Nor should we overlook the evidence that the rabbis intimidated potential witnesses who might have testified in support of the boy's charges — acts that also, under this statute, could have constituted a criminal offense. It is too late to remedy what happened to the Abrahams. But if rabbis who undertook similar actions against other alleged victims were threatened with prosecution under civil rights laws, they might think twice about interfering with the criminal courts.

Another relevant statute is found at Title 18, Section 245(b)(2). This law makes it a crime to "attempt[] to injure, intimidate or interfere with . . . any person because of his race, color, religion or national origin" in that person's attempt to enjoy a benefit of state law, by "force or threat of force." Any Orthodox victim or potential witness who receives a death threat (or a threat of injury) from someone else within the community deserves the protection of this law. That it has not been used for this purpose is probably because, to date, this statute has never been applied to a civil rights violation committed by a person against a member of *his own* religion or ethnic group. So far, in other words, it has been assumed that religious discrimination always works the other way: Christians against Jews, Jews against Muslims, etc. But surely there is nothing sacred about the limited history of this statute. When an Orthodox Jew is threatened by a rabbi or fellow Orthodox Jew because he is a prospective witness in a child sex abuse case (involving a Jewish defendant), the threat is clearly directed against the victim's enjoyment of a state benefit — i.e., access to police, state prosecutors, and the courts — and what is more, is aimed at this target specifically *because he is an Orthodox Jew*. Unquestionably, the culprits making these threats against fellow Orthodox Jews believe they are preventing, or avenging, a violation of the religious law they share with their victims, and *would not have threatened anyone other than an Orthodox Jew for a parallel act*. It follows that they have *singled out* their victims because of the victims' religion — and that should be enough to subject them to the same legal consequences as an anti-Semite who threatens a Jew for using the courts or some other service provided by the state.

Even now we are not finished with our review of federal civil rights law; there is still one statute to go. Section 242 of the same Title 18 renders it criminal for a state official — or someone who conspires with a state official[38] — to deprive anyone of legal or constitutional rights "by reason of his religion, nationality, color, or race." As we have seen, there may have been such prohibited collusion between rabbis determined to stop Hafner's prosecution and officials of the Brooklyn district attorney's office. Even if this could never be proved in the Hafner case — again, it is too late for that — there is certainly reason to believe that such illegal conspiracies have marred other child sex abuse cases arising in Orthodox communities. Under this statute, both the private individuals and the officials they corrupt can be charged with a federal crime. Is there, then, any reason they should not be prosecuted in such a case? After all, this part of the federal law is meant to protect all rights secured by the Due Process clause of the Fourteenth Amendment.[39]

One can plainly see from this legal survey that methods of containing Hafner-like abuses are already available to state and federal prosecutors. Laws exist, but so far have not been used for the purpose. That should change; it is up to prosecutors, and the people they represent, to see that it does. At the same time, legislators are free to draft additional laws if the existing ones are found wanting.

The question is not really how rabbinic tampering with the criminal justice system can be stopped; it is whether public officials understand the necessity of stopping it and are prepared to take the needed action, regardless of the unpopularity this may earn them with some influential Jewish figures. What is at stake is nothing less than the integrity of the justice system. Our public officials cannot continue to look the other way while one sort of justice prevails among non-Jews and another is practiced in some Jewish communities. When our public officials are determined not to tolerate special treatment for Orthodox rabbis who abuse children — or when they know that their constituents will not tolerate it — the practices that have led to that special treatment, as in the Hafner case, will become relics of the past.

CONCLUSION

It is easy — but meretricious — to rationalize the rabbinic interference in the Hafner case by appealing to a "tradition" of Jewish unease about secular police forces. That there is a long history of such unease, that it has been invoked to justify abuses that compromise both the justice system and the legitimate role of the beth din, are certainly not in question. But it would be a great mistake to soft-pedal this history as a species of religious "tradition" when it is, as we have shown, little better than a corruption of it.

On the contrary: those who care most about Jewish tradition should feel the sharpest need to rescue it from the ugly manqué that prominent rabbis made of it in the Hafner case, and that, to borrow Elliot Pasik's words, was "a great shame and stain on all of us."

The authors, themselves Orthodox Jews, deny that reform and tradition are contradictory. Jewish history abounds with examples of the two working hand in hand. This is at it should be. As the eminent critic Hugh Kenner commented in an analysis of the role of the past in shaping the present:

> Tradition is not a bin into which you relegate what you cannot be bothered to examine, but precisely that portion of the past . . . which you have examined scrupulously. You cannot admire, you cannot learn from, you cannot even rebel against what you do not know.[40]

The spread of knowledge and understanding about both child sexual abuse committed by rabbis and the tactics by which these offenses have been concealed can only aid us in developing a saner and healthier future in traditional Jewish communities.

Otherwise, all we will have to look forward to is a continuation of the Hafner paradigm. And surely no one would wish to repeat the wrongs that case visited on the Abrahams, including the insults added to the family's injuries even after the dropping of the abuse charges against Rabbi Hafner. A month after clearing the rabbi, the five-member rabbinic court met again to issue an unusual written "blessing" to Rabbi Hafner, declaring that the charges against him were "false and based on falsehood" and asking God to compensate him for any losses incurred through his involvement in the legal system. "After all," commented Rabbi Rottenberg to the authors, "Rabbi Hafner has to marry off his children."

Henna White, Hynes's liaison to the Orthodox community, tried vainly to put the best face on what had happened when she spoke to the authors, claiming that she had heard about the Hafner case "everywhere I go" (presumably in Orthodox circles), and adding that she hoped the Abrahams' willingness to pursue their son's charges would "change things."

"She's full of baloney, in my opinion," retorted Mrs. Abraham. She and her family, after being publicly humiliated in the Bobov community, had had enough of official expressions of sympathy unmatched by official action. (What will happen when she "marries off" her son?)

"The man will strike again," she told the authors. "And when he strikes again, and somebody else gets hurt, that's when it will hit them."

1. Mordechai Glick, "Dealing with 'Orthodox' Child Molesters: A Response to the Community's Response" [letter to the editor], *Jewish Press*, February 4, 2000, pp. 87–88.

2. Rabbi Yosef Blau, posted to Canonist.com, September 19, 2006.

3. The authors investigated this case while under contract with *New York* magazine to write a lengthy feature article about it. Due to the sudden resignation of a key editor, the article was not published. Throughout this chapter, quotations not otherwise cited are from statements made directly to one or both of the authors during that eleven-month investigation, which commenced the second week of January 2000 and concluded in mid-December 2000. The authors remain grateful to *New York*, and to its former editor Maer Roshan, for encouraging the research into this case.

4. The authors researched this case according to the professional standards of journalism. In addition, all interviews were conducted in accordance with the strict standards of the IRB (Institutional Review Board) process for studying human subjects, even though this research was not part of a funded project. In fact, the results of this research are reported in a special double issue of the *Journal of Child Sexual Abuse*, 17(3/4), September/October 2008. The authors have not used the real name of the victim or of his family members; we also provided anonymity to other sources who asked that their names be withheld. There were numerous interviews, many of them long, often at late hours of the night, to accommodate the prayer and teaching schedules of the rabbis who agreed to be interviewed. The authors followed a careful procedure for interviewing subjects. Before each interview they reviewed with one another a list of prepared questions; following each interview, they compared notes via detailed e-mail and phone discussions. Some interviews were conducted jointly by the authors. For some subjects (victim's family members, community members, the alleged offender's wife, rabbinic supporters), interviews by a single author were often deemed preferable, particularly where having two interviewers could have induced unnecessary stress in the subject.

5. Susan Rosenbluth, "Abuse in the Orthodox Community and the *Beit Din*," *Jewish Voice and Opinion*, July 2006, p. 16.

6. In fact, though most rabbinic authorities agree that child sexual abuse is a serious crime, another view has been reported: according to one published article, some rabbis assert that a boy cannot claim to have been sexually abused under Jewish law unless he was subjected to homosexual penetration. See Robert Kolker, "On the Rabbi's Knee: Do the Orthodox Jews Have a Catholic-Priest Problem?" *New York*, May 22, 2006. Rabbi Isaac Mann, a teacher of Talmud at the Academy of Jewish Religion, in a personal communication with the authors, disputed such a position, pointing out that Jewish courts have long claimed the authority to regulate improper conduct of all kinds in their role as guardians of the Jewish community.

7. "Severe Prohibition and Serious Warning," *Der Blatt*, June 8, 2000, p. 8.

8. *Hoshen ha-Mishpat* 388:9.

9. The history of Jewish law on this subject is discussed in detail in chapter 5.

10. Jacob Neusner, "Rabbis and Community in Third Century Babylonia," in *Religions in Antiquity*, edited by J. Neusner (Leiden: E.J. Brill, 1970), p. 447.

11. Rabbi Herbert Bomzer, speaking on ABC's *Nightline* on October 11, 2006, singled out informing as a capital crime and insisted that even the victim of child sexual abuse should first go to "the Jewish authorities" who attempt to "handle it internally."

12. Anonymous, *The Rebbes: The Lubavitcher Rebbe Shlita* (Kfar Chabad, Israel: Chish Printing, 1993), pp. 13–14.

13. Michael Winerip, "Yeshivas Wield Political Power," *New York Times*, February 4, 1994, p. A16.

14. Rabbi Dratch's arguments may be found in chapter 5.

15. In another and (up to a point) typical case, Stefan Colmer, an Orthodox Jew who allegedly sexually abused several boys, was protected by a Brooklyn rabbi who discouraged the alleged victims from speaking to police. The authors became aware of the case in 2007 and worked with police and with those close to the alleged child victims. Eventually two of them came forward, and, in early 2008, Colmer, who had fled to Israel, was extradited and formally charged on several counts of sexual abuse. See John Marzulli, "10M Bail for Man Accused of Molest," *Daily News*, January 9, 2008.

16. Public Summary of the Report of the NCSY Special Commission [on Baruch Lanner], December 21, 2000, pp. 1, 10–12 (report available on the Web site of The Orthodox Union, http://www.ou.org/); Gary Rosenblatt, "Stolen Innocence," *Jewish Week*, June 23, 2000, p. 1.

17. A letter from Rabbi Shlomo Zalman Auerbach to the *Beth Din Tzedek* of Jerusalem regarding the case of Avrohom Mondrowitz was reviewed by two sources, who described it to the authors; the authors are still attempting to obtain a copy of the letter itself. See e-mail from Avrohom Mondrowitz to Michael Lesher, February 20, 2003. Mondrowitz now faces extradition to the United States to stand trial on these charges after over twenty years of rabbinic inaction or cover-up. His case is described in chapter 6.

18. See, e.g., Rosenbluth, "Abuse in the Orthodox Community and the *Beit Din*," p. 12.

19. See chapter 6, note 9.

20. When the facts were first revealed to the press, the D.A.'s spokesperson claimed that the office was not aware it had directed federal authorities to drop their efforts to bring Mondrowitz back to the United States for trial, though documents clearly showed that it had (see following note).

21. See Stephanie Saul, "Tripping Up the Prosecution," *Newsday*, May 29, 2003, p. A6; Nathaniel Popper, "Victims Press Brooklyn D.A. to Seek Abuse Suspect's

Extradition from Israel," *Forward,* July 28, 2006, pp. 1, 7. The Mondrowitz case is discussed in detail in chapter 6. Since at least two members of Hynes's Jewish Advisory Council told the authors "the community" did *not* want to see the case prosecuted, there can be little doubt who was behind this astonishing behavior by a public prosecutor in dealing with such serious charges.

22. Stewart Ain, "Sex Abuse Suspect Charged in Fraud Case," *Jewish Week,* August 24, 1990, p. 7.

23. Hella Winston and Larry Cohler-Esses, "No Sex Charge for Kolko; Boys' Parents Foiled by DA," *New York Jewish Week,* April 18, 2008, pp. 1, 20–21.

24. Hella Winston and Larry Cohler-Esses, "DA Struggles to Explain Kolko Plea Deal," *New York Jewish Week,* May 2, 2008, pp. 18–19, 31.

25. Emphases supplied by the authors.

26. This was not the only time a rabbinic tribunal sealed a significant part of its record in a child abuse case. In 2003, victims and critics of Rabbi Baruch Lanner sent a letter of protest against Rabbi Mordecai Willig, who had headed a beth din investigating various charges against Lanner. The letter was sent to four synagogues in New Jersey that were sponsoring a symposium on Jewish parenting featuring Rabbi Willig as the guest speaker. In it, the victims and advocates criticized Rabbi Willig "for sealing the tribunal's findings and doing nothing 'to remove (Lanner) from the children' . . . , claiming that he [Willig] withheld for more than a decade a religious tribunal ruling that found Lanner guilty of sexual abuse." Ana M. Alaya, "Victims: Rabbi Failed to Protect Children," *Star Ledger,* January 31, 2003, p. 38.

27. The Lanner case, according to news reports, also involved an attempt to force an alleged abuse victim to disown his accusation. The *Bergen Record* reported that the panel of rabbis who convened in 1989 to hear testimony from Lanner's alleged victims "acted in a hostile way toward accusers, and forced one of them to publicly recant his allegations." John Chadwick, "Group Opposes Lecture by Rabbi," *Bergen Record,* January 31, 2003, p. L-2.

28. Amy Neustein and Michael Lesher, "A Single-Case Study of Rabbinic Sexual Abuse in the Orthodox Jewish Community," *Journal of Child Sexual Abuse,* 17(3/4), September/October 2008, pp. 70–89; reprinted in *Betrayal and Recovery: Understanding the Trauma of Clergy Sexual Abuse,* edited by R. McMackin, T. Keane, and P. Kline, (London: Routledge, 2009, chapter 5, pp. 72–91.

29. Irving Greenberg, "Rabbis Can Help by Speaking Out," *Moment,* April 15, 1990, p. 49.

30. Avi Shafran, "Blogistan," *Yeshiva World,* December 28, 2007, http://www.theyeshivaworld.com/article.php?p=13342.

31. Tzvi Frankel, "Blogs: Transgressing a Major Sin 'In the Name of Heaven,'" *Jewish Observer,* December 2007, pp. 32–33.

32. Elliot Pasik, posted to UOJ (Unorthodox Jew), http://theunorthodoxjew.blogspot.com, November 21, 2006.

33. Oscar Wilde, *The Importance of Being Earnest*, in *The Play: A Critical Anthology*, edited by Eric Bentley (New York: Prentiss-Hall, 1951), p. 164.

34. Mark Dratch, *Published Minutes of the RCA Roundtable*, April 1992, pp. 1–18; see also Mark Dratch, "Domestic Abuse is a Community Issue," on the Web site of JSafe: The Jewish Institute Supporting an Abuse-Free Environment, http://www .jsafe.org/resources.htm, January 19, 2006.

35. See chapter 5.

36. Reported on theunorthodoxjew.blogspot.com, June 17, 2008. The authors have independently confirmed the authenticity of the study, the published results of which are not expected for several years.

37. See *Bounds v. Smith*, 430 U.S. 817, 821, 97 S. Ct. 1491, 1494, 52 L. Ed. 2d 72 (1977); *Bill Johnson's Restaurants, Inc. v. NLRB*, 461 U.S. 731, 741, 103 S. Ct. 2161, 2169, 76 L. Ed. 2d 277 (1983).

38. *U.S. v. Price*, 383 U.S. 787, 794, 86 S. Ct. 1152, 1156–57, 16 L. Ed. 2d 267 (1966); see also *U.S. v. Lynch*, 94 F. Supp. 1011 (N.D. Ga., 1950), *aff'd.*, 189 F.2d 476, *cert. denied*, 342 U.S. 831, 72 S. Ct. 50, 96 L. Ed. 2d 629; *United Steelworkers of America v. Phelps Dodge Corp.*, 865 F.2d 1539, 1540 (9th Cir., 1989), *cert. denied*, 110 S. Ct. 51, 107 L. Ed. 2d 20 (1989), *citing Dennis v. Sparks*, 449 U.S. 24, 27, 101 S. Ct. 183, 186, 66 L. Ed. 2d 185 (1980).

39. *U.S. v. Lanier*, 520 U.S. 259, 272 note 7, 117 S. Ct. 1219, 1228 note 7, 137 L. Ed. 2d 432 (1997).

40. Hugh Kenner, *The Invisible Poet: T. S. Eliot* (New York: McDowell, Obolensky, 1959), p. 117.

ROBERT WEISS

Pedophiles & Penitence

Whom to Banish, Whom to Support — Helping
Jewish Communities Make the Right Choices

INTRODUCTION

When a sexual offender abuses a child, our response is understandably unambiguous: *Do something with these sick people. Keep them out of my neighborhood. Lock them up and throw away the key!* And though our revulsion toward the sexual offender and his actions is certainly justifiable, the growing cultural tempest this issue has engendered, compounded by media sensationalism and bad politics, has steadily worked against the goal of keeping offenders from offending. Effective protection of the vulnerable requires an emotionally unencumbered view of the problem and its solutions, some measure of detachment, and a willingness to look beyond our own abhorrence of the sexual offense. Clear factual insight into the perpetrator, his behavior patterns, and potential treatment or containment options will encourage more effective community decision making and management of this disturbing problem than reactive responses based on fear, contempt, or political gain. It is toward this *solution-focused* understanding of the sexual offender and his behavior, both in the Jewish community and beyond, that this chapter is directed.

WHAT TO DO?

Late in 2006, a Southern California Methodist church was presented with an interesting dilemma.[1] A registered sexual offender, John L., recently released from prison and on probation, had moved nearby and wished to become a member of the congregation. John went directly to the pastor, explained his offender history, and asked the pastor to tell him whether or not he would be welcome there. He stated that part of his emotional healing and reform — toward not returning to his previous offending — required being actively involved in a healthy community with a strong religious affiliation. Further, John wished to be completely open and transparent regarding his offending history from the beginning to prevent any uproar or confusion regarding his intent.

What is this pastor to do? If he rejects John outright, he risks depriving him of a religious affiliation that might serve as a pillar of John's emotional stability and sexual abstinence. If he takes John into the fold without informing the congregation, he risks keeping information from his community that might prevent a future offense should John re-offend. If the pastor informs the congregation of John's request and history, then how is it decided if he might join the community: by whom and under what terms?

This recent event points out some of the complex dynamics that sexual offenders present to our religious and secular community organizations. These groups must come to terms with the fact that sexual offenders cannot simply be locked up and sent away forever, a solution that is neither viable nor useful. Increasingly, as our awareness of the problem grows and the sexual offender becomes more visible on Internet watch lists and the like, community leaders are being asked to take a defendable stand on "the sex offender issue." This difficult task requires them at the very least to be armed with fact-based answers to questions such as:

1. What is a sexual offender?
2. Which sexual offenders are likely to re-offend and which are less likely to do so?
3. What is considered the most useful form of treatment and monitoring for which type of offender?
4. If someone in a position of power and influence is found to have acted out sexually, can he return to a position of authority and, if so, under what circumstances?
5. How can community leaders (secular and religious) help keep their communities safe from sexual perpetrators?
6. What should be done if the best course for offender prevention comes into conflict with strongly expressed community concerns?

7. What is considered an effective course of treatment to keep a sexual offender from re-offending?

WHAT IS A SEXUAL OFFENSE?

Some common terminology is defined below:

Child sexual abuse is the sexual assault of a minor or, according to the American Psychological Association, sexual activity between a minor and an older person in which the dominant position of the older person is used to coerce or exploit the younger.

Sexual offender is a legal term. Under the law, a sexual offender is a person who has been criminally charged and convicted of, or has pled guilty to, a sex crime. Offenders may also be identified through the child welfare system. Most offenders are likely to be known to the victim, and 95 percent are male.

Sexual or child predator is a social term, having no legal or clinical function. The media often uses it, as it has an incendiary, provocative quality. The term "sexual predator" can be applied to a person according to the observer's individual beliefs, and does not necessarily denote criminal or pathological behavior. For example, an adult male who cruises a bar looking for consensual sex from an adult female could be considered a sexual predator by some but not by others.

Child molester is a general psychological term. "Child molester" describes an adult who is sexually attracted to children (pre- and postpubescent), but the term typically refers to one who has acted out these attractions.

Pedophile means someone sexually attracted to prepubescent children, whether or not they have acted on it.

Ephebophile means someone exclusively sexually attracted to postpubescent children, whether or not they have acted upon it.

The legal definitions of "sexual offense" and "sexual offender" vary considerably depending on the place the act occurred. For example, a nineteen-year-old male caught having sexual intercourse with a fifteen-year-old female can be brought up on felony charges as a sexual offender in certain states of the United States, while in other states, allowing for parental consent, he might legally marry her. As the same sexual behavior can be deemed a felony in one state, a misdemeanor in another, and legal activity in some, it is more productive, for our purposes, to define sexual offending from a clinical rather than a legal standpoint.

From a clinical or therapeutic standpoint, a "sexual offense" is any sexual act that is undertaken *without the full consent of both parties*. For example, the exhibitionist, driving onto a college campus and openly masturbating in his car, hoping for a response from some young woman walking by, is an offender. Since the woman passing by his car has not agreed to a sexual act with him, his uninvited genital display is a nonconsensual act of sexual offending against her. Similarly, the fritter, rubbing his body, hands, or genitals against peoples' buttocks or breasts on crowded buses or subway trains, has not asked those people if it would be acceptable for him to touch them in this intimate fashion. His sexualized touch, without their permission, is his offense.

The child molester or pedophile is a sexual offender, because our culture understandably views children (and mentally, emotionally, or physically dependent adults) as not having the full capacity and/or ability to consent to such acts. Therefore, the thirty-three-year-old soccer coach who gradually lures several of his fourteen-year-old female players into sexual acts is offending against those children, as we do not regard those girls as having the emotional maturity, insight, or knowledge to consent fully to being sexual with an adult. Further, we see the coach as having exploited the power intrinsic to his professional role by asking the girls to be sexual with him.

In clinical treatment, we also view those who exploit a position of power to initiate sex with adults as sexual offenders, even though these people often violate ethical and moral standards more than legal ones. Examples of this type of offending might include a physician being sexual with a patient, a boss with a secretary, a rabbi with a congregant, or a family attorney soliciting sex from a vulnerable female client. Abusing the trust inherent in an emotionally powerful or influential role in order to coax, coerce, or seduce someone into a sexual act is exploitative. Complicating this definition of offending, however, is the need for a contextual view of such situations. For example, the thirty-two-year-old unmarried male college teacher who openly initiates a romantic or sexual relationship with a like-minded twenty-six-year-old female student presents a very different scenario from the thirty-two-year-old unmarried college teacher who secretly initiates sexual and romantic relations with every female student available to him, or, for that matter, from the thirty-two-year-old married college teacher who abuses his professional role by secretly having sex with many of his female students, while self-righteously deploring such conduct to his wife, family, and community.

Understanding the motivations, behavioral patterns, and suggested treatment of nonviolent sexual offenders — like all those described above — is the focus of this chapter. Specifically under consideration are those who exploit a power differential to have sex with minors or vulnerable, dependent adults. Anyone functioning in a role that naturally places another in a dependant position, who then exploits that role to obtain sex — teachers, therapists, camp counselors — is our subject. The author has chosen to exclude from discussion rapists, sexual mutilators, or perpetrators of intrafamilial and sibling incest, as there remain other remedies for those categories of offenders (incarceration in the criminal justice system or family court dispositions on juvenile delinquency, visitation, and custody) that exist largely outside the purview of any given community.

CHILD OFFENDING: A PUBLIC EXAMPLE

In 2006, the network television program *Dateline NBC* explored and filmed a series about child sexual offenders entitled *To Catch a Predator*. Though both exploitative and sensational, the series nonetheless raised public awareness of the dangers the Internet presents to minors, while also offering a fascinating snapshot of the kind of person who might seek out sex with a minor. The premise of the TV show was simple: adults posed in Internet chat rooms as bored young adolescents, aged twelve to fourteen, whose parents were away from home. These decoy "children" responded to anyone who attempted to establish an online connection with them. It wasn't long before adult men began to "stream in these chats" — that is, to strike up intimate relationships with those who they thought were children — turning the conversation toward lurid and pornographic subjects in an attempt to entice these "boys" and "girls" into sexual liaisons. NBC rented several suburban homes where these supposed children invited the adult perpetrators to meet them. These houses were rigged with cameras, a film crew, and waiting police officers. The show proceeded to film the perpetrators, as they appeared one at a time, seeking sex with a minor boy or girl. At several of these locations more than fifty potential perpetrators a day showed up, men of every age, class, race, and socioeconomic group: college students, day laborers, retirees, army veterans, professionals, construction workers, and more. Upon entry each man was confronted by *Dateline* producer Chris Hansen, who, standing there with detailed, written logs of the lurid chat communication, challenged each man to explain his presence. All of this was captured on film. Once understanding that he was being filmed for television, each man would quickly exit, only to find the police waiting outside to arrest him.

What motivates someone to show up at a setting so fraught with danger, both to himself and a child? If fifty men line up seeking sex with a minor, do they all show up with the same motivation and intent? How many of these men have done this before? What kind of danger to children does each man represent at home or at work? What fantasy inspires a man to put so much at risk for the sake of a fleeting sexual liaison? Despite having been caught, filmed, and arrested, which of these men are likely to attempt to sexually act out with a minor in the future and which will have "learned his lesson"? Though all engaged in a similar activity, sexual exploitation of a child, each of these men likely had differing motives, interests, justifications, and approaches to their sexual offending behavior. And while it might feel satisfying to condemn them all to life in prison, it is imperative that we find more productive solutions. Only through gaining insight into an individual offender's psychological profile and specific offender type can anyone hope to manage his sexual behavior and ensure that he does not return to it.

WHO OFFENDS?

To begin to address some of the questions above, it may be useful to review a few common misconceptions or myths about child sexual offenders.

MYTH: Offenders are mostly "dirty old men."
FACT: Most offenders report having committed their first offense by age sixteen.

MYTH: Children must always watch out for strangers.
FACT: While teaching children to avoid strangers enhances their general safety, the vast majority of child sexual offenders (likely 85–90 percent) are known to their victims prior to the offense.

MYTH: Offenders are monsters.
FACT: The majority of nonviolent sexual offenders are law-abiding, working citizens and neighbors with no prior history of illegal behavior or arrest.

MYTH: They are incurable.

FACT: There are many types of offenders, and their recidivism rates vary depending on whether or not they receive treatment and what type of offender they are. Given proper treatment and monitoring, the majority of child sexual offenders do not re-offend.

MYTH: The majority of sexual offenders are caught and convicted.

FACT: Only a small fraction of those who commit sexual violations are apprehended and convicted for their crimes. Most convicted sex offenders eventually are released to the community under probation or parole supervision.

MYTH: All sex offenders are male.

FACT: The vast majority of sex offenders are male. However, females also commit sexual crimes. Approximately 5 percent of all sexual offenders are female.

MYTH: Youths do not commit sex offenses.

FACT: Adolescents are responsible for a significant number of rape and child molestation cases each year.

MYTH: Children are being snatched and molested in increasing numbers.

FACT: The number of U.S. children actually "snatched" by an unknown predator has remained constant over the past thirty years — around three hundred children annually. The vast majority of U.S. children who "disappear" are either runaways or are taken from their homes by a known family member.

With some of the myths behind us, let's take a look at the different types of child sexual offenders who most often present for evaluation, sentencing, or treatment, along with a general description of how each type approaches his offending behaviors. In essence, there are three primary types of child sexual offender, each with differing motivations, behavior patterns, and interests.[2] These types are: the dedicated or fixated child offender; the situational or regressed child offender; and the addicted offender.

The sample cases below review each type of offender, along with his typical lifestyle, sexual interests and history. This will help create a background for the discussion to follow, regarding treatment, monitoring, and appropriate community response. As their stories demonstrate, each type of offender approaches his deviant sexual activity from a different emotional standpoint.

In various ways he justifies, rationalizes, and minimizes his actions, thereby *giving himself permission* to act out sexually with a child or dependent adult. While each individual varies somewhat in his degree of pedophilic desire, pattern of sexual acting out, specific life stressors, emotional stability, and emotional/intellectual abilities, within each offender type there are typical motivations and behaviorial similarities. Perhaps a clearer understanding of the internal world of the offender will help reduce knee-jerk reactions to his behavior and engage a higher level of critical thinking toward balancing our children's safety with the rights and management of offenders. The various types of child sexual offenders are listed and discussed below, with fictional composite stories used as a device to elucidate their thoughts and behaviors by type. We begin with the most challenging type of child offender.

The Dedicated or Fixated Child Offender

Jake N. was referred for a sexual offender assessment by a local rabbinic association after multiple complaints were made to the administration of the religious school where Jake has been employed as a coach for over five years. Jake is thirty-eight, Jewish, single, and has no children of his own. He is a physical education teacher for a large, private Conservative Jewish school and also spends his summers as a sports educator/counselor at a nearby Jewish camp. Jake lives alone and has few close adult friends. After having graduated from college, Jake moved to a state several hundred miles from his family and returns to see them annually for holidays and family events. Religiously involved, he attends synagogue services weekly, and though he often volunteers his free time to work individually with boys preparing for bar mitzvah, he rarely takes part in larger, adult community social activities. Jake tends to shy away from adult peer relationships and appears a bit uncomfortable around people in general. Being single, he often feels pressured by other adults to date women and be personally revealing — both of which he avoids. Jake spends most of his work and free time with his students, feeling more like a kid himself than an adult.

He is highly regarded as a teacher; several of his students report that "coach understands me better than any other adult." Jake is highly encouraging of the children and can often be found working with them late into the evenings and on weekends. As athletic director, he frequently recommends and chaperones events and weekend trips that take the kids off campus to out-of-state athletic events.

On multiple occasions, when traveling with students to out-of-town athletic events, Jake insisted on sharing beds in small motel rooms with his twelve- to fifteen-year-old male students; in fact, he required his young bedfellows to sleep naked. If a child objected (and several did), Jake would say, "Better two to a bed than no uniforms next year!" — claiming that he was only responding to the school's limited budget. Recently, a male student, uncomfortable with such intimate contact and embarrassed at having to lie undressed next to Jake, complained to his parents and they in turn brought the issue to the attention of the school board. Many similar complaints quickly surfaced, and while none of the children interviewed has acknowledged having been genitally molested, several teens did report that "coach" masturbated in their presence. Jake was understandably suspended from his job and arrested pending further professional and legal evaluation.

Jake is every parent's nightmare: a pedophile who abuses the professional role of child caretaker, coach, or teacher to gain access to children for emotional and sexual gratification. Approximately 10 to 15 percent of all child sexual offenders are of a "dedicated" or "fixated" type, mirroring the description of Jake provided above. Fixated offenders are primarily or solely sexually oriented toward pre- and postpubescent children.[3] Much as a heterosexual person is aroused by opposite-sex adults and a homosexual person is aroused by same-sex adults, fixated pedophiles like Jake are primarily or solely aroused by pre- and postpubescent children of various ages. Fixated offenders rarely have a sincere interest in adult sex, nor do they experience sexual arousal from adults — hence the terms "fixated" or "dedicated." Their arousal pattern appears to be set by early adolescence and is unlikely to change, even with treatment. Not surprisingly, this type of offender will often pick a career role or job choice offering them consistent access to children. They choose this not only because of their sexual interest in children, but also because they feel more socially and emotionally comfortable relating to children than adults. Fixated offenders sometimes do enter into relationships or even marriages with adult women, but do not usually do so due to any genuine sexual or romantic interest in the marital partner. This type of offender often chooses a mate who already has children, which provides him free access to children he can manipulate into having sex.

A fixated offender typically approaches children from the child's perspective, perceiving their sexual exchanges more as acts of kinship than romantic or sexual pursuit. He often shares children's interests and relates easily to them. Though he most frequently molests same-sex victims, he is not considered gay or homosexual, as he is equally disinterested in sex with adult males as adult females. Fixated offenders are the most difficult type of offender to treat and have some of the highest rates of recidivism. Even if given extensive treatment, they are unlikely to adapt healthier, adult-oriented sexual patterns.

The Situational or Regressed Child Offender

Samuel G., a fifty-three-year-old married attorney and father of three children (ages twenty-five, twenty-two and seventeen), was referred for a sexual disorder assessment on the recommendation of his attorney. Sam is under investigation for reportedly having had a physically inappropriate relationship with a female babysitter who was fifteen years old at the time. Beth, the reported victim, is now in her twenties and recently became engaged. She revealed this troubling past experience to her rabbi, saying, "I want to put this shameful secret behind me before I marry." After hearing Beth's story, the rabbi — whose congregation also includes Sam and his family — became concerned that he might have an ethical/legal duty to report the alleged offense to authorities, as Sam's teenage daughter still resides at home and she or her friends might be at some kind of risk. After both anonymously reviewing the matter by phone with local child protection professionals and explaining to Beth that he is required by law to report the information she provided him, the rabbi reported Beth's story to the police.

After the report was made, Sam's wife, Ruth, also reached out to the local Jewish Family Services program because of what she described as "an increasing fear that my husband isn't who or what I believe him to be." Ruth, who had met and married Sam thirty-one years earlier, told the social worker that, before the recent police report, there had been rumors among their friends that Sam was "too friendly" with the one of the teenagers who babysat their children. And though Sam has adamantly denied to his wife, both then and now, that "anything happened," Ruth has not been able to shake the feeling that he is hiding something. When asked directly about her experience of Sam at the time he was involved with their babysitter, Ruth told the counselor, "My instincts told me that something was wrong, Sam seemed too attentive and interested in that girl. He was always offering to give her a ride home, and he would give her little gifts and things. I should have known better."

Sam represents the most common child sexual offender: the "situational" or "regressive" type. It is estimated that 85 percent or more of all child molesters fall into this category. Unlike the dedicated offender, the situational/

regressive type has an enduring sexual orientation toward (and social interest in) his own peer group, rarely demonstrating sexual interest in children or teens until adult life. When heterosexual, this type of offender usually chooses opposite-sex victims and if homosexual usually chooses same-sex victims — reflecting the fact that his sexual acts are more *acts of sexual and relational substitution* than kinship. Intact intellectually and often socially as well, this type of offender can be found among all ages, races, and social classes. He may enjoy a successful career and family life, often not offending until something goes wrong in his world. Regressive-type child molesters turn to a child sexually as a substitute for what they feel they are unable to receive from adult relationships, reflecting their own developmental immaturity and interpersonal insecurity. Their offending can be seen as a maladaptive attempt to cope with life stressors, relationship conflicts, or losses. Often married or in another primary relationship, the situational offender's sexual interest in children and/or minor teens tends to be temporary and/or opportunistic. His offending behavior is episodic, tending to wax and wane depending on his exposure to emotional stressors (job loss, financial stress), involvement with hyperstimulating sexual material, or repeated opportunities to offend (wife starts evening classes so he is now frequently home alone with the babysitter, etc.), or some combination of these.

In the example above, Sam was discovered, as a result of intensive psychosexual evaluation, to have started offending with Beth just as he hit midlife and his wife got a full-time job, thereby becoming physically and emotionally less available to him. He was unable to articulate to his wife his distress, feelings of abandonment, and emotional needs; instead, he rationalized that his hurt feelings justified him in turning to a relationship with a vulnerable minor, Beth. This was a reflection of his limited emotional health. Many offenders like Sam may fantasize about this type of sexual acting out, but only come to engage in it when disinhibited by drug or alcohol use. (Alcohol abuse and drug dependency are often identified as precipitating factors to this type of sexual behavior.) Fortunately, this type of offender responds well to treatment and with appropriate intervention, the right type of therapy, and long-term monitoring is unlikely to re-offend.

The Sexually Addicted Offender

Rabbi Daniel G. was asked by his temple's governing board to leave his job at the synagogue and subsequently was referred for a psychosexual evaluation following his secretary's discovery of thousands of pornographic images saved to his work computer, some of which were identified as child porn (females aged twelve to sixteen). This event, and the rabbi's subsequent arrest, came as a complete shock to his community, as Daniel had served for over ten years as an active, committed, seemingly selfless leader. His congregation has always experienced him as an extraordinarily personable and engaged role model who unquestioningly put aside his personal priorities to focus on those in need. As rabbi, he took phone calls and pages around the clock, and had been known to get up in the middle of the night to visit sick or troubled members of the temple if they were in need. As the father of five young children, when not responding to the demands of a challenging job, he seemed quite focused on being a role model for a stable and consistent home life. During the High Holidays, or when the needs of his temple were particularly great, many in his congregation wondered whether Daniel even took time to sleep or eat.

Though clearly dedicated to helping others, Daniel seemed somewhat oblivious to what he himself might need — as evidenced, for instance, by his not having taken a vacation in over five years. Self-care appeared a low, even unknown, priority for the rabbi. Throughout the years, many in the community had praised both Daniel and his wife, Sara — the latter for seamlessly managing to care not only for five children, but also for this man who always seemed to do more for others than he did for himself. Since his arrest, community feelings about the couple ranged from disbelief to unfounded fears for the safety of the community's children. His wife has moved, along with the children, into her parents' house, as she is unsure if Daniel might act inappropriately with them in some way. Daniel, on the advice of his attorney and therapist, has checked into an inpatient sexual disorders treatment facility.

Until recently, the emphasis of most sexual offender assessment and treatment was directed solely toward the offending behavior itself. Today, clinicians incorporate a broader focus, one that takes into account the entire range of an offender's sexual behavior. This shift, along with the marked increase in problems now appearing among those compulsively viewing Internet porn, has sparked an interest in a category of offender that is inclusive of his entire sexual repertoire. It is becoming increasingly apparent that 60 percent or more of those who sexually offend have other, nonoffending areas of their sexuality that can be defined as compulsive, addictive, or fetishistic. These types of addictive sexual behaviors may include but are not limited to:

- compulsive masturbation with or without porn use
- Internet and video porn use
- online sex with web cams or in chat rooms
- sadomasochism and fetishes
- involvement with prostitutes, sensual massage, and/or escorts
- multiple affairs and serial adultery
- frequenting strip clubs and/or adult bookstores
- anonymous or public sexual experiences

Sexual addiction affects a much larger percentage of the general population than does sexual offending. Some research estimates that as much as 3 to 5 percent of the general population may have an active sexual addiction problem. But, unlike offenders, sexual addicts most often have no direct victims and their repetitive sexual behaviors when involving other people are nearly always consensual. A behavioral or process addiction, most closely resembling compulsive eating or gambling, sexual addiction is characterized by:

- a loss of control over the sexual behavior(s) — i.e., more frequently engaging in it than desired or without the conscious ability to stop engaging in it
- escalation of the sexual behavior(s), either in time spent engaging in it or the type of activity
- irritability or anger if asked to stop the sexual behavior
- negative consequences directly related to the sexual behavior, such as relationship, legal, financial, or other problems
- continued sexual acting out despite prior or ongoing negative consequences directly related to it

Rabbi Daniel is a sexually addicted offender. Following an extensive psychosexual evaluation he was found to have longstanding patterns, going back as far as his adolescence, of compulsive porn use with masturbation. He disclosed in his evaluation that prior to marrying and becoming a rabbi he frequently visited sensual massage parlors and paid for sexual activity, while also dating girls who were his peers. Though it had been a struggle, he had managed to avoid direct physical contact with anyone other than his wife after marrying her. Nonetheless, by the time he was caught, Daniel was spending upward of two to three hours daily viewing porn from his work and home computers, having done so for many years. Not surprisingly, Daniel's sexual acting out had increased in concert with his lack of self-care and his focus on putting everyone else's needs before his own. The less he allowed himself the time to rest, reflect, and care for himself, the more he justified to himself being entitled to view porn consistently. Despite the obvious disconnect between his given profession and his sexual behavior, Daniel would frequently rationalize it to himself by thinking, "With all I give and do for everybody else, I deserve to be able to have pleasure and fun for myself."

Eventually, viewing pornography became his primary means of self-care. Since adolescence, Daniel had used sex as a means of emotional self-soothing, which is a key element of sexual addiction. A circular thought process kept him acting out for so many years, as the more frequently he viewed and masturbated to porn, the more he would end up trying to compensate for the ensuing guilty feelings by doing more for others. And though Daniel truly had never been sexually attracted to young teens or children, when his addictive patterns inevitably escalated, along with his deep feelings of shame and hypocrisy, so did the intensity of the types of images he was viewing and the frequency with which he viewed them. Nonfixated sexual offenders whose offending is preceded or paralleled by sexually addictive/compulsive behavior are, for the most part, good candidates for successful treatment. And though Daniel may have a lifelong struggle with his desire to act out sexually in one form or another, effective evaluation, treatment, and monitoring can offer him the freedom from ever again feeling compelled to view child pornography or other illegal sexual material.

RESPONDING TO AN OFFENSE
OR POSSIBLE OFFENSE

First Responders

In the religious and secular life of a community, those in leadership positions are asked daily to make decisions on behalf of those they serve. Most of these choices, though meaningful, are often relatively mundane, ranging from where to hold a holiday event to how best to distribute funding. This daily financial and logistical decision making is what maintains the structure of a given community or organization. But having to decide what to do when someone in or near the community is accused of sexually violating another person, or is found to have done so, is likely beyond the job description of even the most educated community leader, whether volunteer or salaried. So, when situations like these do come to light, they are most often passed from the individual decision maker to a larger entity for evaluation and direction. Thus an executive board, a community service organization, or a synagogue's governing committee can often end up having to decide the best course of action in such a case, often without an accurate assessment of risk, in situations typically rife with suspicion, legalities, rumor, fear, and bad feeling. Consider the following example.

Sam is a senior drug and alcohol counselor at a nonprofit Jewish recovery residence, an entity governed by the local synagogue. Sam is also the eldest son of a prominent cantor in a nearby Conservative Jewish community. Eighteen months into his employment, a female resident complained that she had seen Sam "peeking into the bathroom" when she was in the shower. Once the news got out, several other women came forward, reporting having felt "uncomfortable" when Sam performed an after-hours room check, that he frequently lingered to talk with them when they were in night clothes or already in bed. One woman stated that a sixteen-year-old resident reportedly had found Sam going through her underwear drawer when she returned unexpectedly early from a family visit, but the story could not be substantiated because the girl was no longer living there.

Most residents stated that Sam was a kind, empathic counselor, but it also seemed common knowledge that he had a "tendency to flirt." When confronted by his superiors regarding these concerns, Sam denied having ever done or said anything that could be considered inappropriate. He excused his actions by framing them as "just doing my job and being helpful," and offered highly plausible, reasonable explanations for each of the reported incidents. After gathering the initial information, the managers of the house found themselves at odds with the senior synagogue members over the handling of this matter. While the recovery house management, having had a long-term relationship with Sam, tended to believe his story and wanted to retain him in his current position, perhaps with a few stronger boundaries, the synagogue committee members directly responsible for overseeing the recovery house felt that Sam should be fired. Neither set of managers had any prior experience with this kind of concern, nor was there any direct proof of Sam's guilt or innocence. To further complicate matters, the synagogue's board president, whose opinion would have normally helped to resolve this type of disagreement, was an old friend of Sam's father, and for his own reasons appeared reluctant to take any action at all.

The situation described above illustrates the multifaceted organizational and personal challenges often faced by decision makers when reports of a possible sex offense are made. And though "Where there's smoke, there's fire" is an apt metaphor when someone in an organization receives multiple complaints involving behavior of a sexual nature, the degree to which there is a problem and how best to handle that problem are usually hard to determine. In addition to the personal issues, this scenario also presents potential legal liability concerns for those in authority. For example, should the recovery house staff win out and keep Sam as a counselor, perhaps giving him a warning, who will be responsible and/or liable if Sam violates a female resident in some manner at a later date? On the other hand, is there really just cause to fire Sam in circumstances that could readily be viewed more as gossip than as fact? After all, Sam is working in a program populated by newly sober drug addicts. What if these rumors were started in an attempt to undermine Sam's authority and no sexual problem actually exists? In order for the organization to move forward in a considered manner, the following questions require an accurate answer:

1. Did Sam engage in any sexually inappropriate behavior as described above, and if so, to what degree?
2. Has Sam acted out any sexual improprieties other than those already mentioned?
3. If a problem is found, does Sam simply need some workplace boundary correction and education or is further action required?
4. Is Sam a perpetrator?
5. Does Sam require some form of treatment or therapy for these issues? If so, what is recommended and what is the expected outcome/prognosis?

Careful Evaluation

Situations like Sam's are fraught with risk on many levels, and it is in the best interest of the synagogue to consider obtaining both legal and psychological advice. It is prudent for any organization or community decision maker responsible for appraising situations like the ones described in this chapter to make full use of outside professional support and direction. Rather than taking on the task of gathering the necessary information and attempting to determine the best course of action themselves, local rabbinical councils, Jewish family-service organizations, attorneys, and other professionals are well advised to refer the person in question for a formal psychosexual assessment.

In Sam's case, outside counsel could give advice on the information to be obtained and the steps to take if a decision is made to fire Sam. On the other hand, should the decision makers decide to retain Sam, due to his skill set and/or his personal relationship with the organization, an accurate, nonbiased psychosexual assessment should be obtained. A well-organized *assessment* and *return-to-work evaluation* will serve to clarify fact from fiction objectively and offer suggestions for avoiding any future risk. Such assessments are based on extensive interviews, along with established, reliable psychological testing, to evaluate accurately whether the person did or did not engage in the problem behavior and if he or she did, to what degree. Polygraphs are often employed as an adjunct to the history taking and testing to assure the truthfulness of the evaluee.

Although a psychological assessment and testing battery provided by a general psychologist is useful in evaluating most mental health problems, psychological concerns related to problematic sexual behavior are best evaluated by a specialist. Most large urban areas have local clinics or individuals who specialize in the assessment of these types of sexual problems, and suggestions about finding such professionals can be obtained from the Association for the Treatment of Sexual Abusers (www.atsa.com), the Safer Society Foundation (www.safersociety.org), and the Society for the Advancement of Sexual Health (www.sash.net), among others. In order to gain an accurate and complete overview of the presenting concerns, those providing the assessment will require full support from those making the referral, as well as full documentation of all current and past reported concerns, when available — such as police reports, victim accounts, etc. In addition, the evaluee must be told that his honesty and cooperation are a part of what is being gauged.

A comprehensive and properly prepared sexual offender evaluation and/or return-to-duty assessment, prepared by a skilled professional, should offer a great deal of specific information not only about any alleged sexual offenses that may have already occurred, but also some direction toward appropriate next steps. Information about the alleged offender offered through such a report is likely to include:

\ general psychological functioning
\ sexual and relationship history
\ family and social history and current structure

\ sexual deviancy, if present
\ personality concerns and sociopathy, if any
\ honesty of reporting (determined by polygraph or like method)

It should also provide:

\ a full picture of past, current, and potential sexual acting out concerns
\ guidelines for treatment (if needed)
\ guidelines for potential return to work, home, and/or community
\ potential hazards for return to home or community

Who Decides?

When a sexual offense is alleged to have taken place, it is advisable for a large board or organization to form a smaller committee to be specifically responsible for overseeing the investigation and evaluation of the situation, gathering any professional reports or recommendations, and providing any required ongoing monitoring.

Due to the extremely confidential nature of these situations, these carefully chosen committee members are typically the only people with access to all of the facts and reports related to a given situation. They are charged with obtaining and maintaining all pertinent legal, personal, personnel, and psychological reports and are likely to be the liaison between the accused offender and his workplace or the larger community. This small group can arrange to have the individual formally evaluated, gather all the necessary releases of information, and ensure that any legal or psychological findings and recommendations are fully carried out. An individual, committee, or group of this type must have access to all pertinent materials and must be fully empowered to follow through on whatever is recommended.

The creation of such a group establishes a central place, within the larger organization, for these types of issues to be handled confidentially and consistently. While most who are found to have sexually offended in the workplace are dismissed, if not prosecuted, there are cases where the individual may be able to return to duty partially or fully following treatment, with specific on-site monitoring, psychological evaluation, and ongoing reporting in place. Requirements are likely to be placed on the offender who is returning to duty — rules calling for continuing oversight by a designated individual responsible to the aforementioned committee or perhaps by one of the group members themselves.

Over the last century, many differing methods, alone and in combination, have been attempted to keep the sexual offender from re-offending. The results of these methods range from very little change to highly successful outcomes. And though we cannot fully or accurately predict who will re-offend and who will not, those exhibiting the criteria below are less likely to achieve treatment success over the long term:

\ Having multiple victims
\ Having diverse victims (different ages, races, etc.)
\ Having victims who were strangers
\ Having a history of offending as a juvenile
\ Having a history of abuse or neglect, and/or early long-term separation from parents
\ Antisocial personality and/or chaotic or antisocial lifestyle
\ Being unemployed or severely underemployed
\ Having substance abuse problems

Brief descriptions of the most-utilized sex offender treatment modalities are discussed below, along with caveats regarding their efficacy.

1. *Psychodynamic psychotherapy.* This form of what might be considered traditional therapy encompasses a wide range of approaches based on interpersonal interaction. It considers the offending sexual behavior as symptomatic of internal emotional conflicts, which can be resolved through achieving awareness and better understanding of the underlying issues. Through such introspection, the offender is expected to arrive at better controls over his sexually inappropriate behavior. *This has proved the least effective method for achieving change.*

2. *Chemotherapy.* With the use of various antiandrogenic hormones, such as Depo-Provera, treatment has been demonstrated to have a moderating effect on sexual aggressiveness and to enhance self-regulation of sexual behavior. It does offer some promise as a chemical control of antisocial sexual behaviors, particularly in the more severe or violent offender and/or those with intellectual or developmental deficits. *This method is useful for some types of offenders, but is only partially effective, since sexual drive is primarily in the mind, not the body.*

3. *Behavior modification.* This treatment addresses specific behaviors

associated with the sexual offense and uses conditioning exercises based on learning principles. This modality attempts to change the subject's sexual preferences by pairing them with aversive stimuli and replacing them with more socially acceptable sexual behaviors. *This method, used as a sole form of intervention, is only minimally effective because the desired result consistently degrades and extinguishes over time.*

4. *Cognitive-behavioral therapy, relapse prevention, psycho-education, and client monitoring.* This combination of therapy methods is used by mental health professionals who view most sexual offending behavior as stemming from early neurobiological, social, and developmental deficits (often caused by childhood abuse and/or neglect) and as symptomatic of a severe childhood attachment disorder. Treatment consists of a combination of reeducation and resocialization with the confrontation of the offender's denial and defenses, in addition to an underlying conviction that sexual acting out represents the offender's unconscious and misguided attempts to achieve healthy emotional stability, relational connection, and "self-soothing," rather than a conscious desire to cause harm. Treating professionals are aware that, for some offenders, sexual acting out represents a repetitive manifestation of early, unresolved childhood sexual trauma. The goal of this form of treatment is to alert the offender to his specific individual life stressors and help him find ways of reducing them, while teaching and encouraging more productive and nonoffending coping skills. This combined therapeutic method also teaches offenders self-observance of sexual compulsivity and helps to satisfy the goal of "relapse prevention" by training the subject to recognize the warning signs of characteristic behavior that may result in the commitment of sexual offenses. *This combined method, with an emphasis on relapse prevention, has proved the most effective treatment for the largest population of offenders, those who are described as nonfixated and nonviolent and have the intellectual capacity to integrate these therapies. However, the caveat here is that this form of treatment is only minimally effective with violent, sociopathic, and/or fixated sexual offenders.*

Although the definition of a "successful" treatment outcome may vary from person to person, at the minimum, clients who have completed sexual offender treatment should:

\ Experience their desire to sexually act out as intellectually undesirable

\ Work diligently not to commit any offending behavior, though they may always have some emotional and/or sexual interest in offending

\ Recognize their sexual problems, and the antecedents for those problems, through a thorough knowledge of their sexual disorder and its symptoms

\ Admit all of their problem behaviors, sexual and otherwise

\ Be open with family members and diligently honest with those providing treatment

\ Accept responsibility for what they have done and how it may have affected others

\ Realize their sexual offending behavior is pathological and harmful

\ Acknowledge that they must gain control over their behavior and accept specific limitations and accountability

BALANCING MODERN-DAY TREATMENT MODALITIES WITH COMMUNITY CONCERNS

As our ideas and beliefs about human psychology, sexuality, and motivation have changed over time, so has offender treatment methodology. The development of this methodology is, of course, far from complete. A few of today's methods would still be somewhat familiar to systems of long ago: we have moved from the literal castration of extreme offenders — a treatment option used in the United States well into the twentieth century — to chemical castration (the use of hormonal injections and the like), which is employed today with serious, violent, and repeat offenders. And we are far from having any kind of definitive treatment method for any one type of sexual offender.

It is important to note that most sex offender research, treatment outcome studies, and published reports related to sexual offenders have come from examining subjects who are already inside the penal system. This leaves us with little understanding of the necessary elements of any long-term treatment and maintenance of the much larger, nonimprisoned offender population. Clearly, there is much work and research yet to be done. Significantly, treatment success depends as much on the *individual offender's* continuing desire and commitment to stop his sexual acting out, and to remain free of it over time, as it does on the treatment method itself. Here is where Jewish community support can make a difference in the success of the treatment outcome for a recovering sex offender.

This is no easy task. In this complicated and dangerous area, as much as we all would like to have decisive solutions at hand, the reality is that treatment success — when and if it occurs — is obtained day by day, on a case-by-case basis. Given this reality, our communities owe nothing less to their members than the rigorous monitoring of each case and the careful fashioning of responses that fit each one. On the one hand, when an offender's treatment shows promise, being too quick to banish the offender from the community can lead to a relapse, with tragically preventable results. On the other hand, if as a community we are too lenient, or lenient in the wrong cases, we may be placing children at risk.

This delicate problem can only be solved through an educated response by all members of the community — rabbis, teachers, parents, neighbors, etc. — to deviant or offending sexual conduct. This chapter is intended to provide the lay reader with the benefit of insights learned over time by clinicians working steadily with nonviolent sex offenders. Since sex offenders do not represent a homogenous group, the community's response must be tailored to the individual case. When Jewish communities and their leaders understand more about the complexity of sexually aberrant behavior, we will be an important step closer to bringing about a healthier community response to the sexual offenders among us — and this in turn will lead to more educated decisions about whom to banish and whom to support.

NOTES

1. Andrea Hsu, "California Church Debates Accepting Sex Offender." *All Things Considered*, National Public Radio, March 29, 2007. Available at www.npr.org/templates/story/story.php?storyId=9213698.

2. Adapted from A. Nicholas Groth, William F. Hobson, and Thomas S. Gary, *The Incest Offender, the Victim, the Family: New Treatment Approaches* (New York: Mental Health Association of Westchester County, 1985/2002).

3. Ibid.

PROFESSOR DANE S. CLAUSSEN

Epilogue

MEDIA COVERAGE

The careful reader of this book will spot references to the news media throughout it — the news media broke this story, the news media buried that story, the news media were supposedly sensationalist on another story. Even when the news media are not mentioned in a given case or chapter, they are conspicuous by their absence: if Jews were going to be attacked by non-Jews (this fear is mentioned several times), how would such an attack be known of at all if it weren't for the news media?

It has been true for decades in all but small towns that if something isn't covered by the news media, then it doesn't exist — if no one hears a tree fall in a forest, it made no sound. Mass communication researchers even have a term for this — "symbolic annihilation," describing what happens to events, individuals, institutions, or other subjects that receive very little or no news coverage.

Thus, this book's contributors find and note various faults in news media coverage of the sexual abuse of Jewish children. It is indisputable that the news media's most egregious faults (more likely in the U.S. papers and magazines than in their foreign counterparts) have been their minimal amount of coverage of this issue — both in the metro New York region and nationally — and how long they took to get around to covering it. Let's look for a moment at how journalists work and think, so that we may better understand why it is that U.S. news media haven't covered this important story enough — either often enough or in enough depth.

Journalist Competence and Related Problems

Journalists have numerous widespread practices and routines that would at least partially contribute to their minimal coverage of sexual abuse in the

Jewish community, and that also resulted in the news media taking far too many years to cover sexual abuse in the Catholic Church. First, consider how journalists decide whether something they hear constitutes news or not. In the Catholic Church scandals, many journalists had heard everything from thirdhand rumors to firsthand reports for years, but they waited to cover the sexual abuse until lawsuits were filed, priests were indicted and arrested, church officials made public statements related to the matter, and so on. For journalists, it doesn't matter that most civil lawsuits never go to trial (they are withdrawn, thrown out, settled out of court, etc.), that a high percentage of arrested persons are arraigned on lesser charges, and that a high percentage of those arrested never go to trial. Regardless of the outcome, papers filed in court at the minimum give journalists a document to quote (as if such is more credible than an oral claim), in the same way that U.S. journalists increasingly quote and don't question public and corporate officials, even when the journalists know they are being lied to. Ironically, accurate quotes have become critical, while the *truth* of what is in those quotes seems to matter less and less.

Second, daily newspaper newsrooms in the United States are divided into beat reporters (assigned to cover specific news areas) and general assignment reporters. Among beat reporters, who could and should cover child sexual abuse in a religious community, one must ask: is that a story for a religion reporter, a cops and criminal courts reporter, a legal affairs reporter, or someone else? (The Catholic Church scandals had to be covered by multiple reporters, either working together and/or each writing stories on different angles, which eventually included several dioceses declaring bankruptcy.) Even when a newspaper has relevant designated beat reporters (note: the vast majority of the nation's 1,430 dailies do not have a religion reporter), reporters can try to pass the buck on these stories, fight over whose story it is, let it fall through the beat-reporting-system cracks, or cover it in teams. Each outcome is possible, but only the last one is likely to produce a high-quality result and then only at large metro dailies with big and sufficiently competent staffs.

Third, some evidence suggests that a certain number of reporters are not eager to cover stories that are "distasteful," to say the least. In truth, journalists do not choose the religion beat, or even choose to write about cops and courts, in order to write about children's sexual abuse. Similarly, at least some editors are not eager to publish such stories. Did all mainstream daily newspaper editors who happened to be Catholic cover the Catholic Church scandals as vigorously as possible? One would have to say no. And surely a news story's predicted negative backlash by itself, regardless of its topic, may result in less — and less explicit — news coverage. For instance, David Carr, a *New York Times* media columnist, admitted in his July 7, 2008, column, "When Fox News is the Story": "I have choked a few times at the keyboard when Fox News has come up in a story and it was not absolutely critical to the matter at hand." And that's just business, not religion!

Again, I am well aware that my point here is directly contrary to the assumption that many Americans make that U.S. news media are willing, even eager, to be sensationalistic. Such rhetoric, of course, lumps all news media together, missing the point that the *Philadelphia Inquirer* is not the *National Enquirer*, and, for example, television news is, on average, much more sensationalistic, much more superficial, and sometimes just downright silly as compared with typical newspaper coverage. It also must be pointed out that news media are largely in a no-win situation covering any child sexual abuse, let alone such abuse that has religion, partisan politics, public education, or other hot-button issues connected to it. As Joyanna Silberg and Stephanie J. Dallam correctly put it (chapter 4) and Robert Weiss's introduction confirms (chapter 9), "There is an almost physical disgust and revulsion many people feel when the topic of child sexual abuse is raised." If the subject itself, almost by definition, is sensationalistic, then news media will be accused of sensationalism merely by covering it, regardless of how hard those news media try to make a story dry by leaving out the sordid, albeit critical, details of accusations.

Fourth, journalists are creatures of habit, tradition, and standard practices and procedures, including (particularly relevant for the purposes here) covering the same types of stories in the same way and going back to the same sources over and over again when that is possible. Thus, it took a long time for Jewish children's sexual abuse to get on U.S. news media's radar screen for the first time, and news coverage of Catholic Church scandals made it easier, in all kinds of ways, to cover those in the Jewish community. One can quite reasonably and seriously wonder whether Jewish children's sexual abuse would have received what little coverage it has if the Catholic Church scandals hadn't broken first.

Fifth, general interest, mass circulation newspapers must rely on specialized media to truly keep up with what is going on in various reporting beats. For example, medical/health reporters must skim the *Journal of the American*

Medical Association (JAMA) and the *New England Journal of Medicine*. Sports reporters read, watch, and listen to a lot of other sports news media. Business reporters read the local business weekly journal and such national news media as *Fortune, Forbes, Business Week*, etc. And so on. Mass communication researchers refer to this process as "intermedia agenda-setting." (Most of it happens from the "top" down; in other words, the *New York Times*, the *Wall Street Journal, Time*, and other elite national news media, usually based in New York or Washington, have a disproportionate influence on other, smaller, U.S. news media.) In the case of the Jewish (as opposed to the Catholic) child sexual abuse story, metro New York City religion reporters almost surely were monitoring various Jewish local, regional, and national publications. And, as Amy Neustein details in this book's introduction, the Jewish media rarely covered the story until 2007, a year after a *Nightline* broadcast on it and five years after Neustein and Michael Lesher together wrote a *Jewish Exponent* column on child sex abuse and documented in my book, *Sex, Religion, Media*, how U.S. Jewish news media had failed to cover the story.

Small Jewish Population

One probable reason why sexual abuse in the Jewish community receives very little coverage by U.S. news media may be, frankly, because Jews compose only about 2.5 percent of the U.S. population (and Orthodox Jews, the primary subject of this book, less than that), while 25 percent of the U.S. population are Catholic (a ten-to-one ratio), and about 50 percent of the U.S. population identify themselves as at least nominally Protestant. Among U.S. minority groups in terms of nationwide population, Jews are far down the list, after the disabled (19 percent), Latinos, African Americans, gay/lesbian/bisexual/transgendered (GLBT), Asian Americans, and Muslims. In only ten states do Jews compose more than 2 percent of the population: California, Connecticut, Florida, Illinois, Maryland, Massachusetts, Nevada, New Jersey, New York, and Pennsylvania; and in only one of those states (New York) does the Jewish population exceed 5.7 percent. Thus, for example, the popular notion of heavy Jewish populations in Florida (4.1 percent) and/or Arizona (1.7 percent) is simply not accurate. Generally, and with exceptions tied only to specific major news events, minority groups in the United States receive minimal news media coverage, and in the case of the GLBT community, news media usually cite sources (such as the Family Research Council, American Family Association, etc.) hostile to its mere existence or at least to equal legal rights. Again, this is an explanation, not a defense, of U.S. news media behavior.

Stonewalling the Media

Loel M. Weiss and Mark F. Itzkowitz, in chapter 1, observe, "Investigators and reporters will not give up the search for truth because you do not cooperate." Well, yes and no. Journalists are not supposed to give up a search for truth because sources and potential sources are not cooperating; moreover, uncooperative sources are often taken by most journalists as a sign that they are onto something important. But today's reality is that daily newspaper staffs are being slashed in cost-cutting layoffs, buyouts, and hiring freezes; many investigative reporting positions have simply been eliminated. The slack is not being taken up by local or national television news, which always has had limited staff, time, and expertise, or by magazines, World Wide Web sites, wire services, or anyone/anything else. And, thus, if a story is very difficult to obtain, and a reporter could be working on stories that are as important as, or more important than, the one that is difficult to get, some stories will just not get covered these days. But it still is a bad bet for Jewish leaders to assume that if they stonewall the news media well enough and long enough, that the mainstream news media will go away — even in the absence of arrests and arraignments and/or civil lawsuits. And this is especially true in the Internet age (addressed below).

SOLUTIONS

It would be beneficial to all parties concerned in these sex scandals if all key parties were as savvy about how the news media work and how to work with them as Weiss and Itzkowitz apparently are, as suggested by much of their chapter. But we know that hasn't been true and won't be true, based on what is recounted (and not) in the other chapters. So allow me to make a few suggestions.

The Jewish community should not pay any attention to, as Weiss and Itzkowitz put it, "hostile press coverage in Ku Klux Klan, Nazi, and Islamic publications (*Jews for Allah*), taking advantage of the scandal to assure their readers that Jews inherently are evil and sexually debased." Such publications have extremely small circulations, they will not cover Jewish news accurately or objectively (nor publish corrections and probably not letters to the editor, either), and one also cannot shut them down or even successfully sue them for libel. (A key part of U.S. libel law is that one's reputation must be damaged by a party with enough credibility that its libels would be taken seriously by a reasonable person; thus, because a reasonable person would not give credibility to KKK, Nazi, or anti-Semitic Muslim publications, such publications are legally "libel proof.") Thus, they are best ignored; to do otherwise gives them too much credibility and fosters unnecessary paranoia in the Jewish community.

The Jewish community needs to be extremely cautious about imputing allegations of anti-Semitism to general interest, mass circulation/market newspapers, magazines, television broadcasts, etc., as occurs when news media cover sex abuse scandals (see, for example, the end of chapter 2). David Broder, the so-called dean of the Washington press corps, has famously put it, "There just isn't enough ideology in the average reporter to fill a thimble." To which I would add: there aren't enough strong opinions about any religion (as contrasted with opinions about individual religious leaders, such as politically involved Protestant televangelists) in the average reporter to fill a thimble. Are U.S. journalists professionally incompetent? Sometimes. Not competent enough? Frequently. Anti-Semitic? Come on.

Various leaders and experts who want to get information and ideas out through the news media need to be careful that they are dealing with *professional journalists in the news media* and not with members of other mass media outlets. For example, Barbara Blaine made a foreseeable mistake, which she realized only in hindsight, in going on *Geraldo* to talk about the Survivors Network of those Abused by Priests (SNAP). Talk shows, from Bill O'Reilly's to Oprah Winfrey's, are not news broadcasts and O'Reilly, Winfrey, and virtually all such others make no pretense of calling themselves journalists or of subscribing to any journalistic processes or ethics. (Likewise, *Dateline NBC's* *To Catch a Predator* broadcasts, noted in this book by Robert Weiss, were intentionally sensationalist entertainment programs trying to pass themselves off as investigative journalism. However, they were doing something that almost no journalists do [sting operations] and failing to do what real journalists do: report and write a fleshed-out story with documents and numerous other sources, expositions of causes and effects, statistics, etc.) Fortunately, Blaine's later experiences dealing with real journalists apparently were much better, as evidence by the 850 articles about pedophile priests in the *Boston Globe* alone. One also must remember that news media coverage can be a two-edged sword, and is only *part* of a multitactic process for making progress; for example, Blaine found out that Catholic bishops sometimes respond to negative press coverage both by ignoring it and by executing their own, even dishonest, public relations strategies.

As importantly, perhaps even more importantly, the Jewish community, both as individuals and in groups, needs to be careful about what kind of assumptions it makes about how the public interprets what is in the news media. Erica Brown, in chapter 3, for instance, although stressing the importance of high moral standards for leaders, cautions us about the facile assumption that "private sin easily translates into public betrayal.... [W]hen we move unfairly from a leader's public service to his inner life, we are no longer capable judges of behavior." I agree: my reactions, like those of many other Americans, are tempered by a more complex or nuanced approach to evaluating a leader's transgressions. And yet, as stated repeatedly in this volume, Jewish authorities have assumed that news media accounts of children's sexual abuse by Jewish leaders would reflect poorly on the entire religion; thus they often have engaged in intimidation of victims, suppression of evidence, manipulation of officials, and stonewalling of news media. They apparently never "got the memo" over the past thirty-five years that the cover-up of a crime is *always* more damaging in the long run than the crime itself. (See, e.g., Richard Nixon and Bill Clinton.)

All of us (but for the purposes of this book, notably Jewish leaders) need to remember, as Rabbi Mark Dratch puts it, "The Internet has been a rich resource of information and advocacy, and blogs have given voice to many who were previously silent or alone." (Amy Neustein and Michael Lesher note in chapter 8, "No amount of blog banning will reverse it [education on sexual abuse].") Chapter 6, written by Lesher as sole author, points out that blogs have been "particularly valuable in the Orthodox Jewish community because the anonymity they offer protects individuals from public shaming if they broach a taboo subject — like child sex abuse." What this means is that covering up the sexual abuse of Jewish children is now more difficult than ever, because the Internet has made it possible for information and support to become widespread, regardless of attempts at cover-up.

The Jewish press, like almost all U.S. minority news media, needs to make even more of an effort to professionalize and modernize what stories it covers and how it covers them (without going the route of, for example, the *Advocate*, which has gone from being the GLBT community's *Time* magazine to being its *People* magazine).The Jewish and general interest, mass market news media need to learn, or at least remember, that covering child sex abuse in an accurate, objective, professional way is not sensationalistic — while bracing themselves for the fact that a substantial percentage of the audience will think that it is, regardless of how a story is written and perhaps regardless of how far the story is from the top of the front page. Likewise, all news media, both general interest and Jewish, need to remember that neither Catholics nor Jews are separate or above the law; in other words, the fact that both Jews and Catholics have their own religion-based judicial systems is completely irrelevant to constitutional judicial systems, either federal or state. Public officials do not have the option to delegate government-mandated judicial proceedings — civil or, especially, criminal — to the Catholic Church or to local Jewish communities.

Journalists, Jewish leaders, and prosecutors and other involved lawyers must focus on science and social science of the highest rigor when discussing in court, for the news media, and the general public the causes and effects of sexual abuse of children. This means, among other things, avoiding uniquely Freudian theories and/or methods for which there is very little or no evidence. (Note, for example, that Robert Weiss [chapter 9] confirms, "Psychodynamic psychotherapy . . . *has proved the least effective method for achieving change"* in a sex offender [italics in original].) Care must also be taken not to state or imply that studies that have not been conducted pursuant to rigorous (social) scientific method may be relied upon by politicians, lawyers, Jewish leaders, victims, journalists, psychologists, or others — especially anyone with authority or credibility involved in the aftermath of child sexual abuse.

Journalists in particular, because they can expose the practice for the public and put pressure on prosecutors, should act on the knowledge that rabbinic courts, like ecclesiastical courts in the Roman Catholic Church and the Episcopal Church (usa) and quasi-judicial processes in various Protestant churches, are not adequate substitutes for government investigations, government prosecutions, and government prisons. Neustein and Lesher note the "severe limitations under which such tribunals necessarily labor when they try to adjudicate a violent crime like child abuse. Rabbinic courts are, in fact, largely impotent to stop a criminal. Lacking a police force . . . they cannot arrest suspects, compel the production of information or evidence, detain a suspect pending the outcome of a trial, or even punish an offender in the event he is found guilty." (Even if rabbinic courts had those powers, when did U.S.

criminal justice get "outsourced" by government to anyone, let alone religious organizations? As someone who has never lived anywhere in which the Jewish community has such political clout, I am shocked that it would need to be suggested, as Neustein and Lesher do in chapter 8, that "district attorneys can establish policies that bar prosecutors from relying on religious courts to take over their function." As Neustein and Lesher have demonstrated, the subverting of the criminal justice system by rabbinic courts causes immediate and substantial constitutional questions. A district attorney who relies on religious courts in a criminal case should be reported to the state attorney general, the state supreme court, the state bar association, and the general public through news media.) Separation of church and state does not mean that religion is above any law of general application, especially not criminal law — a fact that the U.S. Catholic hierarchy also has tried to obscure and avoid.

Finally, journalists, educators, leaders, and others have to be careful not to appear to be antisex while clearly being anti–sexual abuse. For example, Weiss provides a list of characteristics of sexual addiction that would make it fairly easy to separate those who are sex addicted from those who are not: "loss of control over sexual behavior(s) . . . escalation of sexual behavior . . . irritability or anger if asked to stop the sexual behavior; negative consequences directly related to the sexual behavior . . . [and/or] continued sexual acting out despite prior or ongoing negative consequences directly related to it" (chapter 9). These criteria must be emphasized, along with the statistic that "3 to 5 percent of the general population may have an active sexual addiction problem," regardless of whether one thinks that is a relatively large or relatively small number. Like the frequent discounting of "binge drinking" studies because they use a "binge" criterion so low that they indict a large minority, if not a majority, of all university students (and a significant percentage of other Americans), "sexual addiction" rhetoric that focuses too heavily on behaviors such as "Internet and video porn use" or "fetishes" is not likely to be taken seriously by large percentages of the twenty-first-century U.S. public. In other words, to catch and maintain either public or news media attention, the focus here needs to be on the consequences to individuals and on societal or institutional causes.

What I am requiring of journalists here, and suggesting to all key parties involved in child sexual abuse cases in the Jewish community, is a tall order. However, it is in keeping with the responsibilities that the news media have to the public (and to persons with a direct and personal interest in these stories) and that all of us have to all children and to all crime victims — made all the more critical when they are one and the same.

DANE S. CLAUSSEN, PHD, MBA, is professor and graduate programs director, Department of Journalism and Mass Communication, Point Park University, Pittsburgh, Pennsylvania; and editor, *Journalism and Mass Communication Educator*, Association for Education in Journalism and Mass Communication, Columbia, South Carolina. He is author of *Anti-intellectualism in American Media*; editor of *Sex, Religion, Media* and two books about the Promise Keepers; and a former newspaper editor and publisher.

CONTRIBUTORS

BARBARA BLAINE, Esq., MDIV, MSW, founder and president of SNAP
    (Survivor Network of those Abused by Priests), a national advocacy
    group for survivors of clerical sexual abuse
ERICA BROWN, PHD, scholar-in-residence, managing director for education
    and leadership, the Jewish Federation of Greater Washington
STEPHANIE DALLAM, RN, MSN, research associate for the Leadership
    Council on Child Abuse and Interpersonal Violence, Baltimore,
    Maryland; nurse practitioner specializing in pediatric trauma; former
    nursing instructor
MARK DRATCH, Rabbi, founder of JSAFE (Jewish Institute Supporting
    an Abuse-Free Environment); chairman of the Rabbinic Council of
    America's Task Force on Rabbinic Improprieties; instructor of Jewish
    Studies at Yeshiva University, New York, New York
MICHELLE FRIEDMAN, MD, board-certified psychiatrist; director of
    pastoral counseling at Yeshivat Chovevei Torah (YCT) Rabbinical School,
    New York, New York
MARK ITZKOWITZ, Esq., general counsel and member of the board of
    Temple Beth Am, Randolph, Massachusetts
MICHAEL LESHER, Esq., MA, author; columnist; investigative reporter;
    lawyer; legal editor; and advocate for abused children, northern
    New Jersey
AMY NEUSTEIN, PHD, sociologist, author, and public speaker on
    intrafamilial child sexual abuse and clergy sexual abuse; founder of
    Help Us Regain the Children Legal Research and Advocacy Center,
    Fort Lee, New Jersey; member of the Editorial Board of the *Journal of
    Child Sexual Abuse*
JOYANNA SILBERG, PHD, board-certified clinical psychologist; executive
    vice president of the Leadership Council on Child Abuse and
    Interpersonal Violence; coordinator of trauma disorder services for
    children at Sheppard Pratt Hospital in Baltimore, Maryland

LOEL WEISS, Rabbi and spiritual leader at Temple Beth Am, Randolph, Massachusetts

ROBERT WEISS, LCSW, practicing clinical social worker; executive director of the Sexual Recovery Institute, Los Angeles, California

crime scene, in temple, 26
CSI: Crime Scene Investigation, 36
C-SPAN, 179

Dallas Jewish Family Services, 78
Dallas Morning News, 172, 175, 191
Dateline (NBC), 234–235, 258
Davitt, Kevin, 207, 212
DePaul University, 220
Detroit News, 172
Dickinson, Emily, 72
DNA tests, 21
Dorff, Elliot, 94
Dratch, Mark, 153, 203, 219

Ehrman, Mordechai, 210
Elyashiv, Yoseph Shalom, 115–116
ephebophile, 232
evangelical religion, xvii
ex post facto limitations, 144. *See also*
    Mondrowitz, Avrohom

Faculty of Comparative Religion, xx
FaithTrust Institute, xi–xii, 52, 53
False Memory Syndrome Foundation,
    88–89
false witness, commandment not to
    bear, 24
Farkas, Moshe, 208, 209, 213, 214. *See
    also* Hafner, Solomon; Brooklyn
    district attorney: Hafner case
Federal Bureau of Investigation (FBI),
    158
federal civil rights laws, 222
Feinstein, Dovid, 207. *See also* Hafner,
    Solomon
Ferenczi, Sandor, 86. *See also* Freud,
    Sigmund
Ferentz, Lisa, 83–84, 85, 94, 96
first responders, community leaders as,
    243–244

Flynn, Archbishop Harry, 176. *See also*
    Catholic Church: U.S. Conference of
    Catholic Bishops' Ad Hoc Commit-
    tee on Sexual Abuse
Fortune, Marie, 52–53, 59n7. *See also*
    FaithTrust Institute
Forward, 144
Fox, Debbie, 78, 98–99. *See also* Aleinu
    Resource Center
Freedom of Information Act (FOIA),
    requests, 134, 156, 184
Freud, Sigmund, 85–86
Freudian theories, 260

Gauthe, Gilbert, 166
Giller, Esther, 97
Glick, Mordecai, 198, 204
Goldstein, Ariela, 78
Greenberg, Irving ("Yitz"), 3, 216–217
Gregory, Wilton, 177, 178, 180. *See also*
    U.S. Conference of Catholic Bishops
Grimm, Katherine, 200, 206, 214

Ha-aretz, 153–154
Hafetz Hayyim (Yisrael Meir Kagan,
    Rav), 112
Hafner, Solomon, 197–200, 205, 207, 212,
    224, 225
halacha (Jewish law), xvii, 18
Hamilton, Marci, 211. *See also* Brooklyn
    district attorney: State v. Kolko plea
    bargain
Hansen, Chris, 235. *See also* Dateline
    (NBC)
Hely, Charles, 38
hillul ha-Shem (desecration of God's
    name), 42, 111, 114, 116–118, 146
Hirsch, Samson Raphael, 68–69
Holtzman, Elizabeth, 132, 133, 135, 136
Hynes, Charles ("Joe"). *See* Brooklyn
    district attorney

informers, 7
Institutional Review Board (IRB), 226n4
intermedia agenda setting, 256
Isserles, Rabbi Moshe, 115

Jacobs, Phil, 77, 84, 90, 96–97
Jarecki, Andrew, 89–90
Jaus, Rhonnie, 208
Jewish Community of Greater Boston, 19, 25
Jewish Exponent, 256
Jewish Family Service of Los Angeles (JFS), ix, x, xi, xii, 78, 98
Jewish Observer, 217. *See also* Agudath Israel of America
Jewish Press, 2, 159, 198. *See also* Mondrowitz, Avrohom
Jewish Voice and Opinion, 200. *See also* Brooklyn district attorney: Hafner case
John Jay College of Criminal Justice, 179. *See also* Catholic Church: National Review Board
Journal of Child Sexual Abuse, 216, 226n4
JSafe (The Jewish Institute Supporting an Abuse-Free Environment), 55. *See also* Dratch, Mark

Keating, Frank, 177. *See also* Catholic Church: National Review Board
Kehoe, Patricia, 131–132, 153
Kelly, Tina, 153
Kenner, Hugh, 225
kiddush ha-Shem (sanctification of God's name), 42. See also *hillul ha-Shem*
Kolker, Robert, 139–140, 141
Kolko, Yehudah, 139, 141, 149, 210–211, 228n23

Lanner, Baruch, 1, 6, 7, 204, 228nn26–27. *See also* National Council of Synagogue Youth (NCSY)
lashon hara (gossip), 24, 25, 94, 110–111, 112, 113
Leadership Council on Child Abuse and Interpersonal Violence, 89, 90
Lev, Rachel, 93
Litwin, Steve, 147, 148–149. *See also* Colmer, Stefan
Loftus, Elizabeth, 89. *See also* False Memory Syndrome Foundation
Lori, Aviva, 153–154
Love Your Neighbor and Yourself: A Jewish Approach to Modern Ethics (Dorff), xii–xiii
Loyola University (Chicago), 220

Mahony, Cardinal Roger, 170–171, 172, 174, 187–188. *See also* SNAP: NCCB, publicity stunt
Maimonides (Rambam), 63, 65, 105–106, 115
malpractice insurance, for temple employees, 28, 29, 31
mandated reporter, of child abuse, ix, 15, 18–19
Mandel, David, 157. *See also* Mondrowitz, Avrohom: Ohel Children's Home and Family Services
Manhattan Children's Advocacy Center, 206. *See also* Grimm, Katherine
Marcovitz, Richard, 1
marit ayin (appearance of impropriety), 29
Markwitz, Adele, 206, 214
McFadden, Cynthia, xxi, 133, 145
McKelvey, Gerald, 157. *See also* Mondrowitz, Avrohom: Ohel Children's Home and Family Services
McKenna, Jeremiah, 150

mesirah (informing or traducing), consequences of, 111, 114, 115, 116, 201, 202, 203

Moment, 3

Mondrowitz, Avrohom: arrest in Jerusalem and potential extradition, 2, 130, 132, 152, 154, 155, 156; Badatz of Yerushalayim (Beth Din Tzedek of Jerusalem) Harav Shlomo Zalman Auerbach (Aurbach), 138, 227n17; child pornography on computer hard drive, 150–151, 153–154, 158; civil rights victim, considered himself as, 138; credentials (specious) of, 2, 9n4; deportation requested, 133, 135, 136; extradition requested, 132; extradition treaty, new, 148–149; fugitive from justice, 1–2; gifts to children by, 131; indicted by Brooklyn grand jury, 2, 129, 132; (*see also* Brooklyn district attorney: State v. Mondrowitz, embarrassment to); Israel's Supreme Court, appeal of extradition order to, 156; Lesher as pro bono attorney for victims of, 128, 129; "love-bombing," 127; Neustein's role in seeking justice for victims, 127–128, 129, 131, 133, 139, 145, 150, 151, 154; non-Jewish children as victims of, 128–129, 131; Ohel Children's Home and Family Services, foster child complaint of abuse, 157, 162n38, 209; radio show, hosted by, 131, 137, 209; slander victim, considered as, 155; school for troubled children, administrator of, 131, 209; Shas Party's "special treatment" of, 136; suicide of alleged victim of, 146, 154; "therapy" office of, 131, 132, 141; underground, role of, 130–131, 147, 153; Weiss as outspoken victim of, 127–128, 129, 145, 146

Moral Responsibility Research Project, 220–221

motzi shem ra (spouting lies and spreading disinformation), 111

Ms. magazine, 87

m'sirah. See *mesirah*

Nachmanides (Ramban), 107

National Conference of Catholic Bishops (NCCB), 170–171, 172, 174. *See also* Pilarczyk, Archbishop Daniel; SNAP: NCCB, publicity stunt

National Council of Synagogue Youth (NCSY), 1, 9n8

Nefesh (international network of Orthodox Jewish health care professionals), 3, 198

Nevison, Howard, 1

New York Eyewitness News, 144, 146

New York Jewish Week (Jewish Week), 1–2, 92, 144, 204, 210–211

New York magazine, 1, 139, 141, 210

New York Post, 144, 149, 162n38

New York Times, 130, 132, 152–153, 154, 180, 202, 256

Newsday, 137, 140, 141

Nightline (ABC), xxi, xxiii, 1, 144–145, 148, 256

non-Jewish authorities: oversight of Jewish schools, 218; taboo to bring claims of child sex abuse to, 199, 200–201; tape recording of *beth din* kept away from, 214. *See also* Pasik, Elliot

North Shore University Hospital, 213. *See also* Schaffer, Sylvan

O'Toole, James, 67, 68

Oedipal theory, 86. *See also* Freud, Sigmund; seduction theory

offender, child: dedicated or fixated,
237–239; sexually addicted, 240–
243; situational or regressed,
239–240
Ohel Children's Home and Family
Services, 157, 162n38, 209. *See also*
Mondrowitz, Avrohom
Orthodox Union, 1

Panetta, Leon, 177. *See also* Catholic
Church: National Review Board
papal infallibility, xviii. *See also* Catholic
Church
Pasik, Elliot, 217–218, 221, 225, 228n32
Patriot Ledger, 21, 22, 27
Pell Grant fraud, 202–203. *See also*
secular authorities, mistrust for
pikuach nefesh (saving a life), 94. See
also *lashon hara*
Pope John Paul II, 188, 189, 190. *See also*
Catholic Church
post-Holocaust reaction, xviii
"The Problem of Sexual Molestation by
Roman Catholic Clergy: Meeting
the Problem in a Comprehensive
and Responsible Manner" (Doyle,
Peterson, and Mouton), 176
Proverbs, Book of, 72
psak (ruling of a rabbinic court), 138.
See also Mondrowitz, Avrohom:
Badatz of Yerushalayim
psychodynamic psychotherapy, for
sexual offenders, 248, 260
Puccio, Deanne, 208

Rabbeinu Gershom, 115
Rabbeinu Yonah ben Abraham of
Gerondi, 108
Rabbi Moshe Isserles. *See* Isserles,
Rabbi Moshe

Rabbinical Assembly, 28
Rabbinical Council of Greater Baltimore, 78, 93, 94
Radbaz (Rabbi David ben Solomon ibn
Zimra), 115
religion reporter, 254
Rivera, Geraldo, 166, 258
rodef (pursuer: someone in pursuit of
another with the intention of committing harmful acts), 107, 116
Rosenberg, Bernhard, 7
Rottenberg, Chaim, 207–208, 212, 213;
scolding *beth din* witness who
believed the child, 214; imitating victim's mother's distressed reaction to
beth din ruling, 215. *See also* Hafner,
Solomon; Brooklyn district attorney:
Hafner case
Russell, Diana, 87–88

Safe School System, 93. *See also* Fox,
Debbie
Safer Society Foundation, 246
Salamon, Michael, 3
Salter, Anna, 95
Saul, Stephanie, 137
Schachter, Herschel, 116
Schaffer, Sylvan, 213. *See also* Hafner,
Solomon; Brooklyn district attorney:
Hafner case
Schick, Marvin, 3
Schmetterer, Jerry, 144
secular authorities, mistrust for, 202–
203. *See also* Pell Grant fraud
seduction theory, 86. *See also*, Freud,
Sigmund; Oedipal theory
Sex, Religion, Media (Claussen), 2,
256
sexual trafficking of children, xix
Sgroi, Susan, 86